The Absolute
beneath the Relative
and Other Essays

By the same author:

Stanley L. Jaki

The Absolute
beneath the Relative
and Other Essays

UNIVERSITY
PRESS OF
AMERICA

University Press of America

The Intercollegiate Studies Institute, Inc.

Copyright © 1988 by

The Intercollegiate Studies Institute, Inc.

University Press of America,® Inc.

4720 Boston Way
Lanham, MD 20706

3 Henrietta Street
London WC2E 8LU England

British Cataloging in Publication Information Available

Co-published by arrangement with
the Intercollegiate Studies Institute, Inc.

Library of Congress Cataloging-in-Publication Data

Jaki, Stanley L.
The absolute beneath the relative and other essays.
Includes bibliographies and index.
1. Science. 2. Science—Philosophy. I. Title.
Q171.J356   1988   500   88-20771
ISBN 0–8191–7182–4 (alk. paper)
ISBN 0–8191–7183–2 (pbk. : alk. paper)

All University Press of America books are produced on acid-free paper.
The paper used in this publication meets the minimum requirements of
American National Standard for Information Sciences—Permanence of Paper
for Printed Library Materials, ANSI Z39.48–1984.

Contents

Preface vii

1. The Absolute beneath the Relative:
   Reflections on Einstein's Theories 1

2. The Impasse of Planck's Epistemology 18

3. The Metaphysics of Discovery
   and the Rediscovery of Metaphysics 43

4. God and Man's Science: A View of Creation 56

5. Brain, Mind, and Computers 70

6. The Role of Physics in Psychology:
   The Prospects in Retrospect 85

7. Order in Nature and Society:
   Open or Specific? 102

8. Scientific Ethics and Ethical Science 123

9. The Physics of Impetus
   and the Impetus of the Koran 140

10. The Last Century of Science:
    Progress, Problems, and Prospects 153

11. Science and Censorship: Hélène Duhem
    and the Publication of the *Système du monde* 173

12. Monkeys and Machine-guns:
    Evolution, Darwinism, and Christianity 188

13. The Demythologization of Science 198

14. Science and Hope 214

Index of Names 230

Preface

Warning voices have been raised in increasing number about the anarchy toward which modern life is moving. Much less has been said about the fact that fashionable thinking about science has been greatly instrumental in propelling us in that fearsome direction. A careful look at science could effectively reverse that trend. Such is the chief claim of this collection of essays. They should help the reader in various ways to gain insight both into the making of science and into the true merits of a climate of thought usurping the label scientific.

The exploitation of science for spurious ideologies and social programs has for its most popular form the claim that Einstein's relativity made everything relative (Ch. 1). Other forms, less widely spoken about, are no less pernicious, though not necessarily easy to recognize. No less a scientist than Planck failed to perceive the threat which is posed by the prevailing philosophy of quantum mechanics to sound thinking about reality and causality, a lesson that cannot be meditated upon often enough (Ch. 2). Again, it is still to be realized that beneath the glitter of scientific discoveries, increasingly numerous and distractingly spectacular, there lies an unpretentious but indispensable philosophy or love of wisdom (Ch. 3).

Only with that wisdom on hand shall one see the stunning witness which modern science, and cosmology in particular, brings to the created character of all things, the universe (Ch. 4). The same wisdom receives a firm vote also from a careful look at the scientific investigation of the inner universe or the mind, both in brain research and in computer theory (Ch. 5), and in respect to the method to be used in psychology (Ch. 6). A judicious look at science is of no less help in viewing true social openness as the very opposite to unspecified freedom (Ch. 7). Quite similar will appear the gist of the relation of ethical norms to science, especially when analyzed through its long history (Ch. 8).

Among the many constructive lessons which society can derive from the study of the history of science, one is available from a look at the present-day ferment of the Muslim world (Ch. 9). Another is on hand from a survey of scientific progress during the past hundred years (Ch. 10). Still another can be gathered from a major scandal of modern scientific life that has been carefully kept under cover for several decades (Ch. 11).

A collection of essays on science could not, of course, be complete without an essay appraising the deeper aspects of debates, very heated nowadays, about evolution (Ch. 12). The next-to-last essay presents the various forms in which science can become the kind of ideology that calls for a demythologization (Ch. 13). In the concluding essay the reader will find a survey of various conditions under which alone can science, this most powerful facet of modern life, be a source of hope (Ch. 14).

Notes have been added to the essays that originally saw publication without them. Only minor changes were made in the text of these fourteen essays published over a period of almost twenty years. No less than an earlier collection of my essays, *Chance or Reality,* this collection too has been the beneficiary of the interest of Mr. Gregory Wolfe, Publications Director of Intercollegiate Studies Institute.

S.L.J.

1

The Absolute Beneath the Relative: Reflections on Einstein's Theories

Einstein's work on relativity was not yet completed when it began to be taken for the scientific proof of the view that everything is relative. Such a view, widely entertained on the popular as well as on the academic level, is now a climate of thought. A stunning proof of this is a full-page advertisement in the September 24, 1979, issue of *Time* magazine.[1] It proclaims, under the picture of Einstein, in bold-face letters the message: EVERYTHING IS RELATIVE. The basic rule in advertising, it is well to recall, is a reliance on commonly accepted beliefs, on generally shared cravings, hopes, and fears, or, in short, on the prevailing climate of thought.

First published in *The Intercollegiate Review* (Spring/Summer 1985), pp. 29-38. Reprinted with permission.

The claim that something absolute may be lurking beneath relativity theory, may therefore be surprising, though not original at all. That Einstein's Relativity Theory implies elements and considerations that are absolutist in character was voiced by Planck as early as 1924 in an address "From the Relative to the Absolute,"[2] which quickly acquired world-wide publicity. Somewhat earlier Einstein himself began to make statements about the indispensability of metaphysics[3] which gave no comfort to positivists and empiricists, so many supporters of the view, in one sense or another, that there is nothing absolute and that therefore everything is relative. It could not have therefore come as a surprise to Philipp Frank that, as he lectured on relativity at the meeting of German physicists in Prague in 1929, a participant publicly warned him about the absolutist character of Einstein's ideas.[4] Frank refused to take heed for the rest of his life. The main proof of this is Frank's *Relativity—A Richer Truth,* a book distinctly insensitive to the perspective in which Einstein viewed relativity in particular and the philosophy of physics in general.[5]

The essence of that warning given at that Congress to Frank was that Einstein fully agreed with Planck that physical laws describe a reality which is independent of the perceiving subject. Doubts on that point were no longer permissible in 1931 when there appeared in print Einstein's contribution to the Maxwell commemorative volume, a contribution which began with the famous declaration: "Belief in an external world independent of the perceiving subject is the basis of all natural science."[6] Twenty years later, when the Vienna Circle regrouped itself in the United States, renewed efforts were made by spokesmen of the Circle, such as Reichenbach, to elicit a word or two from Einstein on behalf of their own "relativist" interpretation of Einstein's relativity. Einstein did not encourage them, though being aware that in turn, as he put it, they would charge him with the "original sin of metaphysics."[7] In his last essay on relativity, written in 1950, Einstein stated nothing less than that every true theorist was a tamed metaphysician, no matter how pure a positivist he fancied himself.[8]

In those statements Einstein denounced positivism, endorsed a realist metaphysics, and professed his belief in the objectivity of physical reality. Those statements (and many others that cannot be quoted here) were so many public and emphatic indications of his belief that there was something absolute beneath the relative. Yet, one would look in vain for any substantive trace of those statements in the books and articles written on relativity by Frank, Carnap, Reichenbach, Feigl, all members of the Vienna Circle, who in the 1950s and 1960s captured, in the USA at least, the role of authoritative spokesmen on behalf of Einstein in particular and of science in general. Their systematic silence on many a relevant statement and fact was only part of the strategy pursued by them. Instead of strategy, the word crusade would be more appropriate. Reichenbach himself warned that logical positivism should be looked upon as a crusade and not as an abstract philosophizing.[9] Intellectual crusades have their inner logic to which logical positivists were not immune. Or, as Herbert Feigl admitted two decades ago: "Confession, it is said, is good for the soul. Undoubtedly we [logical positivists] made up some facts of scientific history to suit our theories."[10]

Such a confession, rather incriminating for positivists, logical or other, who profess to be respectful only of facts, is hardly a spontaneous one. It is most likely triggered when a carefully contrived and nurtured make-believe or illusion is suddenly punctured. As to the long-cherished balloon of Einstein's positivism, it received a particularly stinging blow through the publication, in 1968 and 1969, respectively, of two extensive studies by Prof. G. Holton, "Mach, Einstein, and the Search for Reality," and "Einstein, Michelson, and the Crucial Experiment."[11] Neither of these massively documented essays is without some shortcoming. Although in Einstein's formulation of special relativity the experiment of Michelson and other experiments devised for the detection of the ether played no crucial role, they were familiar to Einstein and played some role in his reasoning. As to Einstein's departure from and opposition to Mach concerning reality, Holton did not quote two letters of Einstein which are particularly expressive in this respect and will be discussed later.

It would be rather naive to assume that such and similar documentations, nay Einstein's own statements repeated over four decades, would be effective in discrediting the climate of thought in which an allegedly exclusive respect for facts supports the tenet according to which everything is relative, and especially all values are relative. The ludicrous worshiping of "facts alone" and its invitation to unabashed selfishness, if not dishonesty, once the concomitant relativization of values is taken full advantage of, were already immortalized in Dickens' *Hard Times*. Clearly, the climate of thought in question had existed long before Einstein's relativity was cited on its behalf. Of the long story of the relativization of truth and values in Western thought, let it suffice here to note that pragmatism and behaviorism were catchwords for a long time before it became fashionable to justify them with copious references to a theory of physics, known as relativity.[12] A striking illustration of the relativization of truth and values as it asserts itself in our own days is that "crazy quilt of revised judgments"—the concise summary by an anonymous reviewer of the picture which emerges from a fairly recent survey of textbooks on American history. Not that Frances Fitzgerald, the author of that survey,[13] was particularly happy with the systematic discrediting of traditionally shared views on the foundation and purpose of this nation of ours. But she offered a very revealing justification of this unpleasant process: "All of us children of the twentieth century know or should know that there are no absolutes in human affairs." She also specified the source of this knowledge as "the pluralism or relativization of values."[14]

It is a redeeming value of her reasoning that she did not invoke Einstein's relativity as a support, a surprising departure from a standard technique. That the technique is such a standard can be gathered from that advertisement in *Time* which also offered as an unquestioned verity that "in the cool beautiful language of mathematics, Einstein demonstrated that we live in a world of relative values." The statement is as misleading as almost anything that makes for flashy advertisement. As all such advertisements, it reflects a tone of thought, or at least an unconscious wishful thinking—otherwise it would not have been seized upon by a highly professional advertising agency.[15] Interested in quick profit, such agencies are not the ones to prove in the language of mathematics, or in any language, that all values are relative.

To find the answer to this question a few hours of reading of Einstein's essays, or a consultation with anyone familiar with his writings and not blinded by positivism, would have been sufficient. Einstein never tried such a demonstration and certainly not in the cool and beautiful language of mathematics. This is not to suggest that Einstein offered no clues to his own thinking about values or that he was original or consistent in this respect. He merely voiced an old cliché when in the Foreword, which he volunteered to Frank's

Relativity—A Richer Truth, he specified man's instinctive avoidance of pain as *the* source of value judgments and of ethics itself. On this basis the relativity of values could only be a foregone conclusion.[16] It is, of course, well known that for all his dismissal of religion and of belief in a personal God, Einstein insisted on the unquestionable superiority of the Judeo-Christian perspective in which unconditional value is attributed to each and every human being. But his insistence was incompatible with mechanistic evolutionism which he also endorsed, although it provides, as has already been pointed out by such a protagonist of Darwin as T. H. Huxley, no room for "higher" and "lower."[17]

To his credit, Einstein consistently avoided basing his views on values and ethics on his theory of relativity and on mathematics. This shows something of his instinctive greatness, because history knows of some misguided men of science (Maupertuis and Condorcet, for instance) who tried to construe ethical theories from manipulating quantities.[18] As to his own theories, which, as will be seen, were more than mere mathematics, he stated emphatically four years before his death: "I have never obtained any ethical value from my scientific work."[19] To be sure, he made a few memorable utterances concerning freedom and oppression, but his general trend was to avoid involvement in human affairs. He declined the presidency of Israel with a reference to his lack of familiarity with personalities and society. Tellingly, his autobiography opens with the remark that he had never regretted that he had left behind the customary human world and moved into the strange, depersonalized world of science.[20]

Clearly, "the absolute beneath the relative" should, in connection with Einstein's theories, be sought in a direction different from what leads to values and ethics. Of the three main theories of Einstein—Special Relativity, General Relativity and Unified Field Theory—the first, on a cursory look at least, does not give a clue as to what the direction might be. The article in which Einstein formulated Special Relativity in 1905 had become the victim of a stereotyped reading. In the crudely superficial version of that reading, Special Relativity is an effort to explain the Michelson-Morley experiment. According to the moderately superficial version, Special Relativity "has its roots in the questions: Where are we? How are we moving?" An example of this latter version is the article "Relativity" by B. Hoffmann in *Dictionary of the History of*

Ideas, an article which starts with the foregoing questions.[21] Both readings can claim for their support one and the same phrase which, after a reference to electromagnetic induction and to the unsuccessful experiments aimed at discovering any motion of the earth relative to the ether, suggests that "the phenomena of electrodynamics as well as of mechanics possess no properties corresponding to the idea of absolute rest."[22] However, the explanation of the unsuccessful attempts had already been given by the Lorentz transforms and by the contraction postulated by FitzGerald. As to the absolute rest, its critique had already been offered two hundred years earlier by Berkeley on purely kinematic grounds. There had to be some specific and novel rationale in Einstein's handling two well-worn topics. The clue to this is given in the phrase which immediately follows the one just quoted above. There Einstein goes beyond the question of absolute rest with the remark that the null-results of those experiments rather suggest that "the same laws of electrodynamics and optics will be valid for all frames of reference for which the equations of mechanics hold good."

In itself the phrase is rather ambiguous: in the light of Einstein's train of thought leading to General Relativity and to Unified Field Theory, the phrase is a classic case of the inability of a genius to say explicitly what was truly in the back of his mind. Had Einstein italicized the word *same,* he would have strongly intimated that his principal concern was neither the explanation of the Michelson-Morley experiment, nor the problematic character of absolute rest. It was rather the *sameness* of the laws of electrodynamics, which the opening phrase of Einstein pointedly introduced as "Maxwell's electrodynamics." This electrodynamics had a special place in Einstein's thought. In his autobiography he referred to it as the "most fascinating subject" available in his student days.[23] Actually, he viewed it as the most fundamental subject in physics. The proof of this is his contribution in 1931 to the volume commemorating the centenary of Maxwell's birth. There, in surveying the latest developments of physical theory, including quantum mechanics, he claimed it as a certainty that ultimately physics will return to carrying out "the program which may properly be called as the Maxwellian—namely, the description of physical reality in terms of fields, which satisfy partial differential equations without singularities."[24]

The singularities implied by the context where the material

points (particles) which in Newton's physics represented the bed-rock of reality. They were replaced by fields in Maxwell's theory which, of course, did not mean the elimination of such singularities as constants and boundary conditions. But the notion of a field could not function as the post-Newtonian foundation of physics if it was the function of a particular frame of reference. Its independ-ence of any frame of reference could only be safeguarded if Max-well's equation retained the same form regardless of the frame of reference in consideration. This, however, implied the postulate of the constancy of the speed of light regardless of the motion of its source. Such is the ultimate justification of that postulate about which Einstein felt it necessary to note in his 1905 paper that it was "only apparently irreconcilable with the former" principle, which he unfortunately labeled "Principle of Relativity." The label, per-haps the most unfortunate in the entire history of physics, made him oblivious to the fact that he failed to reconcile fully two appar-ently contradictory points. One was the principle itself, which on a cursory look stated the relativity of all positions and motions. The other was the speed of light, endowed, as being not relative to the motion of its source, with an absolute character. His claim that be-tween these two points there was no basic irreconcilability made sense only if the expression "same laws of electrodynamics" meant the sameness of these laws in a somewhat different but certainly far deeper sense. He should have spelled out that if those laws retained their original form regardless of the frame of reference to which they were related, it was only because they reflected an objective, invariant, absolute cosmic order and reality.

Such was the gist of Einstein's explanation of Lorentz's trans-forms, which had already explained the null result of the Michelson-Morley experiment, but through which (and this was the all-important point not emphasized by Lorentz) Maxwell's equations retained the same form even when related to a frame of reference which moved at constant velocity with respect to another. That in 1905 Einstein himself was not entirely clear or explicit as to what was the real driving force behind his reasoning, is a secondary mat-ter.[25] The important thing is that his mind was in the grip of that driving force. It was the attractiveness of a specific vision of nature and of a most fruitful scientific interpretation of it.

The vision was that of a cosmic reality, fully coherent, unified and simple, existing independently of the observer, that is, not relative to him, and yielding its secrets in the measure in which the mathematical formulae through which it was investigated, embodied unifying power and simplicity. In the case of Special Relativity there was already a most unexpected and unintended yield, the absolute energy content of a mass at rest, given in the now historic formula $E = mc^2$.[26] Although at that time experimental evidence on behalf of that formula was ambiguous, Einstein upheld its validity by referring to the broad theoretical foundation on which it rested. The foundation was much broader than it appeared to be. The proof of this is his first essay on General Relativity, running over fifty pages, which was already in print in 1907.[27] Clearly, if Special Relativity had not been far more than the explanation of the null result of the Michelson-Morley experiment and an answer to the questions of where we are and how we move, Einstein would not have faced up to the problems of General Relativity while the printer's ink was still fresh on his Special Relativity. His real concern was the elaboration of a cosmic view in which physical reality was a totality of consistently interacting things, an absolute in the sense that its existence was not relative to any observer, and absolute also in the sense that if the observer's knowledge of reality was properly scientific, the laws in question had to remain as invariant as the universe is invariant. Indeed, Einstein himself suggested that Special Relativity should have been called the theory of invariance.

On the face of it, General Relativity is a further exercise in relativization. The impossibility of specifying any frame of reference as privileged over any other that move with respect to one another with constant velocity is extended in General Relativity to all frames of reference that are accelerated with respect to one another. The three classic observational consequences of General Relativity (the gravitational red-shift, the gravitational bending of light, and the precession of the perihelion of planetary orbits, observable in the case of Mercury) implied not only relativization but also equivalence or unification, namely, the equivalence of gravitational and inertial masses. That the thrust of General Relativity was indeed unification became all too obvious with the appearance in 1917 of Einstein's memoir, "Cosmological Considerations on the General Theory of Relativity."[28] Instead of 'considerations' Einstein should have perhaps written 'consideration.' The considerations he specified (the value of the total mass of the gravitationally interacting matter, the value of the radius of that totality, or the universe, the curvature of space-time) are well known. What is hardly ever recalled is the fact that all such considerations rest on one basic consideration: the power or ability of General Relativity to treat in a scientifically consistent manner the totality of material particles endowed with gravitation. That ability made scientific cosmology possible for the first time.

There were, of course, cosmologies before Einstein. Their scientific insignificance is not primarily the outcome of the relatively meager data that were available about the cosmos prior to the twentieth century. What makes those pre-Einstein cosmologies scientifically insignificant is that (with the exception of one proposed by Lambert) they were not free of a basic theoretical defect of which there was a sufficient awareness already in Newton's time. The defect concerns the infinity paradox which plagued the notion of the idea of an infinite universe whether it was homogeneous or hierarchical. The idea of a homogeneous infinite universe is usually connected with Newton's name. The basis of this connection is that the idea began to be mentioned by some scientists only from his time on. Although Newton, as it appears from his letters to Bentley, did not seem to think that an infinite homogeneous universe of stars is gravitationally impossible, he never departed from his early belief that the universe is finite whereas space itself was infinite.[29] Indeed, no protest was heard either from Newton or from others when in 1714 Addison attributed to Newton this idea of a finite universe in infinite space and praised it as the notion most worthy of reason and of God. Addison did so in the pages of the *Spectator*[30] which was read all over Europe.

Contrary to clichés in most histories of cosmology and science, the finiteness of the universe was the prevailing view until the early part of the nineteenth century. But as Lambert already pointed out in 1761, such a finite universe had to collapse gravitationally unless all its parts revolved around a center, possibly an enormously massive body. The rotating finite universe proposed by Lambert was hierarchically organized,[31] an organization which had already been proposed by Kant a few years earlier who argued the infinity of a hierarchically organized universe without realizing that his universe had to have an infinitely massive body at its center.[32] Earlier, Halley tried to save the infinity of the universe by suggesting that the distribution of stars was not homogeneous.[33]

He considered the optical part of the problem but not the gravitational one. In 1823 Olbers also failed to consider the gravitational paradox as he tried to solve the optical paradox by a recourse to the absorption of starlight in interstellar space,[34] a procedure already suggested in 1731 by Hartsoeker,[35] and in 1743 by Chéseaux.[36]

There was no echo when in 1872 Zöllner showed both that an infinite homogeneous universe was contradictory and that the only consistent way of treating the totality of gravitationally interacting matter was to take it to be finite in a four-dimensional non-Euclidean space. No major discussion followed when in 1895 Seeliger suggested a change in the inverse square law of gravitation to avoid the gravitational contradiction which arises in an infinite homogeneous universe. Needless to say, the slightest change in the inverse square law made impossible the explanation of planetary motions. In 1901 Kelvin summed up the paradox of an infinite universe in a concise formula, but he skirted the gravitational aspect and solved the optical aspect on the ground that the light coming from beyond the Milky Way was wholly negligible.[37] No discussion ensued when Charlier tried to save infinity in 1911 by assigning to the universe a hierarchical structure which, by implication at least, denied infinity to it.

What these glimpses into pre-Einsteinian cosmology should suggest is that glaringly defective arguments were taken in stride as long as they were proposed in defense of the infinity of matter or space or both. Behind this non-scientific attitude there must have been lying some non-scientific motivations. They derived from the fact that it was tempting to take infinite homogeneity as a necessary form of existence, that is, something which explained itself and was its own sufficient raison d'être. The shock therefore was considerable when in 1922 Einstein emphatically argued at the Sorbonne on behalf of the finiteness of the total mass of the universe.[38] Further refinements of estimates of the average density of matter, which calls for that finiteness of the total mass, did not fail to corroborate Einstein's argument. Einstein, of course, was fully aware that it was possible to construct four-dimensional world models that could accommodate an infinite amount of matter, and even with a homogeneous distribution. Einstein, however, brushed aside these models as insignificant, although he himself devised one, according to which the world lines were helically cylindrical.[39]

A universe embodying three-dimensional Euclidean homogeneity appears so natural to perception as to be taken for a natural or necessary form of material existence. A universe resembling either a spherical net or a saddle-like hyperbolic surface with no edges must strike one as a very specific and hardly a necessary form of existence. When faced with such a singular form of existence, one can hardly avoid facing up to the question: What makes the universe so specific? Of course, the universe need not be cylindrical in order to prompt this question. It is enough to think of the value of the space-time curvature which the universe actually has. It is a strange specific number, different from 0 which is the curvature of the intrinsically impossible homogeneous Euclidean universe. This 0 is a symbolic indication that such a universe, like 0, is a figment of imagination, bordering on mere nothing. A positive number, such as 0.8 or 1.6, standing for the space-time curvature, must strike one very differently. Looking at such a curvature should do what is done by a look at the tag of a dress, a tag carrying the measurement and price of the dress. Such a tag cannot help evoke the existence of a dressmaker.

Einstein himself was prompted to such considerations. His General Relativity, the first consistently scientific treatment of the universe as the totality of gravitationally interacting entities, reassured him in his previous instinctive conviction that the universe was real and fully rational. This was one of the reasons why he rejected the philosophy of Kant for whom the notion of the universe was a bastard product of the metaphysical cravings of the intellect. Once the notion of the universe was made out to be intrinsically unreliable, Kant could argue that any step from the universe to the Creator was also unreliable. But once the notion of the universe was fully vindicated by General Relativity, Kant's argument and his whole criticism of natural theology lost whatever credibility it could marshal.[40] Einstein was most conscious of the full force of this implication. In a letter written four years before his death to his life-long friend M. Solovine, Einstein insisted that it was not permissible to go beyond the universe to its Creator. The letter was a reassurance given by Einstein to Solovine that Einstein, the cosmologist, had not become a believer in a personal God and Creator. He foresaw that his cosmology would be exploited by priests and theologians. "It cannot be helped," Einstein wrote to Solovine. "I add this," Einstein continued, "lest you think that weakened by old age I have fallen into the hands of priests."[41]

Once the universe as a totality of consistently interacting things is recognized as such, all efforts to relativize everything reveal their futility at once. Tellingly, the most convincing proof of that totality, the 2.7°K cosmic background radiation, reminded some experts on relativity that the expansion of the universe was a non-relativist frame of reference.[42] At any rate, if not priests, at least some basic aspects of their theology must have been in the back of Einstein's mind for a reason relating to his efforts to work out a Unified Field Theory.[43] Twice, in the late 1920s and late 1940s, Einstein thought that he had achieved his goal. As is well known, he failed in both cases. But even if he had succeeded, only gravitation and electromagnetism would have been united and only on the macroscopic level. He did not think that Relativity and Quantum Theory could be united, except by replacing Quantum Theory with something else. He never worked on nuclear forces and was dead by the time the so-called weak forces came to be widely recognized. But with his Unified Field Theory he made a most notable effort toward a goal which has lately exerted a special fascination on cosmologists. The goal is the demonstration on theoretical grounds (mathematical and philosophical) that the universe (from atoms to galaxies) can only be what it is and nothing else. Einstein himself dreamed of a unified theory so simple that even the good Lord would not have been able to fashion the world along any other lines.

To his credit, Einstein never entirely parted with the humble recognition that the ultimate word in science belongs to facts, that is, to the observational verification of theories. Indeed, he did say around 1920 that if only one of the three classic proofs of General Relativity were to be disproved all General Relativity would turn into "mere dust and ashes."[44] Others, Eddington for instance, who were animated by the vision of a final theory, were not so mindful of the primacy of facts. A scientist is hardly mindful of facts when he declares before an audience of 2000 that within a few years, but certainly sooner or later, he or others will come up with a theory which shows why the family of elementary particles and therefore the universe can only be what it is and nothing else.[45] A mere recall of the fact that science can never be sure that it knows all the facts should suffice to dispose of such a brash dream. The intrinsic merits of the goal of devising an ultimate physical theory should also seem nil as long as the theory is sufficiently mathematical, which such a theory certainly has to be. Now Gödel's incompleteness theorem states that the proof of consistency of any non-trivial set of mathematical axioms can be found only outside that set, and in that sense no mathematical system can be an ultimate system. In other words, whereas General Relativity forces us to admit the realistic character of the notion of consistently interacting things, as a valid object of scientific cosmology, the application of Gödel's theorem to cosmology shows that a disproof of the contingency of the universe is impossible. The mental road to the extracosmic Absolute remains therefore fully open.

These points have been repeatedly made in several of my publications since 1966.[46] Apparently some in the scientific and philosophical community want to learn only what they want to hear, and therefore choose to ignore the tie between Gödel's theorem and cosmology. It is, of course, no surprise to me that the contingency of the universe is not pleasant news to a scientific humanism which claims that man is a mere accident, in no way subject to something transcendental to the entire universe. Such a humanism is more powerful in our times than it has ever been. This is why *Time* felt it natural to proclaim under Einstein's picture that everything is relative. The only message befitting Einstein's picture would have been a warning that the absolute is lurking everywhere beneath the relative. But *Time* is very human and so are our times, indeed all times. To this rather defective humanness of the times proper reflections on Einstein's work may bring a much needed corrective. Failing that, there will be no slowing down of that culturally destructive merry-go-round which witnesses the absolutization of the relative by those who are busy relativizing the absolute.

[1]The advertisement, facing page 64, was on behalf of *Time* itself.

[2]The address, "Vom Relativen zum Absoluten," has been a part of the best known collection of Planck's addresses, *Wege zur physikalischen Erkenntnis: Reden und Vorträge*, from its first edition (1933) on. A somewhat free English version is available in M. Planck, *Where is Science Going?* (New York: W.W. Norton, 1932), pp. 170-200. In that address Planck emphasized the absolute value of energy in terms of the formula $E = mc^2$ and the independence of the total four-dimensional space-time manifold from the observer.

[3]See G. Holton, "Mach, Einstein, and the Search for Reality" (1968), in *Thematic Origins of Scientific Thought* (Cambridge, Mass.: Harvard University Press, 1973), p. 243.

[4]Reported by Frank himself in *Einstein: His Life and Times* (New York: A. Knopf, 1947), p. 215.

[5]London: Jonathan Cape, 1951. The book certainly reveals the futility of the efforts of a pragmatist to vindicate universal validity for a democratic way of life on the basis of the "relativity of knowledge." The offspring of that relativity were, according to Frank, "not only modern science, but also liberal Christianity and reformed Judaism" (p. 20), a statement which gives away its true character to anyone mindful of the chronic inability of both liberal Christianity and of Reformed Judaism to proclaim anything absolute.

[6]A. Einstein, *The World as I See It* (New York: Covici-Friede, 1934), p. 60.

[7]See his "Reply to Criticisms," in P. A. Schilpp, ed., *Albert Einstein: Philopher-Scientist* (Evanston: Library of Living Philosophers, 1949), p. 673.

[8]"On the Generalized Theory of Gravitation," in *Ideas and Opinions by Albert Einstein* (New York: Crown, 1954), p. 342.

[9]"The whole movement of scientific philosophy is a crusade. . . . What I'm doing aims as directly at social consequences as the programs of those who call themselves 'social reformers.' " Statement reported by C. Schuster in M. Reichenbach and R. S. Cohen, eds., *Hans Reichenbach: Selected Writings, 1909-1953* (Dordrecht: D. Reidel, 1978), vol. I, pp. 56-57.

[10]H. Feigl, "Beyond Peaceful Coexistence," in R. H. Stuewer, ed., *Historical and Philosophical Perspectives of Science* (Minneapolis: University of Minnesota Press, 1970), p. 3.

[11]The latter too is reprinted in Holton's *Thematic Origins of Scientific Thought*, pp. 261-352.

[12]Relativity was still a novelty for many a physicist in the 1920s, which saw the publication of *Relativity in Man and Society* (New York: G.P. Putnam's Sons, 1926) by A. Bentley, with its ch. 2, entitled: "The Term 'Einstein'—Its Meanings." The next two books, though separated by a World War, a continent, and opposite theses, have one small but revealing detail in common. In his *In Quest of Morals* (Stanford University Press, 1941), H. Lanz quotes (p. 19) H. Weyl on behalf of his claim that relativity supports philosophical and ethical relativism, who is also quoted, but in the opposite sense, in H. Wein's *Das Problem des Relativismus* (Berlin: W. De Gruyter, 1950), p. 26. No relevance is accorded to relativity (and no mention of Einstein is made) in three epistemological rebuttals of relativism: G. Rabeau, *Réalité et relativité* (Paris: Marcel Rivière, 1927); H. Spiegelberg, *Antirelativismus* (Zurich: Max Niehans, 1935); G. D. Kaufmann, *Relativism, Knowledge and Faith* (Chicago: University of Chicago Press, 1960). The following two books are relevant also because of the title of this essay. In *Relativisme* (Paris: Kra, 1930), a little known work by A. Maurois, there is a chapter, "L'Absolu dans le relatif" (pp. 69-76), devoted to the impossibility of "complete" relativism, though with no reference to Einstein or rela-

tivity. Both Einstein and relativity are prominently in view from the very start in *Il n'y a d'absolu que dans le relatif* (Paris: J. Vrin, 1975) by R. Levi.

[13]*Time,* Sept. 10, 1979, p. 68, in a review of *America Revised: History Schoolbooks in the Twentieth Century* (New York: Little, Brown, 1979) by Frances Fitzgerald.

[14]Ibid., p. 69.

[15]That such is the case is palpably shown by another full-page advertisement on behalf of *Time* (Nov. 12, 1979, p. 124) which, under the picture of two famous ballet dancers, carries the caption: "News, like beauty, is often in the eye of the beholder."

[16]Einstein was not unaware of this possibility, but to make matters worse, he tried to save the norms of ethics from pure arbitrariness with a reference to "the psychological and genetic point of view." *Out of My Later Years* (New York: Philosophical Library, 1950), p. 110. In doing so he only presented himself as an easy target to any skillful debater who has been granted the basic philosophical premises of Darwinism.

[17]See *More Letters of Charles Darwin: A Record of His Work in a Series of Hitherto Unpublished Letters,* ed. F. Darwin and A. C. Seward (New York: D. Appleton, 1903), vol. I, p. 360.

[18]For details, see my *The Relevance of Physics* (Chicago: University of Chicago Press), pp. 376-78.

[19]Quoted in P. Michelmore, *Einstein, Profile of the Man* (New York: Dodd, 1962), p. 251.

[20]*Albert Einstein: Philosopher-Scientist,* p. 5.

[21]New York: Charles Scribner and Sons, 1968-74; vol. III, p. 74.

[22]"On the Electrodynamics of Moving Bodies," in *The Principle of Relativity: A Collection of Original Memoirs on the Special and General Theory of Relativity by H. A. Lorentz, A. Einstein, H. Minkowski and H. Weyl,* with notes by A. Sommerfeld, translated by W. Perrett and G. B. Jeffrey (1923; New York: Dover, n.d.), pp. 37-38.

[23]*Albert Einstein: Philosopher-Scientist,* p. 33.

[24]"Clerk Maxwell's Influence on the Evolution of the Idea of Physical Reality," in A. Einstein, *The World as I See It,* p. 66.

[25]Inattention to this point lies at the root of that controversial chapter on relativity in E. T. Whittaker's *A History of the Theories of Aether and Electricity, Volume Two: The Modern Theories 1900-1926* (London: Thomas Nelson, 1953), pp. 27-77, in which Einstein appears a minor figure in comparison with Poincaré and Lorentz.

[26]After writing in 1905 the energy content of a mass as being equal to L/c^2 and in 1906 as E/V^2, he finally put in 1907 the energy E as being equal to μc^2, still not exactly the now standard notation.

[27]"Ueber das Relativitätsprinzip und die aus demselben gezogenen Fol-

gerungen," *Jahrbuch der Radioactivität und Elektronik* 4 (1907), pp. 411-62.

[28]*The Principle of Relativity,* pp. 177-88.

[29]See A. R. and M. B. Hall, *Unpublished Scientific Papers of Isaac Newton* (Cambridge: Cambridge University Press, 1962), p. 138.

[30]See the issue, July 9, 1714. An equally important witness is Voltaire in the uncounted editions of his *Elémens de la philosophie de Newton* (1738) and in its partial enlargement in his booklet, *La métaphysique de Newton ou parallèle des sentimens de Newton et de Leibniz* (Amsterdam: chez Jacques Desbordes, 1740), in which he emphasized the infinity of space and the finiteness of matter with a reference to the authority of Newton (p. 2).

[31]Lambert did so in his *Cosmologische Briefe.* See my translation, *Cosmological Letters on the Arrangement of the World-Edifice,* with an introduction and notes (New York: Science History Publications, 1976).

[32]For details see the introduction of my translation of his *Allgemeine Naturgeschichte und Theorie des Himmels* or *Universal Natural History and Theory of the Heavens* (Edinburgh: Scottish Academic Press, 1981).

[33]For a reprint of his two papers, see my *The Paradox of Olbers' Paradox* (New York: Herder and Herder, 1969), pp. 249-52.

[34]For a discussion and a reprint of his paper, see *ibid.,* pp. 131-43 and pp. 256-64.

[35]He did so in his *Cours de physique* (The Hague: chez Jan Swart, 1730), p. 235.

[36]For a reprint of Chéseaux's paper, see my *Paradox of Olbers' Paradox,* pp. 253-55.

[37]See my "Das Gravitations-Paradoxon des unendlichen Universums," *Sudhoffs Archiv* 63 (1979), pp. 105-22, and my *The Milky Way: An Elusive Road for Science* (New York: Science History Publications, 1972), pp. 275-77.

[38]Typically, the French physicist, E. Borel, was willing to grant only the "convenience" of the finiteness of mass in his exposition of Einstein's theories, *L'espace et le temps* (Paris: F. Alcan, 1922). See its English translation, *Space and Time* (London: Blackie and Son, 1926), pp. 226-27.

[39]"Cosmological Considerations on the General Theory of Relativity," in *The Principle of Relativity,* p. 179. It should be revealing that Eddington, in his *Space, Time and Gravitation: An Outline of the General Relativity Theory* (Cambridge: Cambridge University Press, 1920) objected to Einstein's world-model on the ground that it reinstated absolute space-time (see p. 162)!

[40]For the inconclusiveness of Kant's criticism of the cosmological argument, see my *The Road of Science and the Ways to God* (Gifford Lectures, Edinburgh, 1974-75 and 1975-76; Chicago: University of Chicago Press, 1978), pp. 121-22 and pp. 379-80.

[41]Letter of March 30, 1952, in A. Einstein, *Lettres à Maurice Solovine,* reproduites en facsimile et traduites en française (Paris: Gauthier-Villars, 1956), pp. 114-15. For longer excerpts in English translation from this and Einstein's preceding letter to Solovine, see my *Cosmos and Creator* (Edinburgh: Scottish Academic Press; Chicago: Regnery-Gateway, 1980), pp. 52-53.

[42]See P. G. Bergmann, "Cosmology as a Science," in R. J. Seeger and R. S. Cohen, eds., *Philosophical Foundations of Science* (Dordrecht: D. Reidel, 1974), pp. 181-88, who speaks of the "breakdown of the principle of relativity with respect to the background radiation" (p. 185).

[43]The same was realized very early by Einstein: "This point [the moment of the Big Bang] is thus de facto preferred. . . . Naturally this does not constitute a disproof, but the circumstance irritates me," he wrote to De Sitter on June 22, 1917. See *Nature,* Oct. 9, 1975, p. 454.

[44]A statement made by Einstein in 1920 during a lecture given in Prague which was attended by young H. Feigl who recalled it many years later. See *Historical and Philosophical Perspectives of Science,* p. 9.

[45]Professor Murray Gell-Mann, at the Twelfth Nobel Conference, October 6, 1976, held at Gustavus Adolphus College, St. Peter, Minnesota.

[46]Such as *The Relevance of Physics,* pp. 128-30; *The Road of Science and the Ways to God,* p. 456; *Cosmos and Creator,* pp. 49-50; and "From Scientific Cosmology to a Created Universe," *Irish Astronomical Journal* 15 (March 1982): pp. 253-62.

2

The Impasse of Planck's Epistemology

Classical physics emerged in a context of explicit epistemological presuppositions. They were put forward—it is enough to think of Galileo's evaluation of the respective merits of primary and secondary qualities and of Newton's unabashed Cartesianism in the Queries of the *Opticks*—in a tome which suggests not only the bearing of physics on epistemology but a radical subordination of epistemology to physics. About the emergence of modern physics few beliefs have become more widespread than the one according to which quantum theory and relativity have revolutionized not only physics but epistemology as well. No small role has been played in

First published in *Philosophia* (Athens), 15-16 (1985-86), pp. 467-88. Reprinted with permission.

that respect by headlines, often inspired by statements of prominent physicists. The headline, "Physicists redefine reality," in the August 25, 1981 issue of *The Economist,* could hardly have been more epistemological.[1] Quite a few physicists believe that they can do more with reality than merely redefine it. That material reality is the product of space-time geometries and that even the whole universe issued out of a non-commutative algebraic operator, or, more picturesquely, out of a mere quantum flip, are the not-too-esoteric forms of some prominent physicists' belief that reality is the product of their mind.

The ability to produce reality by mere thought, and even the mere competence to redefine reality, would more than ensure the superiority of physics over epistemology. All-important as such a superiority may appear, it may not be referred to in contexts which deal with the professional advancement of a physicist. In today's frantic race for prestigious chairs, research grants, memberships in scientific academies, let alone for a Nobel Prize (and even for a quantum, that is, a half, a third, or a mere fourth of it), among the qualifications advanced on behalf of a physicist none would relate to the presumed epistemological value of his work. This pattern—a clear evidence of professional purism—is not at all new. It played a part in the process which saw most physicists quietly discard their erstwhile title, "natural philosophers." Planck clearly broke the rules of that purism when in 1910 he urged the Prussian government that Einstein be made a member of the Berlin Academy partly because of his work's bearing on epistemology.[2]

Nothing is more tempting than to look for explanation in the cultural and social context for Planck's departure from unwritten rules. In a Prussia, which almost a hundred years earlier almost begged Hegel to accept the chair of philosophy in Berlin so that the spirit of the nation might thereby be redressed and reinvigorated,[3] philosophy elicited greater awe than elsewhere in the Western World. Philosophy further gained in esteem in that newly-formed Reich which strove to put the German intellectual and scientific heritage on a pedestal comparable to French and British grandeur. The effort was highly successful even abroad. It became a byword in the Third Republic that German schoolmasters were ultimately responsible for the outcome of the war of 1870. As to Britain, its leading philosophers around 1900 did not like to recall, as noted by William James, the incomprehension which their predecessors professed with respect to Kant.[4] American colleges, eager to become universities, sent their younger faculty above all to Germany to learn the art of scholarship and looked at Lotze, who launched Neo-Kantianism, as the leading spirit of the day. In the First Reich the rise and flourishing of Neo-Kantianism, which reached its zenith around 1910, was an aspect of the creation of a pantheon of the heroes of the German mind.

Although Planck was an unabashed patriot who, as will be seen, shared his times' admiration for Kant, his attention to epistemology, of which his recommendation of Einstein was a proof, had roots more personal than social. More than thirty years earlier Planck, who could have made a good career as a mathematician or as a musician, chose physics precisely because physics appeared to him as the most effective tool for securing a solid *Weltanschauung*. The choice was all the more personal because young Planck was emphatically advised by a noted physicist against choosing physics for a career. He would have undoubtedly met with slight ridicule had he disclosed his budding conviction that physical research, if done properly, could lead to the 'absolute.'[5] Indeed, around 1880, when Planck, aged twenty-two, stood between his doctorate and his *Habilitationschrift*, a quest for the 'absolute' could not find much echo with German scientists. They for the most part were engaged in research geared to technological application or in experimental *tours de force* aimed at greatly increasing the precision of measurements. The latter attitude was facetiously embodied in Kohlrausch's often-quoted readiness to measure with perfect accuracy anything, be it the flow of rainwater in the gutter,[6] hardly a venture issuing in epistemological reflections. The relatively few physicists interested in theory sided with Kirchoff's methodological positivism which again was no prompting for pursuing philosophy and *Weltanschauung* unless in the sense of putting both beyond the pale of intellectual respectability, or, at best, keeping them as objects of courteous lip service. Even in that form philosophy was resented by Ernst Mach, who from the 1880s on exerted an increasing influence on German physicists. He never failed to urge that, in constructing physical theory, they should consider only what was directly observable, that is, sensory, and in that sense non-metaphysical.

Within such a professional milieu Planck's ambition to reach the 'absolute' through physics had to appear something to be kept to himself. Nor did he seem to have any clear idea at that time as to what was implied philosophically by that search for the 'absolute.' During his years in Kiel (1885-89), which started his professional career, he felt that his research program was compatible with Mach's philosophy,[7] a judgment hardly indicative of philosophical or epistemological perspicuity. While within a decade or so he had fully cured himself of Machism and opted for Kant, for whom he kept a deep reverence to the end, he never wanted to appear in the mantle of a philosopher. He firmly believed that it was as a physicist that he had waged a crusade during his last forty years on behalf of the 'absolute,' by which he often meant an objective universe. In a much deeper sense than he suspected, he was right in his belief.

Had Kantianism or Neo-Kantianism been effective in inspiring commitment to the 'absolute,' Planck would not have felt the need for a crusade on behalf of an ideal form of physics, a crusade above all aimed at the world of physicists. That crusade forms part of a story, which stretched from Planck's initial commitment to the physical absolute through his weaning himself from antirealist (Machist) theories of physics to his campaign on behalf of an absolute causal order in nature, which in turn was the background of Planck's final grappling with a subtly personal Absolute. It is a story in which Planck's commitment to his notion of the ideal form of physics (science) and his scientific creativity acted as motivation and safeguard, a story told elsewhere.[8] The story shows all too well that taking physics for epistemology calls for the same unlimited play of the force of logic that is displayed time and again in major philosophical systems. Once objective reality was given a recognition in Planck's unconditional manner, a specific train of thought exerted itself, even though some philosophical presuppositions, incompatible with that recognition were simultaneously at work.

Had Planck, the epistemologist, been basically a Kantian and a consistent one, he would have by instinct reached Kant's conclusion that God was merely an idea within him,[9] precisely because the universe as spoken by Kant was but such an idea. But the universe, being supremely objective for Planck the physicist, not only prevented him from being trapped in an idealist ego, but also made him, in the long run, move beyond the universe. This thrust of a truly objective universe is noticeable in most varied and telling contexts. It should seem telling indeed that a Henry Adams, who was raised in an ambience which "solved the universe so thoroughly" that none of the major problems that agitated mankind since times immemorial seemed "worth discussing," came to recognize that if he "were obliged to insist on a Universe, he seemed driven to the Church."[10] Einstein for one felt the need to ease with the remark, "I had not yet fallen in the hands of priests," the anxiety of a friend who worried about a possible theological impact on Einstein of his cosmological thought.[11]

Not so far reaching is, of course, the central problem for Planck the epistemologist to be considered here. In a superficial sense, the problem is the extent to which Planck should be considered the founder of modern physics. Nobody would call in doubt that he was the first to enunciate in 1900 the notion of the "quantum of action" as a universal and real feature of the physical world. Yet it fell to others (Heisenberg, Schrödinger, and Born) to construct around 1926 the science of quantum mechanics, which in view of its enormus success was once described by Schrödinger as "the Lord's quantum mechanics."[12] Planck was not the first to propose something much less, namely, the propagation of electromagnetic radiation in quanta and, contrary to the stereotyped view, he was not even the first to propose its quantized emission or rather generation. His theories of black-body radiation, of which he offered at least two major versions between 1905 and 1920, did not imply a break with classical concepts.[13] Within the framework of those theories, to quote a remark of his from 1905, "the introduction of the *finite* energy quantum h is an additional hypothesis, foreign to the . . . theory."[14] In fact, for all his pride in discovering h and for all his firm belief in its physical and universal significance, he was never at ease with it. "I hate the discontinuity of energy," he wrote in 1915, "even more than the discontinuity of emission."[15]

In his Nobel Prize acceptance speech, delivered in June 1920, there was a distinct touch of pleasure mixed with apprehension. He could but register his satisfaction over the fact that the "quantum of action" made possible the explanation of phenomena ranging from the photoelectric effect through the variation with temperature of the specific heat of solids, to the vast world of spectral lines. That not he but others were responsible for all those feats was acknowledged by him with a generosity untainted by any trace of jealousy. His apprehension related to what in his eyes was a very great price to be paid for all that his discovery led to. The quantum of action was imposing the need to recast "physical ideas which since the foundation of the infinitesimal calculus by Leibniz and Newton, were built on the assumption of continuity of all causal relations."[16] Planck here could but think of the fact that he derived his famous formula not through "integrating" the various modes (energy states) of ideal resonators but through the process of "summation." The latter foreclosed that mathematical continuity which is implied in going to the limit in infinitesimal calculus.

The quantum of action, which emerged on the horizon in 1900, was by 1920 no longer a new element to be fitted into a structure with hardly any change in it. After two decades of proving its immense usefulness, the new element required the undermining of the structure itself. To Planck's brooding question, "at what place and to what degree will this happen?" physics gave an answer within half a dozen years, an answer that became the accepted view, a dogma, to almost all concerned. The nature of the answer was foreconditioned in that phrase of Planck about "the continuity of all causal relations," a phrase much more significant than Planck would have suspected. Therein lies the source of the problem which became an insoluble impasse in Planck's epistemology as well as in the prevailing epistemological interpretation of modern physics. The chief instructiveness of Planck's epistemology lies in that connection.

In speaking of Planck's epistemology several reservations are in order. They are imposed by the fact that Planck was not a philosopher, not even a serious student of philosophy, but a working physicist. As in the case with almost all physicists, Planck did not work out a philosophical system. His only detailed and fairly systematic articulation of philosophical (epistemological) themes is an address he gave on February 17, 1923. By then he was in his 65th year, hardly the age to start in philosophy or anything else. The address, a long public lecture delivered in the Berlin Academy of Sciences on causality and free will,[17] is still to be given its due by historians of the philosophy of modern physics. Planck worked into that lecture philosophical considerations which he had voiced briefly in the previous fifteen years in half a dozen lectures that dealt with the ideal form of physical science in the light of new discoveries and advances.[18] The same lecture also contained several new philosophical reasonings which Planck later reiterated with minor variations. Analysis and appraisal of the lecture are helped by its simple structure and, last but not least, by the clarity of Planck's style which is often presented as model of exposition.

The starting point of the lecture was the plain admission on Planck's part that his reason for discussing the topic derived from his interest in physics and especially in its reliability as the most exact of all sciences. It cannot be emphasized enough that Planck was interested in philosophy only insofar as the cultivation of physics called for philosophical reflections. Moreover, and this is a no less important point, about physics Planck had a very definite idea. It was by no means an original idea with him. Long before him (it is enough to think of Galileo and Newton) many physicists held that the essence of physics was the investigation of causal processes taking place in a physical universe existing independently of the physicist's reflections. Of course, by the time Planck came to the scene a philosophy of mechanistic causality was no longer an invariably shared part of the physicist's conception of his work. Formalism, positivism, economism, and even mere commodism (it should be enough to recall the names of Lagrange, Kirchoff, Mach, and Poincaré) were receiving more and more votes from leading physicists. The thermodynamics of irreversible processes invited antimechanistic views, a point articulated with great persuasiveness by Duhem.[19] Mechanists or not, physicists were at one in stressing the ability of physical theory to predict future occurrences, an ability which Planck emphatically took for the evidence of mechanistic causality. He was fond of referring to that ability with a reference to that superior spirit to whom, as Laplace once memorably stated, no future physical event would be hidden because all physical parameters determining the present were fully known to him. While in Laplace's rendering that knowledge of the future was restricted to physical events, in Planck's version (and this should be indicative of his commitment to mechanistic causality) it included all mental phenomena and even the acts of will.[20]

Defense of the reliability of physics amounted therefore to a defense of causality. Such was even in Planck's admission a narrow perspective. He should have rather referred to its shallowness, and all the more so because he could see merit in viewpoints of distinctly greater philosophical depth. Thus he did not dismiss out of hand the view that "philosophy must precede every special science" and that it was contrary to the dictate of reason "if one of the special sciences were to take up the treatment of general philosophical questions."[21] There could, however, be no point in retaining some measure of competence for philosophy in connection with causality if it was true that causality could not be vindicated by philosophy of which Planck recognized only an abstract (rationalist) and an empiricist version. An impasse was therefore in sight already at the end of the first part of Planck's lecture where he gave a survey of the problem of causality in those two schools of thought which for him represented *all* philosophy. He knew not of a third school, a school of philosophical realism, a school called for by that emphatic assertion of Planck that by causality he meant above all causality in the *real* world.[22] The business of reality rested in Planck's eyes with physics alone. The narrowness of this view was intimated by the fact that what he asked from philosophy was not so much a proof of the fact of causality, but whether causality could be scientifically ascertained in all circumstances and on all levels. Clearly, what Planck wanted to secure was a very narrow aspect of causality implied in a very specific type of physics whose exclusive validity was by 1923 threatened not only by statistical mechanics, but even more so by considerations which the emission and propagation of electromagnetic radiation in the form of quanta kept inspiring.

Planck's spirited attachment to that very specific if not oblique sense of causality (strict predictability of future events, in each and every case, by the methods of mathematical physics) was hardly an invitation to philosophy. That he could not see philosophy as the source of answer to the question of causality could also be gathered from his conclusion that causality was not a necessary element of human thought. He reached that conclusion on the ground that the human mind could imagine all sorts of contradictory and non-causal situations, non-sequiturs, and sheer fantasies. It wholly escaped Planck that if this proved anything, it proved only that the mind was more than a mere logic machine and that this alone secured the possibility that he himself could take such a look at the question of causality which was not a predetermined series of reasonings and therefore a meaningful topic to consider.

Planck the philosopher hardly distinguished himself as he surveyed the answer of philosophies to the specific question whether causality was unrestrictedly valid. The rationalist or deductive approach to causality he saw exemplified in the Greco-Scholastic school, in Descartes, in Spinoza, and in Leibniz. Planck seemed to be satisfied with at least that aspect of Spinoza's system according to which the divine was identical with everything to such an extent as to exclude the possibility that even a miracle might break the chain of causality. That the Spinozean system did not allow for the existence of particular things, the very things which physics was supposed to investigate,[23] was not considered by Planck. About Leibniz, Planck remembered only his monadology without warning that monadology foreclosed interaction (and therefore causality) among individual things, so many monads or strictly isolated entities in ultimate analysis. Planck did not as much as hint about the realist strain in Leibniz, a strain harking back to Leibniz's familiarity with some of the very foundations of Scholastic philosophy, which prompted his famous question: "Why is there something rather than nothing?"[24] Planck's rendering of Descartes makes one wonder whether Planck knew of him except by hearsay. He stated as Descartes' starting point that the universe was God's free creation and therefore miracles were possible. Such a rendering was certainly characteristic of Planck's deep uneasiness about the breaking of the causal chain but rather distortive of Descartes' philosophy, the essence of which was that God had to create (if he created at all—Descartes the philosopher was very different from Descartes the Christian) the actually existing world because one could, through Descartes' method, convincingly derive its main features from a priori considerations.[25]

As to Planck's rendering of "Greco-Scholastics," one has to be somewhat, though not overly, indulgent. Planck was the product of a cultural ambience in which the precept, *catholica non leguntur* (books written by Catholic scholars need not be read), was voiced even by such luminaries as Harnack, Planck's predecessor as perpetual secretary of the Berlin Academy. By 1923 Neo-Scholasticism in Germany produced not only a vast number of meticulously documented historical studies of scholastic philosophy but also some high-level popularizations[26] which gave so many lies to Planck's assertion that "in the historical rationalist school" (Scholastics) one was faced with a "hybrid attempt of fusing the Greek Prime Mover of Aristotle with the Hebrew Jehovah so that room might be left for supernatural intervention in the causal chain."[27] That Yahweh was the ground of existence for the Scholastics rather than a mere Prime Mover was a notion that did not seem to have ever come within Planck's ken. He opined that in the

Scholastic outlook the First Being was a mere replica of the visible world, so that, to quote Planck's words, "the concept of the Divinity in this case must take its color from the world-outlook either of the individual philosopher in question or of the particular cultural background to which he belongs."[28] The statement clashed head-on with the insistence of all great Scholastics, and certainly with the insistence of Thomas and Scotus, that all knowledge, natural and supernatural, about God is essentially negative.[29] Had Planck informed himself, however modestly, on Scholastic philosophy, he might have seen that the Scholastics, precisely because they believed in creation out of nothing, could extricate even physics from an impasse where it was left by the insistence of Aristotle and other Greek philosophers on the unbrokenness of causal chain, an insistence which Planck tied to their espousal of the principle *ex nihilo nihil fit*.[30]

Planck's lack of interest in the question why the chain itself existed was an all the more revealing feature of his epistemology because he rallied to the defense of objective reality long before Einstein himself was driven to a staunch espousal of the realist position. Planck was a realist not as a philosopher but as a physicist. He failed to perceive that a realist philosophy was implied in his penetrating evaluation of the empiricists' handling of causality. Useful as the empiricist school was in breaking with what Planck called the naiveté of the rationalist school, and oriented as it was toward science, it was nevertheless trapped in solipsism. Sensations, Planck insisted, were entirely subjective and did not entitle one to deduce the existence of an object. The succession of sensations could in no way be construed as an evidence of objective causality, because the force of habit did not in itself explain why the attribution was to be made at all. The empiricists (whether represented by Locke or Hume) could not, Planck remarked, logically argue that their dreams were different from their thinking while being awake. Of course, the empiricists could and did fall back on common sense, but it was not something which they could invoke on the basis of strictly logical inferences starting from the initial presupposition that sensations were the sole primary data.

As one might expect, Berkeley's method of escaping from the solipsism of Locke's sensationism did not find favor with Planck. For one thing, the method was not tailored for ordinary material reality, for another, it was contrived to make possible miracles, so

many breaks in the causal chain which Planck could not coun-
tenance. Quite different was Planck's appraisal of Kant. Whatever
the arbitrariness and dogmatism of some of Kant's assertions, his
teaching was "useful and conclusive in most of its results," so
Planck declared.[31] Such was a position typical of a Neo-Kantian
who preferred to ignore all those results of Kantian philosophy
which made themselves fully felt in Kant's *Opus postumum*. About
the thousands of manuscript pages making up that work, discovered in the 1880s, the standard view then as now was that they
were mere jottings by an increasingly senile Kant and not an
integral part of the task which Kant had set for himself. The
"critical" viewpoint which Kant implemented for metaphysics
(*Critique of Pure Reason*) and extended to ethics (*Critique of Practical Reason*), esthetics (*Critique of Judgment*), and afterwards to
pedagogy and theology,[32] had to be spelled out in detail also for the
sciences if "critical" philosophy was to obtain its ultimate touch-
stone of truth. The result was sheer horror, *Naturphilosophie*,[33]
about which Neo-Kantians preferred the strategy of silence.
Planck, and this should be indicative of his uncritical Neo-Kantianism, never referred to that aspect of Kant's system, nor did he
refer to *Naturphilosophie* as practiced by Kant's successors,
Schelling, Hegel, and others, although it was the target of very
critical and well known remarks by such prominent German physicists as Gauss and Helmholtz.[34]

According to Planck, Kant was the first to point out that in addition to sensations, there was another source of knowledge, the
categories, among them causality, independent of all experience.
Causality, conceived in such a way, imposed on the human mind the
recognition that anything that happens presupposes something
from which it follows according to a law. Such was Kant's way, as
Planck put it, "to jump the wall separating the senses from reality
at some part of it, preferably at the beginning." The jump was
metaphysical and Planck readily admitted that "we cannot avoid
metaphysics if we are to save ourselves from falling into the dead-
lock of solipsism."[35] But to what extent did Planck need metaphysics? Without spelling out the weak aspects of Kant's metaphysical jump to reality, he stated that they could be "strengthened
for all *practical* purposes" (italics added) and thus a compromise
(obviously epistemological) could be worked out.[36] That compromise was in substance the pragmatism contained in the *Critique of*

Practical Reason. That it did not differ at all from the positivists' justification of causality on the basis of its "usefulness" wholly escaped Planck as he closed his survey of the philosophical efforts to do justice to causality. The grand conclusion of that survey was that "the nature and universal validity of the law of causation cannot be definitely decided upon any grounds of purely abstract reasoning."[37] Clearly, Kant could be retained only as the author of *Practical Reason.* Planck's statement that "the transcendental and positivist viewpoints are irreconcilable and they will remain so as long as the race of philosophers lasts," could not therefore be construed in the sense that the transcendental viewpoint was right, however undemonstrable, even if this was what he meant.

Now that philosophy proved itself impotent in reference to causality, one had to turn to the sciences for help. To be sure, the turn was to be mindful of the rights of philosophy, but in the end all basic rights of philosophy were to be handed over to physics. This was implied already in an earlier statement of Planck who conceded causality as being ultimately a philosophical question only on the condition that there should be a collaboration between philosophy and the sciences. The collaboration (as far as causality was concerned) was a mere subjection of philosophy to physics. Or as Planck phrased the *dénouement* of the problem of causality:

> In the case of a definite problem which philosophy recognizes as fundamental and the final solution of which is the business of philosophy alone, but about which philosophy cannot come to a decisive formulation by the use of its own methods, it must seek information from the special branches of science in regard to particular features of the problem at issue. Now if the answer here turned out to be definite and final, then it must be treated as such. It is a characteristic mark of every true science that the general and objective knowledge which it arrives at has a universal validity. Therefore the definite results which it obtains demand an unqualified   acknowledgment and must always hold good. The progressive discoveries of science are definite and cannot permanently be ignored.[38]

Planck's reasoning, which equated a particular feature of a thing with the thing itself, should not be a cause of surprise in view of his idea of a definite progress displayed by physics. The importance of that idea cannot be emphasized enough if one is to have a proper grasp of Planck's epistemology which, as previously noted, was ruled by a very specific and rather exalted notion of physical science. This led to an impasse in Planck's epistemology similar to that of Kant. Planck would have hardly recognized his own predicament had he read Kant's "Enquiry concerning the Clarity of the Principles of Natural Theology and Ethics," written in 1763. There, under the influence of Bishop Warburton's remarks on the atrophying effect on the mind of exclusively geometrical studies, Kant made the very valid and profound statement that nothing harmed philosophy more than its having been cultivated along the lines of geometry, a particular science.[39] Almost in the same breath Kant blinded himself to this insight by suggesting that philosophy should be patterned after physics. Even if Planck had read the "Enquiry," he did not have to remember it in order to write the foregoing passage, a passage crucial for a proper grasp of his philosophical thinking. It was enough for him to agree with the author of the *Critique of Pure Reason* in which the exactness of Newtonian physics served as pattern for metaphysics in particular and philosophy in general. Since Planck had subscribed to the primacy of physics, in respect at least to some essential philosophical questions, the methodical subjugation by Planck of philosophy to physics could only be a foregone conclusion.

The subjugation was complete for all practical purposes. It was of no consequence to state as Planck did, that physics in investigating causality in physical reality presupposed philosophy to make a start. The start was, in Planck's words, a "jump into the region of metaphysics," and a "leap into the transcendental."[40] The leap was not a matter of logic but a fiducial act supported by two considerations. One was that science required much more than the data of senses. The latter not only trapped one in solipsism, but also invited that anthropomorphism which science kept transcending as it progressed. The other was that sense data as such were not logical proofs of the existence of the external world. "It is only through the immediate dictate of our consciousness that we know that this world exists," declared Planck[41] who as a Kantian could not perceive that it was natural for man to know external things and that his own consciousness was merely a reflection of his knowing things. Otherwise consciousness was no less a trap serving solipsism than the data of the senses.

Clearly, whatever priority philosophy (metaphysics) could claim over physics through the indispensability of that act of faith in reality, precisely because the act in question was an act of faith and not a step of plain knowledge, the physicist did not have to remember that priority as he went on cultivating his own specific brand of knowledge. According to Planck, "once the scientist has begun by taking this leap into the transcendental he never discusses the leap itself nor worries about it. If he did, science could not advance rapidly."[42] One justification of this hardly philosophical policy was the inability to attack it on logical grounds. The act of faith or leap of faith was obviously beyond the confines of mere logic. The act represented a surplus which in Planck's rendering was mystical and not rational. Had Planck not been a Kantian idealist but a philosophical realist, he would have said that knowledge of the real is not a mere conceptualization and therefore more than mere logic. As a Kantian he could not see that while logic dealt with the relative domain of two or several concepts, inert in themselves, knowledge of external reality was a dynamic though natural relationship among the thing, the knower, and his knowledge of it. The other justification was the progress of science, by which Planck meant physics above all. "The history of science is at hand to confirm our faith in this truth,"[43] namely, the truth that through science man was progressing toward an ever more genuine grasp of reality. A truth it certainly was but, when claimed by Planck, a mere impasse out of which his Kantianism offered no escape.

Such was a twentieth-century replay, through the discourse of a prominent physicist, of the logic of the Kantian dictum that philosophy should be cultivated along the lines of physics. What this ultimately meant was the surrendering to physics, as will be seen shortly, even in respect to the problem of free will. That this was a Kantian procedure was spelled out by Planck himself:

Having once assumed the existence of an independent external world, science concomitantly assumes the principle of causality as a concept entirely independent of sense perception. In applying this principle to the study of natural phenomena science first investigates if and how far the law of causal relation is applicable to the various happenings in the world of nature and in the realm of the human spirit. Science finds itself here exactly on the same footing which Kant took as the starting point of his theory of knowledge.[44]

The one exception which Planck took to Kant's legislation on causality was minor and rather elusive if not plainly confused. One wonders what Planck meant in saying that "Kant took not merely the concept causality but also to a certain degree the meaning of the causal law itself as an immediate datum of knowledge and therefore universally valid. Specialized science cannot go thus far."[45] The distinction between the "concept of causality" and the "meaning of causal law" is best considered as one of those trivial profundities which abound in the writings of any Kantian philosopher, professional or not.

Planck has now reached the second main part of his discourse where he asked with obvious relief: "How far can science help us out of the obscure forest wherein philosophy lost its way?"[46] Clearly, he was not at ease with philosophy. His questions about causality (do the sciences take causality for an indispensable postulate and do they insist on its validity in all cases?) did not relate to the nature of causality but merely to the use of it by the sciences. In formulating the answer of physics to these questions Planck admitted that the quantum of action posed certain problems. Indeed he felt that it might impose "essential modifications" of the causality principle as implied in Newtonian physics and its relativistic recasting by Einstein. Now if the modifications were "essential," it was hardly rigorous to state, as Planck did, that nevertheless the "quantum hypothesis will eventually find its exact expression in certain equations which will be a more exact formulation of the law of causality."[47] Also, if the law of causality as assumed in Newtonian physics was exact, and it certainly was, what kind of reformulation could make it more exact? That in 1923 Planck felt that most physicists shared his hopes about the future of the law of causality may be understandable, but he was a poor prophet nevertheless. That statistical methods introduced in several new branches of physics allowed in principle an exact investigation could, of course, be granted. It was another matter whether on the atomic and molecular level, where statistical methods had their most important role and where the quantum of action was not a negligible quantity, one could reasonably look for at least theoretically exact measurements. At any rate, Planck took the idea of exact measurement as equivalent to strict causality.

Planck then turned to biology where he registered an ever wider admission of exact chemical interactions. He would have done far more justice to biology had he referred to the unabated struggle of biologists with the notion of teleology. The statement, by then half a century old, of a German biologist that teleology was for any biologist an indispensable companion though not one to appear with in public,[48] could hardly be unknown to Planck. But Planck's mind was too firmly set in the groove of that identification of the measurably exact with the causal and the real to make room for other aspects of the problem. This is well illustrated by his sudden broaching, at the end of his reflections on biology, of the question whether causality was after all a mere hypothesis. Planck's answer was that causality was a very special hypothesis which accounted for the finding of any "definite rule" in any field of science.[49] The "definite" obviously meant quantitatively exact and also verifiable as such.

This identification by Planck of exact, or rather of the exactly measurable, with causal, was very much in view as he discussed the answer of the humanities (psychology and sociology in particular) to the question of the status of causality. As was already noted, he was strongly inclined to take cogitation, however creative, for a predetermined process. Modern psychological research gave, in his view, heavy support to the subjection of mental processes to the law of causality:

> The principle of causality must be held to extend even to the highest achievements of the human soul. We must admit that the mind of each one of our greatest geniuses—Aristotle, Kant or Leonardo, Goethe or Beethoven, Dante or Shakespeare—even at the moment of its highest flights of thought or in the most profound inner workings of the soul, was subject to the causal fiat and was an instrument in the hands of an almighty law which governs the world.[50]

Typically, the difficulty of seeing an unbroken chain in all mental processes was answered by Planck with a reference to a purely physical analogy. If this was already revealing, even more so was Planck's interpretation of the analogy, the uncertain outcome of throwing asymmetrical dice. The uncertainty lay, of course, in our inability, owing to our incomplete knowledge of all quantitative parameters of such a throw, to say nothing of its dynamics, to predict the outcome. Planck described that inability as an inability "to detect the function of strict causality."[51] Planck's dismissal of "absolute chance" might have led him to causality as an ontological question had he not seen in causality above all a mental category. Only on occasion did he attribute to it the status of being transcendental to and independent of the perceiving mind. Even in such cases he quickly fell back on the shallows of exact measurability and observation. Actually, he fell back there not only quickly but almost readily. Once on those shallows, he felt he could answer the objection that free will was therefore a mere phantom. Free will, the ethical responsibility of man, and the inviolability of his ego (person), could be defended, so Planck insisted, because a complete observation (measurement) of one's own acts was a *practical* impossibility, whatever the *theoretical* possibility of a full observation and therefore the rigorous ascertaining of causality. Our freedom was therefore not an ontological principle but a pragmatic precept resting on a mere inability on our part to analyse with full objectivity, that is, to measure with complete precision, all our actions and chains of motivation. To a superior spirit, such as the one described by Laplace, all our so-called free actions could be seen as fully determined. The Laplacian spirit too, although a mystery to himself because his ego could not become his own object, was an open book to a Supreme Wisdom (if there be one, Planck added),[52] whose celestial nature is infinitely above us.

Whether that Supreme Wisdom was free only because as his own subject he could not fully become his own object of observation, Planck did not discuss. Had he done so he might perhaps have caught a glimpse of the manner in which one's notion of the ultimate in being and intelligibility conditioned all of one's philosophical utterances, provided they were consistent. In Planck's case that notion was heavy on the side of "idea" and very light on the side of "being" or reality. Planck's philosophical means of securing reality, such as the "metaphysical leap" and the categories which barred him from *knowing* reality, were markedly idealistic. For Planck the idealist, it was not possible to state that man *knew* reality and that causality was a matter of knowing the real and not a mere matter of categories, let alone of scientific techniques. Idealist philosophy could not encourage him to recognize that his own ability to move his little finger at will contained much more realist evidence both about himself and the world than all the laws of all the sciences. Thus he was helplessly pushed by his favorite theme, measurably deterministic causality, to the extreme where it engulfed man's mind and will. No wonder. Idealism was a vote cast on behalf of a priori categories and "truths" which held the human mind prisoner of its own presumed structure. Within such a framework reality could only be brought back through the schizophrenic device of a fiducial leap in the dark, hardly a step of rationality, and the free will could be salvaged only through the even more schizophrenic precept of a categorical imperative.

The lecture of 1923 provides by far the most systematic exposition by Planck of his reflections on epistemological topics. His two other lectures on causality, delivered in 1926 and in 1932, were mere rephrasing and regrouping of themes developed in the 1923 lecture.[53] They also reveal him as the prisoner of his cherished themes, mechanistic causality and the Kantian precepts of epistemology. As a system, Planck's epistemology offers nothing original; it is not even profound, unless profundity is taken for brave consistency. It is even short on the pregnant phrases which make the reading of Einstein's much shorter philosophical essays a more refreshing experience. Yet Planck's epistemology, especially as portrayed in that 1923 lecture, is worth studying. A survey of half truths, plain errors, blind alleys, hapless impasses is not without its instructiveness especially when they are tied to the name of a great physicist. The pre-eminent position, almost pontifical role, with which leading physicists, especially when decorated with a Nobel Prize, are accredited in our culture is not something to be taken lightly. It makes a very sad reflection on that scientific culture of ours that the inability of scientific expertise to guarantee philosophical expertise comes largely as startling news. And so does any reference to science as a major source of the sprouting up of ever new philosophical systems. The novelty is only apparent. The major philosophical options of our times reflect, though in ever more virulent and accelerated way, that process of being tossed to and fro in which philosophy finds itself since the rise of science. With ever increasing frequency, philosophy is swinging from an aping of scientific exactness to a reveling in the irrational. The story, often told, need not be reviewed here. Perhaps the story would have more constructive strength if more attention were paid there to the philosophizing of leading modern physicists. This is not to suggest that most of the time one could find much texture in that philosophizing, which almost invariably brings out the truth of Einstein's poingnant remark: "The man of science is a poor philosopher."[54]

Such an admission has more mental health to it than the sophisticatedly articulated claims of certain philosophers who largely succeeded in being taken for the authoritative interpreters of modern science. The fumbling of prominent physicists in matters philosophical will not escape a reader with a modest measure of critical sense. Quite different is the case with lengthy treatises, mostly devoted to logical refinements, although even there the same reader should be taken aback by the end results. There reality subtly vanishes, the universe dissolves into a haphazard succession of particles, so many creations of the scientific mind, while that very mind is turned into the inert locus of concepts, none of which is more related to reality than the other. Like the scene of organic evolution and social development, where everything is said to be ruled by a grim struggle for survival and endless revolutions, the domain of science too becomes a mere series of successes which, being purely relative, cannot in the end be taken for a progress and certainly not for that progress which Planck held high.

Against that background Planck's philosophical reflections on science may be a much-needed antidote, whatever the mistaken philosophical framework within which he tried to make his main points. The spirited affirmations by Planck of a fully ordered external world were not inspired by his idealist philosophy but by his deep scientific engagement for a more comprehensive view of physical reality. That reality was for him absolutely given, that is, in no way the creation of the mind, scientific or other. This is why he saw, well before Einstein, the absolutist and objective character of relativity theory.[55] What he failed to see was that impasse into which he unnecessarily led himself by trying to justify with the shibboleths of Kantian tradition the esteem of a fully coherent objective physical reality which science inspired in him. Far from being necessary, the impasse rested on the transparent fallacy of equating that which cannot be "ascertained" exactly that which is not fully "determined" or really caused.

Quantum mechanics was not yet half a dozen years old when that fallacy was pointed out in a prominent scientific journal,[56] though in vain if the continued popularity of the Copenhagen interpretation of quantum mechanics means anything. In an age of logical positivism, a logical distinction, strong enough to lay bare that fallacy, would not offer escape from an impasse about reality. A philosophical appreciation of the real, which Kantianism and its varied offshoots could not provide, was no less required. Blinded by Kantianism, Planck readily took classical mechanics as an assurance that real interaction among real things was not more than the predictability of its mathematical exactness. In doing so Planck deprived himself of the true assurance needed in revolutionary times.

This is the reason why Planck, who was ready to follow up steps leading to a major revolution in physics, remained a "reluctant revolutionary."[57] To be sure, he never spoke of revolutions in science in the self-defeating sense implied in the succession of incommensurable patterns, with the "incommensurable" being taken for ontological incoherence. If the progress of science needed a revolutionary or drastic step, Planck did not recoil from pioneering it. In fact, as he himself recalled, he worked frantically during the closing months of 1900 for snatching victory in a race for the theoretical derivation of the shape of the black-body radiation curve already established on experimental grounds. It was no secret to him that this feat of his would match in significance that of Newton. Years later, when Einstein extended the quantum of emission into a quantum of propagation, Planck, as Einstein recalled, considered the arguments with complete disregard for his own preferences.[58] The true source of his dislike of discontinuity, be it of emission or of propagation or of both, was not so much scientific as philosophical. Unfortunately, those reasons remained muddled as he kept articulating them. In trying to reverse the stampede of those whom he called "indeterminists" he put emphasis not so much on causality as on a special aspect of it, and much less on reality without which causality makes no sense.

Planck must not, however, be judged too harshly. After all, his erstwhile protégé, Einstein, came to perceive in full only in his last years, after growing tired of a long debate with Born, that the real bone of contention between them concerned the status of reality.[59] But there is little to defend in Planck's defense of reality through his advocacy of metaphysical leaps and acts of faith. Such leaps and acts remain pieces of idealist rhetoric when not supported by a philosophy which transcends mere empiricism, and even a so-called "rationalist" metaphysics. Thus Planck's arguments failed to impress the leader and the chief representatives of the Copenhagen school who, if they had any philosophy, gloried in some variation of pragmatism. Nothing was easier for them than to turn the tables on Planck who loved to refer to the fruitfulness of causal thinking in physics.[60] In quantum mechanics, where all basic operations are statistical, probability proved itself useful beyond the most sanguine expectations. It was another matter to use that usefulness as a cover-up for casting doubt on the coherence of the universe at its fundamental level, nay, on existence itself. The gist of that procedure was a systematic refusal to consider questions of ontology.[61] Indeed, in that procedure accidental or chance events stood opposed not to determinate events, but simply to reality itself.[62]

While Planck failed to see this, he sensed something of his opponents' systematic way of sapping, in the manner of parasites, the tree of reality, which pre-twentieth-century scientific thinking still duly revered and which, of course, cannot be exorcised or cut down by any science, however successful. Parasites, it is well to recall, have always formed very successful species. To argue effectively against their kind, parading as scientific philosophers, the cause of reality demanded much more than the sincere zeal for the real which animated Planck, the scientist. The same cause could be only compromised by falling back on the 'Ding an sich' which, with most other results of Kant's philosophy, Planck accepted. Being merely the spurious product of a second or third step in reasoning, the "thing in itself" deprived reality from being the very starting point of that episteme which alone can issue in consistent human understanding.

[1]The headline was prompted by the experiment performed in the laboratories of the University of Paris at Orsay by A. Aspect and his co-workers in 1981. The experiment bore out the truth of Bell's theorem of inequality. The latter contradicts the so-called hidden-variables theories according to which absolutely precise measurements of conjugate variables are possible, in principle at least, on the atomic level. To the credit of the article in *The Economist* (p. 95) it was pointed out there that a Pandora-box might open by siding with the opposite view, which usually implies the philosophy that a thing exists only when it is being thought of.

[2]For excerpts from that document, see R. W. Clark, *Einstein: The Life and Times* (New York: Thomas Y. Crowell, 1971), p. 169.

[3]See F. Wiedmann, *Hegel. An Illustrated Biography,* translated from the German by J. Neugroschel (New York: Western Publishing Co., 1968), pp. 53-54.

[4]W. James, *A Pluralistic Universe* (New York: Longmans, Green and Co., 1909), p. 5.

[5]See the opening paragraph of "Wissenschaftliche Selbstbiographie" in M. Planck, *Physikalische Abhandlungen und Vorträge* (Braunschweig: Friedr. Vieweg & Sohn, 1958), vol. III, p. 374. The physicist in question was Philipp von Jolly, professor at the University of Munich.

[6]Such was Kohlrausch's comment on a remark of A. Kundt. See my *The Relevance of Physics* (Chicago: University of Chicago Press, 1966), p. 237.

[7]"Zur Machschen Theorie der physikalischen Erkenntnis," *Naturwissenschaften* 11 (1910), p. 1187.

[8]In ch. 11, "The Quantum of Science," in my Gifford Lectures, *The Road of Science and the Ways to God* (Chicago: University of Chicago Press, 1978).

[9]*Kant's Opus postumum*, edited by A. Buchenau (Berlin: Walter de Gruyter, 1938), vol. 1, p. 145. There Kant also spoke of man as a being that was God himself (p. 25).

[10]H. Adams, *The Education of Henry Adams* (1918), with an introduction by J. T. Adams (New York: The Modern Library, 1931), pp. 34 and 429.

[11]*Lettres à Maurice Solovine* (Paris: Gauthier-Villars, 1956), p. 115. The letter was written on March 30, 1952.

[12]E. Schrödinger, *What is Life and Other Scientific Essays* (Garden City, N.Y.: Doubleday, 1956), p. 83.

[13]As shown by T. S. Kuhn, *Black-Body Theory and the Quantum Discontinuity 1894-1912* (Oxford: Clarendon Press, 1978), p. 132.

[14]Letter of July 6, 1905 to Ehrenfest: quoted *ibid.*, p. 132.

[15]Letter of May 23, 1915 to Ehrenfest, quoted *ibid.*, p. 253.

[16]"The Origin and Development of the Quantum Theory" (June 2, 1920). See English translation in M. Planck, *A Survey of Physics*, translated by R. Jones and D. H. Williams (London: Methuen, 1925), p. 109.

[17]An almost complete, though in places somewhat free translation of that address, "Causation and Free Will," is given in M. Planck, *The New Science* (New York: Meridian Books, 1959), pp. 65-122. The German original, "Kausalgesetz und Willensfreiheit," is readily available in M. Planck, *Vorträge und Erinnerungen* (Darmstadt: Wissenschaftliche Buchgesellschaft, 1965), pp. 139-68.

[18]Their English translation is available in *A Survey of Physics* quoted above (note 16). The most important of them is the lecture, "The Unity of the Physical Universe" ("Die Einheit des physikalischen Weltbildes"), which Planck delivered at the University of Leiden on December 9, 1908, and in which he made a frontal attack on the subjectivism implied in Mach's sensationism.

[19]Both in a series of essays on the philosophy of physics published during his years in Lille (1887-93) which he later worked into his *La théorie physique: son objet et sa structure* (1906; English translation, *The Aim and Structure of Physical Theory*, 1954), and also in some of his technical publications, such as his "Commentaires aux principes de la thermodynamique" (1892-94) and especially his *Traité d'Energétique* (1911). For details, see my book, *Uneasy Genius: The Life and Work of Pierre Duhem* (Dordrecht, London, Boston: Martinus Nijhoff/Kluwer, 1984; 2d edition, paperback, 1987).

[20]"Causation and Free Will," *The New Science*, p. 116. Planck explicitly referred to Laplace in the same context. Laplace was clearly echoed in the opening sentence of Planck's address, "The Principle of Least Action" (1914); see *A Survey of Physics*, p. 69. In speaking in 1935 in his "Die Physik im Kampf um Weltanschauung" (English translation, "Physics and World Philosophy") in M. Planck, *The Philosophy of Physics*, translated by W. H. Johnston (New York: W. W. Norton, 1936, pp. 24-26) of the subjection to strict physical laws of every bubble in waves breaking on the seashore, Planck may have followed a rephrasing of the Laplacian theme by T. H. Huxley in his reminiscences on the reception of Darwin's theory. See *The Life and Letters of Charles Darwin*, edited by F. Darwin (1888; New York: Basic Books, 1959), vol. I, pp. 553-55.

[21]"Causation and Free Will," in *The New Science*, p. 88.

[22]Ibid., p. 71.

[23]The problem was brought to Spinoza's attention by Tschirnhausen. For their exchange of letters, see *The Chief Works of Benedict de Spinoza*, translated from the Latin, with an introduction by R. H. M. Elwes (1893; New York: Dover, 1951), vol. II, pp. 408-09.

[24]"The Principles of Nature and of Grace, based on Reason" (1714); see *Leibniz Selections*, ed. Philip P. Wiener (New York: Charles Scribner's Sons, 1951), p. 527.

[25]This is why Descartes had to insist in the *Discourse on the Method* that his procedure did not do "outrage to the miracle of creation"; see *The Philosophical Works of Descartes*, tr. E. S. Haldane and G. R. T. Ross (Cambridge: Cambridge University Press, 1911), vol. I, p. 109.

[26]The chief organ of those studies was the series *Beiträge zur Geschichte der Philosophie des Mittelalters* (Münster i. W.). Among the authors of such popularizations were M. Grabmann and C. M. Manser. Even a study of post-World-War-I editions of F. Ueberweg's *Grundriss der Geschichte der Philosophie,* a work which by then had long established itself as a classic, could have given to Planck a far better view on scholastic philosophy than the one he set forth.

[27]"Causation and Free Will," pp. 75-76.

[28]Ibid., p. 75.

[29]As emphatically argued by no less an expert on Thomistic philosophy than E. Gilson in his *The Spirit of Thomism* (New York: P. J. Kennedy & Sons, 1964; Harper Torchbooks, 1966), pp. 77-78.

[30]For details see my *Cosmos and Creator* (Edinburgh: Scottish Academic Press, 1981), pp. 73-75.

[31]"Causation and Free Will," p. 86. It is difficult to see how this could be true if it was also true that "Kant's teaching . . . is to a certain extent arbitrary on account of its strong dogmatic attitude" (*ibid*). This inconsistency was compounded by Planck's subsequent reasoning which stated

the need for metaphysics if one was to avoid solipsism, but which also stated the need to accept a certain measure of compromise with logic, because in order to save causality one had to remain somewhere in the middle between metaphysics and empiricism.

[32]The works relating to those last two fields have been translated into English under the titles, *Kant on Education* and *Religion within the Limits of Reason Alone.*

[33]A. E. Adickes, *Kant als Naturforscher* (Berlin: W. de Gruyter, 1925), vol. II, p. 204.

[34]For details, see my *The Relevance of Physics,* p. 334.

[35]"Causation and Free Will," pp. 84 and 86.

[36]Ibid., p. 86.

[37]Ibid., p. 88.

[38]Ibid., p. 90.

[39]English translation in *Kant: Selected Pre-Critical Writings and Correspondence with Beck,* translated and introduced by P. G. Lucas (Manchester: University Press, 1968), pp. 5-35.

[40]"Causation and Free Will," pp. 93 and 94.

[41]Ibid., p. 94.

[42]Ibid.

[43]Ibid., p. 95.

[44]Ibid.

[45]Ibid.

[46]Ibid., p. 96.

[47]Ibid., p. 98.

[48]The remark is usually credited to von Bruecke. See W. I. B. Beveridge, *The Art of Scientific Investigation* (rev. ed.; New York: Random House, n.d.), p. 83.

[49]"Causation and Free Will," p. 104.

[50]Ibid., pp. 109-10.

[51]Ibid., p. 108.

[52]Ibid., p. 117.

[53]The former, "Physikalische Gesetzlichkeit" (*Vorträge und Erinnerungen,* pp. 183-205), has not yet been translated into English. The other, "Kausalität in der Natur," appeared in English under the title, "Causation in Nature"; see *The New Science,* pp. 259-90.

[54]"Physics and Reality" (1936), in *Out of my Later Years* (New York: Philosophical Library, 1950), p. 58.

[55]Planck did so in 1924 in his lecture "From the Relative to the Absolute," *The New Science,* pp. 123-54.

[56]Letter to the Editor, *Nature,* Dec. 27, 1930, p. 995. Of course, as the letter was written by E. J. Turner, a now completely-forgotten teacher at the

University of Liverpool, his most justified remarks could not make as much as a dent on a rapidly forming consensus.

[57]Indeed, the "most reluctant revolutionary of all times," to recall a felicitous phrase of L. Pierce Williams in his "Normal Science, Scientific Revolutions, and the History of Science," in *Criticism and the Growth of Knowledge,* ed. I. Lakatos and A. Musgrave (Cambridge: Cambridge University Press, 1974), p. 50.

[58]Einstein's words are quoted in A. Hermann, *Max Planck in Selbstzeugnissen und Bilddokumenten* (Reinbek bey Hamburg: Rowohlt, 1973), p. 45.

[59]See *The Born-Einstein Letters: Correspondence between Albert Einstein and Max and Hedwig Born* (New York: Walker and Company, 1971), pp. 216-24.

[60]Already in his first major non-technical address, delivered in Leiden in 1908, "On the Unity of the Physical Universe," a frontal attack on the sensationism advocated by Ernst Mach.

[61]Such is the conclusion of the most comprehensive study on Bohr's epistemology, "The Nature of Quantum Mechanical Reality: Einstein versus Bohr," by C. A. Hooker, in R. G. Colodny (ed.), *Paradigms and Paradoxes: The Philosophical Challenge of the Quantum Domain* (Pittsburgh: University of Pittsburgh Press, 1972), pp. 67-302. See especially p. 208.

[62]As argued and documented in my "Chance or Reality: Interaction in Nature versus Measurement in Physics," *Philosophia* 10-11 (Athens, 1980-81), pp. 87-105, reprinted in my book, *Chance or Reality and Other Essays* (Lanham, Md.: The University Press of America, 1986).

3

The Metaphysics of Discovery and the Rediscovery of Metaphysics

A historian of science owes some explanation to a gathering of philosophers for having accepted their invitation to address them on the general topic of the role of the non-physical in the investigation of the physical. He may be allowed to remind them that half a century ago Harnack advised his students to go to Planck and Einstein, two chief creators of modern physics, for new material in philosophy. Were Harnack, a keen observer of the latest developments, still alive, he would probably refer his students to historians of science. A telling aspect of these developments was intimated when, around 1925, a

Lecture delivered at the Fifty-second Annual Meeting of the American Catholic Philosophical Association, April 1, 1978. Reprinted with permission from its *Proceedings,* vol. LII (1978), pp. 188-96 with additional notes.

historian-philosopher student of a great scientific achievement discovered for himself that the only way to avoid becoming a metaphysician is to say nothing.[1] E. A. Burtt, who made that discovery, pleaded, however, for a metaphysics which is such only in name. Its other advocates, too, do their best to avoid what is truly metaphysical. Indeed, in that "rationalist" metaphysics, as it was qualified by G. Holton, all that is above the physical or beyond the material becomes largely irrelevant.[2]

Burtt's study is separated from Holton's work on the epistemological foundations of Einstein's thought by almost half a century, a period increasingly rich in probings into the fact that science, the study of the material, is not immaterial talk, precisely because it is a continual pointer to the immaterial in the sense in which it matters most. This development may not be well known to philosophers committed to a realist metaphysics. They would do well to pay more attention to the scant measure of familiarity with science on the part of Hume and Kant, who in the name of science reputedly have abolished metaphysics or at least any metaphysics other than one that is rationalist or idealist.

The unwitting starting point of this "scientific" abolition of metaphysics, which had God, soul, and the universe for its chief truths, was Locke. He had been most intent to do philosophy (including some metaphysics) in the spirit of Newton's science, the great novelty of the times. But the trend started by Locke led to undermining those epistemological foundations upon which science relies, tacitly at least, while making its major discoveries. That may not have happened if Locke had been more circumspect. He was more or less aware of the fact that on the basis of Cartesian metaphysics, steeped in innate ideas, no major discovery can be made. Locke was, however, distinctly blind with respect to the empiricists' predicament, possibly because his confidence in Newton's physics rested on the advice he had solicited from Huygens that the mathematics of the *Principia* was reliable.[3] Locke failed to notice that no references to Bacon can be found in Newton's writings. This was a very strange fact, even on a cursory look, because Newton was a member of the Royal Society for which Bacon was the patron saint and the great program giver.

The same fact should not appear so strange once it is recalled that, when pressed late in life for an explanation of his discoveries in physics, Newton spoke of long solitary thinking. The thinking in question was a concentrated groping into the wide unknown on the meagre basis of what is known. That groping bespoke a unique, more than material ability, conveniently called the mind, for which there was no room in Bacon's method of doing science. In fact, Bacon boasted that for making discoveries he had provided a machine the use of which would enable any industrious fellow to become a discoverer. The machine, to quote his words, would "level all wits" and through its use by many all possible discoveries might be completed within a few years.[4] In justice to him he was not always so hopeful.

At any rate, Bacon with this method was only a mirror image of Descartes, who also put at the center of his philosophy a method of ascertaining, as if by machinery, all truths and of securing all discoveries. Actually, the publication by Descartes of *the* method left room only for making minor discoveries. Descartes believed he had already made all the major discoveries that were possible. The fact was that no Cartesian, not even Descartes, made a notable discovery in physical science, a point ruefully noted by d'Alembert around 1730, or a hundred years after the publication of the *Discours de la méthode*. D'Alembert did so as he surveyed the sad state of science in Cartesian France as compared with Newtonian England.[5] D'Alembert's remark is in the preface of a strictly scientific book, in which, by instinct, he avoided the name of Bacon, whereas in d'Alembert's writings of philosophical propaganda Bacon was constantly referred to.

As a scientist d'Alembert might have suspected that there was as little difference between Bacon and Descartes as is the apparent difference between opposite extremes. The non-mathematician Bacon frowned on the use of mathematics in science, whereas the mathematician Descartes left no proper room in science for mathematics. That in his science there was nothing but mathematics was a hollow boast on Descartes' part. The truth was, as noted by the still standard monograph on Cartesian physics written by Muoy half a century ago, that Descartes' mathematical physics is in fact a physics without mathematics. This is why there was not enough room for creative thinking and for discoveries in the method as proposed by Descartes and Bacon respectively. That Bacon wanted his method to be used by everyone, whereas Descartes thought that he alone could use his properly and therefore urged everybody to send observational data to him, made little difference.

The scientific philosophy of Bacon was given its death certificate when Newton's *Principia* made it clear (at least in retrospect) why Hooke, Boyle, and others—to mention only the better known names in the incipient Royal Society—hampered their own scientific talents by paying attention to Bacon's dicta. The illusion about Bacon's greatness lingered on, although it was unwittingly laid bare in 1728 when Pemberton wrote his account of Newton's philosophy and science. In the preface Bacon was mentioned three or four times in every page, but Pemberton rightly noted that Newton followed a middle course in natural philosophy (physics) and that this was the key to his success.[6] That middle course was as far from Bacon as it was from Descartes, the two extremes of which one, empiricism, excluded metaphysics by retaining only the physical, while the other, rationalism, undercut metaphysics by severing it from the physical.

The middle course which Newton, the creative physicist, followed was also equally far from the initiators of the two main trends that claimed science as a basis of philosophy. Neither trend was endorsed by scientists who did make the discoveries. Great scientists of the second half of the eighteenth and of the entire nineteenth century could be very naive in their philosophical dicta, but in their scientific work they were neither empiricists nor idealists. They were middle-roaders by instinct, if not by reflection and philosophical learning. It was not a popular road to follow because the tone of thought had been set either by the idealists, Kant and his followers, or by the empiricists and sensationists. The chief organs of the latter were the Encyclopedists who did their best to bring Bacon back into the scene.

Although not popular, the middle road leading to discovery was easy to find for a genuine scientist as far as idealism was concerned. True, it remained unknown until the 1880s that Kant had spent his last eight years on a project of giving final form to physics on the basis of the pseudometaphysics of his *Critique*. That final form, as revealed in the *Opus postumum*, was sheer subjectivism.[7] But the subjectivism of idealism was already apparent through the writings of Schelling and Hegel. In its form known as *Naturphilosophie* it presented a real threat to German scientists throughout the first half of the nineteenth century. Thus a genuine scientist aiming at making discoveries could easily resist the lure of idealism.

The scientific ineptitude of the sensationist or empiricist trend became all too evident through Auguste Comte's legislation in science. Its most celebrated and best remembered aspect was Comte's rejection of all metaphysics. What is hardly ever remembered is Comte's full awareness of the fact that his positivism, or rejection of all metaphysics, entailed the barring of any new major discovery. He went so far in that respect as to declare that anything beyond the solar system, even beyond the orbit of Saturn, was irrelevant for astronomy. He repeatedly defined cosmology as the study of the system of planets. Such was the antimetaphysical destruction of the material universe and also of science, insofar as all science is cosmology. As to the mental world, its truly scientific investigation was given, according to Comte, in Gall's phrenology![8]

The situation was only apparently better for science when J. S. Mill, a distinctly more sober mind than Comte, formulated scientific method in terms of positivism. To the credit of Mill, he realized that the process of induction, in which empiricists from Bacon on saw the exclusive road to discovery, implied more than the enumeration of facts. That "more" obviously implied something non-empirical which Mill did his best to exorcize. This is why he gave a blatant misinterpretation of Kepler's discovery of the elliptical orbit of planets. According to Mill, Kepler's conclusion did not contain more than what was given in his observations and calculations. Clearly, Mill did not read, in flagrant violation of his positivist precepts, the very positive record left by Kepler about his most complicated mental itinerary leading to a discovery, which made history in science. This slighting by Mill of the discoverer's mind went hand in hand with his degradation of the universe into disconnected sections. He took spiral nebulae for universes which could be so different from our part of the universe as to be governed by laws in which two multiplied by two would not necessarily make four.[9] Such was the disastrous price Mill had to pay for his antimetaphysicism in logic which he considered his stronghold.

The most ambitious and programmatic account during the nineteenth century about scientific discovery was *On the Philosophy of Discovery* by W. Whewell.[10] He fully realized the inadequacies of Bacon's program in which facts were supposed to generate science in automatic, mechanical fashion. Whewell was also enough of an historian of science to realize that the historical reality of scientific discoveries was something far richer than could be pigeonholed into Kantian categories. Whewell saw less clearly the questionable status of imagination in which Kant tried to find—illogically enough as far as his postulates were concerned—that keystone which connects sensations and categories into a knowledge related to reality. Failing to realize that every act of knowing reality is a discovery crediting something more than the senses Whewell could only say of scientific discovery that it comes about when facts or observations are matched with appropriate ideas. The truth contained in this dictum was rather superficial and also ran the risk of turning the whole process of science into a chain of accidental discoveries.

Discoveries, at least future discoveries, were no longer in sight when a variant of unmitigated empiricism was taken by Ernst Mach as the basis for explaining science. The variant was sensationism, or rather an economic arrangement of sensations by the mind, as unwary interpreters of Mach would say. But for Mach the mind as an immaterial metaphysical entity could not exist. No wonder that his refusal to see a legitimate role for metaphysics in science trapped him in revealing statements. He claimed, for instance, that Chinese ideographic writing was the most scientific way of recording ideas.[11] Needless to say, he did not ask why the sensationist, that is, "most scientific" Chinese mind was so unproductive in making scientific discoveries. Again, Mach took the view that if all sensations were available for man, he would not need science because the sensations would group themselves in his perception in the most economic, that is, most scientific way, which would be equivalent to science itself.

The most monumental trap which sensationism held in store for Mach can be seen in the goal which he hoped to achieve by his analysis of the history of mechanics. The goal consisted in securing that framework for physics which would require no revamping whatever in the future. Such was a thinly veiled claim about the impossibility of any major new discovery in the physics to be written by future generations. That the impossibility of major new discoveries was for Mach subtly but intimately tied to the impossibility of metaphysics can be seen from his reaction to major new departures from classical physics as they began to appear on the scene shortly after the turn of the century. Mach's greatness lay precisely in the fact that he was the first to see that Planck's postulating a quantum of energy and Einstein's postulates, especially that of the absoluteness of the speed of light, were classic cases of the role of clearly nonphysical factors or assumptions in the investigation of the physical.

Mach's heated debate with Planck on the question of atoms was the great news in the world of science around 1910. The clash was not so much about the atom, but about that metaphysical strain which Planck, a former follower of Mach, claimed to be part and parcel of man's grasp of intelligibility in physical reality. Around 1910 Mach was also fully conscious of the metaphysical basis of Einstein's special relativity; indeed, he was the first to suspect that general relativity was even more metaphysical in character. Concerning Einstein's relativity, Mach kept his thoughts to himself. On the contrary, Planck was, since 1909 or so, an unabashed champion of realism and metaphysics to such an extent that he saw a chief importance of Einstein's relativity in its contribution to epistemology![12] This may sound unbelievable, but the fact is that Planck explicitly referred to epistemology when he urged in 1910 the Prussian government to give Einstein membership in the Berlin Academy. Einstein himself awoke from his Machist slumber only several years later, but once his awakening was complete, he missed no opportunity to chastize Mach, the philosopher-scientist, and to extol metaphysics in the name of science.

Machists, whose number was very great in the 1920s and 1930s, could perhaps have tolerated Einstein's scathing remark that Mach was a deplorable philosopher, but it cut them to the quick to hear Einstein declare that on the basis of Mach's philosophy one could produce no science but only a listing of data no more informative than the list of names in a telephone directory. Positivists could only be incensed on hearing Einstein's emphatic claim that every two-legged animal is a metaphysician and could only shake their heads in disbelief on hearing Einstein's defiant declaration that precisely because of science he was not reluctant to become guilty of the "original sin of metaphysics."[13] Rationalists, whose specialty is a smug confidence about reason, could hardly take comfort in Einstein's marvelling at the ability of the mind to comprehend nature through the act of scientific discovery. He most likely did not know that Aristotle's metaphysics started with reference to man's ability to wonder; but he knew that his defense of metaphysics put him dangerously close to finding himself an ally of priests.

For all his enduring admiration of Kant, whose *Critique* he read and thought he understood at the age of thirteen (a presumption worthy of a teenager, however precocious, about a very unclear book the chief claim of which was to make everything clear), the mature Einstein's defense of metaphysics far transcended the metaphysics of the *Critique*. By its denial of the validity of the notion of the universe, which is the physical realm in its most comprehensive sense, Kant's metaphysics made impossible any reach beyond the physical or material. For Einstein, the universe as the totality of consistently interacting material entities was a most valid notion, indeed, the culmination of his theory of general relativity.

Like many before him, Einstein too was tempted to derive the actual structure of the universe in some a priori fashion. On more than one occasion he tried to play God in theorizing about the universe. Like all before him, he too failed to achieve the great aim of cosmological apriorism, namely, the demonstration that the universe can only be what it is and therefore it is not contingent. But unlike a priori thinkers before him, Einstein, as a superior scientist, was able to recover his sense of wonderment in the fact of the singular specificity of the universe. The intensity of that wonderment made him realize that a universe, which is wondered at owing to its comprehensibility underivable from a priori notions, is a powerful pointer to the Creator. While unwilling to accept a personal God, a Creator, he was not willing to part with a universe which was not made by science but rather made science possible in the sense of inviting scientists to make more and more sweeping discoveries about the coherent rationality of the universe. About the possibility that "Pfaffen" (a rather pejorative term in German for priests) would capitalize on his view of the universe (he obviously meant that cosmology which has been the citadel of natural theology)—about that possibility he desparingly and scornfully remarked: "let the devil care for that!"[14] In the same breath Einstein assured his puzzled friend Solovine, an admirer of Mach, that there was no way of going beyond the universe. What he could not deny was that the material universe, as viewed by him, inevitably invited that mental step beyond, which is a step toward God, the most non-material being.

Einstein's greatest discovery, the rediscovery of the universe for science (before general relativity it had been impossible to have a scientifically consistent discourse about the universe as such), was also the rediscovery by him of metaphysics. This did not come through a philosophical reappraisal of metaphysical theories as Einstein's information about the history of philosophy was rather meager. The man of science, he once noted, is a poor philosopher.[15] Einstein's words that when you want to know the scientific philosophy of a man of science watch his deeds not his words are valid of Einstein himself: his rediscovery of metaphysics is revealed in his scientific discoveries. They show a most unexpectedly singular world. It is a far cry from three-dimensional Euclidean flatness, widely assumed since Descartes to exist naturally and thus to assure that the world cannot be anything else except what suits a common sense conditioned to three dimensions. In all its major advances, twentieth-century science discovered a strangely singular universe, from quasars and black holes to neutrinos and quarks, which in turn most unexpectedly reinstates metaphysics in its own right. This is the metaphysics which the idealist—Royce, Hegel, Kant, Wolff, Leibniz, and Descartes—turned more often than not into logic-chopping, a fate which at times threatened the metaphysical discourse of Thomas, Bonaventure, and Scotus. It is a *metaphysics steeped in physics,* that is, in the assiduous registering of the physical. Such a metaphysics presupposes practitioners who, like Anteus of old, cannot retain their strength except by touching the ground with their feet at regular intervals.

By "a metaphysics steeped in physics" I mean a metaphysics steeped in the study of the physical. Under no circumstance should one try to derive philosophy from science or metaphysics from physics. That such an effort would be disastrous is attested by the whole history of philosophy, a lesson which Gilson stated in his customarily lucid and incisive way: "All philosophies perish by their science."[16] The true relation of philosophy and of science cannot be better stated than in the words of Oliver Wendell Holmes: "Science is a first-rate piece of furniture for a man's upper chamber, if he has common sense on the ground floor."[17] Common sense can be uncommonly misleading but it can only be corrected by common sense, however unscientific in appearance. Common sense, the perennial guide of metaphysics, will forever remain the supreme guide of physics. This truth is perceived at times even by physicists who present, as Eddington did, the philosophy of modern physics as a final discrediting of common sense philosophy, for Eddington had to admit that all physics is ultimately molar [or macroscopic], because "the observer himself is molar."[18] Therefore the reason why the most abstruse form of creative physics is pregnant with metaphysics is that any non-trivial word about the world of matter is a pointer to what is non-material.

The usefulness of the study of physical discoveries for the metaphysician lies in the fact that in an age of science it would be counterproductive to argue the case of the metaphysical, that is, of non-material perspectives and entities, with no reference to science. Apart from existentialists who despise science precisely because of its metaphysical consistency (the only consistency admissible in non-Christian existentialism is that there is no consistency), all major antimetaphysical trends in modern philosophy try to rest their cases with science. Logical positivists have almost succeeded in creating the impression that they are the sole legitimate spokesmen of science. They certainly do not speak in the name of Einstein, Planck, and Rutherford, that most formidable trio of realism, as Eddington once put it. De Broglie, Max von Laue, Schrödinger and others ought not to be forgotten as prominent physicist-advocates of philosophical realism.

Revealingly, some logical positivists, like Reichenbach, were most eager to enlist Einstein's authority; they almost put words in his mouth to suggest that he had made his discoveries along the dictates of logical positivism, but Einstein refused to encourage them. Their effort is noteworthy for a reason far more important than the weaknesses of resting their case on arguments *ex auctoritate*. Their effort to re-interpret Einstein's creativity was a striking aspect of their much broader strategy about scientific discoveries. That strategy aims at the abolition of discoveries as legitimate topics of scientific explanation. The strategy should seem self-defeating for anyone accustomed to seeing science as a series of discoveries in which one breeds another, though never in a mechanically predictable way which contradicts the creativity of the mind. Yet the strategy is very logical if one's true aim is the elimination of metaphysics. Was it not Carnap who boasted in 1932 that metaphysics had been eliminated as nonsensical?[19] If, however, metaphysics is to be excluded from a so-called scientific philosophy, then discoveries too ought to be disregarded for a very simple reason. In making startling scientific discoveries man patently reveals his ability to see beyond what is immediately given in the physical. Because this ability of man is metaphysical, the metaphysics of discovery imposes the rediscovery of metaphysics.

It should, therefore, cause no surprise that when a logical positivist writes a book on the logic of scientific discovery, the title itself proves to be a monumental misnomer.[20] The contention of such a book amounts not only to the assertion that there is no logical road to discovery, but that there is no logic, that is, reason in the act of discovery. The book in question should have been entitled 'the logic of completed research paper.' Surely, if logical means mechanical, the road to discovery is not logical. For all that, the road of discovery still ought to be rational if its end point, discovery, is to be regarded as rational. That surplus, which the rational represents with respect to the merely logical, will be admitted only by those who are not caught in the solipsistic world of pure logic. They alone know that only reason, insofar as it is more than mere logic, can break through the impregnable shell of solipsism and communicate with others by challenging their rational and real surrender to logical argument. It is that challenge and surrender, acts of real and reasonable beings and not merely propositions of logic, which are implied in each and every discovery.

It is no wonder that logical positivists and all those who resent metaphysics try to divest the act of discovery of its rational significance because that significance has a built-in metaphysical relevance. Since metaphysics has long ceased to be popular, one can understand the popularity of explaining away by sheer logic-chopping the great metaphysical rationality of scientific discoveries or by doing the same with recourse to the slogans of psychology and sociology. Thus, discoveries become revolutions, Gestalt switches, and the like, with the result that the marvel which is science becomes discredited in the process. Such a result is certainly logical, for once the simplest act of knowledge is not recognized as a marvel which reveals the non-physical in the physical, a marvel to which only metaphysics can do justice, then even discoveries, these spectacular and sophisticated processes of knowledge, will fail to reassure the scientists, to say nothing of some philosophers and historians of science, about the coherence of the physical.

Here one cannot help recalling the phrase, by their fruits ye shall know them, and the fact that the phrase was prominently used by Planck in 1908 in his great attack on Mach that sent shock waves through the scientific and philosophical world. The fruits which Planck had in mind were discoveries. By seeing in them genuine fruits, the metaphysician will find himself in line with the best scientific tradition, indeed, he will find himself in company with the very soul of science. Moreover, he will find in those fruits a most nourishing food for thought about what matters most in science as a series of creative discoveries, which leads one to a non-material world lurking beyond a world of matter. That world is the world of God and soul, a world reached through discoveries, scientific and other, about that world which is called the physical universe.

[1]E. A. Burtt, *The Metaphysical Foundations of Modern Science* (1924, 2d rev. ed. 1932; Garden City, NY: Doubleday, n.d.), p. 227.

[2]Holton did so in his essays on the presence of metaphysics in the scientific creativity of Kepler and Einstein, reprinted in his *Thematic Origins of Scientific Thought* (Cambridge: Harvard University Press, 1973). In doing so Holton failed to do justice to Kepler's *Christian* platonism and to Einstein's clear realization that the reality of the universe as implied in General Relativity poses a genuinely metaphysical challenge.

[3]As recalled by J. T. Desaguliers, a member of Newton's inner circle, in his *Course of Experimental Philosophy* (3d ed.; London: A. Millar, 1763), vol I, p. viii.

[4]*New Organon*, Bk. 1, aphorism 61.

[5]D'Alembert did so at the end of the preface to his *Traité de l'équilibre et du mouvement des fluides* (Paris: chez David, l'aîné, 1744), p. xxxii and in his much more accessible *Preliminary Discourse to the Encyclopedia of Diderot* (Indianapolis: Bobbs-Merrill, 1963), p. 79.

[6]See Pemberton's *A View of Sir Isaac Newton's Philosophy* (New York: Johnson Reprint, 1972), p. 23. Henry Pemberton, a young physician, was all the more authoritative on this point because he was in charge of preparing for publication, a work of over two years, the third edition of Newton's *Principia*.

[7]For glimpses on that subjectivism with respect to physics, see my *The Road of Science and the Ways to God* (Chicago: University of Chicago Press, 1978), pp. 124-25.

[8]For details, see ibid., p. 147.

[9]See J. S. Mill, *An Examination of Sir W. Hamilton's Philosophy* (London: Longman, 1865), pp. 68-69. It was in that sense that Mill endorsed "randomness" in separate parts of the universe, in his *System of Logic* (Toronto: University of Toronto Press, 1973), p. 565.

[10]First published in 1860.

[11]E. Mach, *The Science of Mechanics*, tr. T. J. McCormack (La Salle, IL: Open Court, 1960), p. 578.

[12]Planck was most explicit in this respect in the memorandum which he addressed to the Prussian government on behalf of Einstein's candidacy to the Prussian Academy of Science. For excerpts from that memorandum, see R. W. Clark, *Einstein: The Life and Times* (New York: Thomas Y. Crowell, 1971), p. 169.

[13]See "Reply to Criticisms," in P. A. Schilpp (ed.), *Albert Einstein: Philosopher-Scientist* (1949; New York: Harper and Brothers, 1959), p. 673.

[14]For references and further details, see note 41 to Chapter 1 above.

[15]A. Einstein, *Out of My Later Years* (New York: Philosophical Library, 1950), p. 58.

[16]No less incisive is the continuation of Gilson's statement: "All philosophies survive by the metaphysical truth which they contain." See *A Gilson Reader: Selected Writings of Etienne Gilson*, ed. A. C. Pegis (Garden City, NY: Doubleday, 1957), p. 216.

[17]O. W. Holmes, *The Poet at the Breakfast Table* (Boston: James R. Osgood, 1877), p. 140.

[18]A. S. Eddington, *The Philosophy of Physical Science* (New York: The Macmillan Company, 1938), p. 77.

[19]For details and documentation, see my *Brain, Mind and Computers* (1969; 2d paperback edition, Chicago: Regnery/Gateway, 1978), pp. 172-74 and 206-07.

[20]The reference is, of course, to K. R. Popper's widely read *The Logic of Scientific Discovery,* a misnomer already in its more modest erstwhile German title, *Logik der Forschung* ("logic of research").

4

God and Man's Science:
A View of Creation

The organizers of this week's special program of Christian Studies have invited me to speak on "God and Man's Science: A View of Creation." For their suggesting the title, I am most grateful. They spared me the irksome task of having to make a choice. A gain is, however, always a loss. The title chosen stands for a vast topic which puts one at a loss about the always difficult problem of where to begin. Logic demands that the subtitle, "a view of creation," should not be the starting point. Logic may then suggest that we start with the main title, which begins with God.

Lecture delivered at Hillsdale College in October 1983. First published in *The Christian Vision: Man in Society* (Hillsdale, MI: Hillsdale College Press, 1984), pp. 35-49. Reprinted with permission.

Being the ultimate, God is certainly the first both logically and ontologically. However, our knowledge of God is not direct but indirect, that is, inferential. Our direct knowledge is about things and ourselves, which are the grounds of our inferential knowledge about God. There is also to be kept in mind a lesson of modern Western philosophy. Some rationalists, such as Descartes and Spinoza, and some idealists, especially the Hegelians, were wont to begin with God. They invariably lost out on things and ended with themselves, the worst possible outcome.

We are then left with "man's science" as a starting point. The expression "man's science" is not, however, as simple a proposition as it may appear. It may mean, for instance, science about man, a terribly vast subject including anthropology, psychology, and medicine, none of which is my specialty. "Man's science" would much more be related to my own studies if the emphasis were to be put on science as such. In that case, one could deal with the philosophy and history of science. Part of that history is very human. There are indeed very good reasons for uttering the phrase "man's science" in a mournful tone. Some sad aspects of science have been very much in the news and therefore could serve as a starting point.

In some very sad sense, which is very human indeed, science is a very human enterprise. Among other things, science is mercilessly competitive. Science does have its tough entrepreneurs no less than does any branch of business. Stories, such as the story of the double helix, have amply revealed the fierce pursuit of prizes which go only to the very first and never to the best second, let alone to the second best. Enough is also reported through newspapers about the keen competition for research grants, for the funding of new equipment, for new laboratories and institutes—a competition which at times mobilizes the public opinion of entire states and even wider regions. Teams of anthropologists stake out claims for elusive distant valleys with no less rush and jealousy than was the case a hundred years ago with homesteaders in Oklahoma and somewhat earlier with gold diggers in California.

There are also some cases, not too many though increasing in number, which show scientists cheating with their data. The pressure to come up with novel results, the pressure of having another paper published, is too great; to yield to that pressure, the pressure of opportunity, is all too human. Some prominent medical schools and research institutes earned bad publicity in recent years because they failed to prevent such misdeeds, or to detect them soon enough. Science can indeed become very much man's science in a very sad sense.

There is also the ever-present human fallacy of wishful thinking: namely, the desire to see something where there is nothing. The case of those who claim to have seen balls moved by their mere mental concentration on them reveals plenty of the humanness of science in that very sad sense. Other, less known examples are the alleged discovery, early this century, of N-rays, and the claim made about ten years ago of experimental evidence of a very slight difference between the negative and positive electric charge. That some scientists take upon themselves the role of universal sages, pontificating on any and all problems and issues, is further evidence of science being very much man's science—that is, a very human affair.

Another aspect of the humanness of science is more tragic. Three hundred years ago, at the time of Newton, when science appeared robustly on the scene, it was greeted by many as the means whereby paradise may be created on earth. In 1664 Henry Power, a junior member of the Royal Society, celebrated science as the tool for which "there is no Truth so abstruse, nor so far evaluated out of our reach, but man's wit may raise Engines to Scale and Conquer it."[1] A hundred years later Joseph Priestley, an English scientist, fled to the United States in a similar state of mind. He felt that in the virgin fields of this newly born country there would be a better chance of implementing the new and final age of mankind, an age "glorious and paradisiacal beyond what our imagination can now conceive."[2]

These United States of ours have indeed proved a fertile ground for that optimism which saw in science only the harbinger of happiness and prosperity. For the past hundred years, the notion of a rather naive progress could thrive in our midst in coexistence with a doctrine, Darwinism, which in fact offered progress (or mere survival) for only a relatively few and meekly condoned the perishing of the great majority in each class, group, or species, if you wish. Social Darwinism saw its heyday in our country not too long ago. In fact, it still has rear-guard apostles who are not taken aback even by the obvious. Thus Jacob Bronowski exculpated science of any and all responsibility concerning Hiroshima and Nagasaki.[3]

As is well known, because of science, man's science, man can trigger a chain reaction of genetic mutation ruining the entire human race. Because of science, man's science, man can ruin his entire environment and blow himself into outer space on the wings of mushrooming nuclear blasts. The mind-boggling extent to which man has turned the finest inventions of science to destructive purposes cannot be given a better summary than the one given by Captain Ahab of *Moby Dick* about his own tragic course. "All my means are sane, my motive and my object mad."[4]

The end, the scientifically engineered end, may of course come unobtrusively as if by default. No properly organized, internationally sponsored studies are in progress, for instance, about the ultimate impact of rocket exhaust deposited in the upper atmosphere of a height three times the one at which most commercial airliners now fly. That may ultimately result in a layer of carbon dioxide of such concentration as to turn the entire earth into a greenhouse in which the rise of temperature can no longer be reversed.

This is easily overlooked when our attention is drawn from the thousands of space satellites serving military purposes to satellites of purely scientific aim. One of these carrying a telescope made headlines a month or so ago after registering radiation around Vega (26 million light years away), the source of which may be a ring of small particles. The spotting of such a radiation is a most extraordinary achievement. It could, however, be expected that around a fairly young star like Vega there would be a ring or belt of small particles, not much different from a thick gas. Unfortunately, it is also to be expected that such a ring would be readily taken for a proof of a planetary system in embryo, eventually able to carry life, intelligent life included.

The proof in question is a perfect example of another aspect of science which shows how human an enterprise science is, how much science is man's science. While the proof has been presented in countless headlines and reports as wholly reliable, it is in fact as full of holes as is a sieve or a colander. Around the turn of the century it was already demonstrated that a ring of particles can never gather into a single large body or planet. The demonstration was duly printed in a leading scientific journal, reported by prominent scientists in other journals and mentioned in widely read books. Its validity has never been questioned. I told the whole story half a dozen years ago in one of my books.[5] Since that book was published by such an eminent and leading scientific publishing house as John Wiley in New York, it had to be easily within the reach of anyone interested in factual evidence, an interest which is the presumed hallmark of scientific thinking. Why is it then that such an evidence fails to be translated into broad awareness? Why is it that in science, no less than in all other fields of human inquiry and enterprise, there is at work a very selective perception, very much akin to the socio-political pattern known as selective indignation?

The reason is connected with the role which science has come to play in shaping the intellectual atmosphere of our modern, Western intellectual world. That atmosphere is largely the making of the leaders of two generations, straddling the French Revolution. The leaders of the first, or earlier generation, were essentially, though not entirely, dismantlers. Their immediate aim was to dislocate and annihilate the *ancien régime* and whatever was connected with it socially, politically, ideologically, and economically. People like Diderot and Condorcet knew, however, that a purely negative strategy never works. Something positive has to be dangled before the eyes of the so-called educated class, that naive and indispensable tool of revolutionaries for whom the cause of the proletariat is all too often but a convenient cover-up. A central part of that positive program was science, with Comte as its chief interpreter, and leader of the second generation that tried to build on the ruins of the Napoleonic wars. It is certainly ironical, though not at all unexpected, that not much science was contained in that program in spite of its label, positivism.

Positivism also quickly revealed itself as a continuation of a pseudo-religious program hiding behind "scientific" facade. About science Diderot and Condorcet were eager to claim not only that it would usher in a paradise on earth, but also that its rise implied a radical opposition to tradition, that is, to Christianity. A principal claim of those two was in fact that science, born in an anti-Christian, purely rationalist spirit, can fulfill its promises only if Christianity as a social matrix and presence is wholly discredited and discarded. This claim was immensely successful. It has produced an intellectual climate which has for the past 150 years found handy vehicles in not a few bestsellers. They all have been devoted to the contention that science and religion (Christian religion, of course) are utterly irreconcilable.

Such was the gist of the claim of Diderot, and especially of Condorcet, about the origin and rise of science. Is it indeed true that science owes its origin to men that have turned their back on Christianity? Quite the contrary is the truth. The question of any historical origin is, of course, always a bit nebulous. Scholars will forever dispute the exact beginning of the Middle Ages, of the Renaissance, of Classicism, and of Romanticism, or who was the first modern thinker. There is always a hazy margin when it comes to the exact determining of any of the *"isms"* forming the principal chapters of Western intellectual history, or of any history for that matter. No one would, however, say that just because the exact beginning of those *"isms"* is difficult to determine, there was no true beginning for the Middle Ages, for the Renaissance, for Classicism and for Romanticism. In fact, if any of these epochs is viewed against its immediate predecessor or its background, its reality strikes one with overwhelming force, and its origin will be easier to pinpoint.

Much the same applies to the question of the origin of science. The clue to its solution can easily emerge if seen against the background of great cultures that had no science. Among such great cultures were ancient China, India, Egypt, Babylon, and Greece. The case of the Chinese is particularly instructive because of a statement made by Francis Bacon in the early seventeenth century. According to Bacon, science arose at that time because of the impact of three European inventions: gunpowder, the compass, and printing. That Bacon did not speak of the old and Chinese origin of at least two of those inventions, the gunpowder and the compass, is a secondary matter. The principal point is that he had ascribed the origin of science to mechanical inventions. Now if Bacon had been right, one would expect the Chinese of old to have developed science. They did not. Had they done so, we would be today part of a worldwide Chinese empire. Please also recall that at the time of Vasco da Gama the Chinese navy was as good if not better than the Portuguese navy. The Chinese could have easily sailed along the Aleutians or across Midway and the Hawaiian islands and colonized the California coastline. But they did not.

Since the Chinese of old served evidence of a great deal of inventiveness in mechanical skills, it is reasonable to assume that what they lacked was something of an intellectual insight for formulating and developing science. This assumption becomes well-nigh irresistible when we look at what happened in classical Greece. The Greeks failed to develop science, by which I mean an intellectual enterprise in which one discovery generates another discovery and does so at an increasingly accelerated rate. Not that they lacked scientific genius productive of intellectual insights—it is enough to think of Euclid's geometry or of Aristarchus' method of determining the size of the earth, moon, and sun and their relative and absolute distances. Yet, the Greeks of old failed to make any breakthrough in the science of motion or dynamics which is the basis of all physics and which in turn is the basis of all modern exact science.

In speaking of the science of motion, Newton's name naturally comes to mind. Physics in Newtonian physics and even Einstein's physics would be inconceivable without Newton's *Principia*. That book begins with the three laws of motion: the basis of the whole science of mechanics, including rocket propulsion and space travel. Newton, of course, did not care to tell his readers how he arrived at those laws. He did not care because he was a very proud man unwilling to give credit to others, as was all too often the case with other seventeenth-century scientists and authors. Galileo and Descartes are two chief examples of this intellectual stinginess. Had Newton cared to say something about the origin of those three laws, and had he been utterly candid, he might have proceeded something like this: The credit for the third law (force equals mass times acceleration) belongs to me though not in the sense that I had formulated the notion of uniform acceleration. Credit for the latter should go to Galileo. As to the second and first laws, Newton should have made a special effort to be candid. The reason for this was that both those laws could be found in the books of Descartes, of whose reputation Newton was terribly jealous. He did not want anyone to suspect that he owed anything to Descartes. In his later years, Newton spent much precious time on erasing from his manuscripts and notebooks the name of Descartes, lest posterity learn a thing or two.

Had Newton acknowledged Galileo and Descartes, he would have not stated thereby the true origin of the first law and of the law of acceleration of which the free fall of a body is a classic case and primary example. Descartes was not the inventor of the all-important first law, nor was Galileo the inventor of the no-less-important law of acceleration. They could find them (and indeed found them) in several books printed in the 1570s and 1580s, whose authors took them from an earlier tradition, antedating the invention of printing. That tradition can be traced to the fourteenth-century Sorbonne, especially to the lectures of John Buridan and his greatest disciple, Nicole Oresme, who died as Bishop of Lisieux in 1378.

Lecturing in the fourteenth-century medieval universities consisted in reading the books of a prominent ancient author, very often Aristotle, and commenting on the text. This had by then been an old tradition going back to Hellenistic times and in particular to Muslim schools. One of Aristotle's scientific books that was most often commented upon was his cosmology, called *On the Heavens.* There Aristotle most explicitly states that the world is eternal and that its motion, and in particular the daily circular motion of the sphere of stars, is also eternal because the world is and must be un-created, that is, without a beginning. Whatever else the Prime Mover of Aristotle was, he was not a Creator. Aristotle had no use for the idea of creation out of nothing.[6] For Aristotle, the world, the universe, the cosmos, was the ultimate entity, most likely identical in its better or celestial parts with the Prime Mover himself. The cosmos, according to Aristotle, had necessarily to be what it is—in no way could his Prime Mover fashion, let alone create, a different universe.

Newton's first law was formulated by medieval schoolmen in reaction against such and similar statements of Aristotle and of other pagan classical scholars who held those statements to be ab-solute dogmas. The eternity and uncreatedness of the universe was indeed the chief dogma of all pagan religions, old and new, crude and refined. The medieval reaction to that dogma was, as one could expect it, made in terms of the first tenet of Christian Creed, which states the creation of all and in time, that is, in the beginning. How productive and fruitful that reaction was for science can be seen in John Buridan's commentaries on Aristotle's *On the Heavens.* After rejecting Aristotle's doctrine on the eternity of motion, Buridan wrote: "In the beginning when God made the heaven and the earth, He imparted a certain amount of impetus (motion) to the heavenly bodies, which impetus they still keep because they move in a space where there is no friction."[7] This statement, which is esentially equivalent to Newton's first law, reappeared in many medieval lec-ture notes and its equivalent appeared in print many times before Descartes came to the scene.

Since there is no time to discuss the pre-Galilean history of ac-celeration, let us turn to Newtonian science, of which the law of ac-celeration is a pivotal proposition in the form of the well-known force law. That law and the first two laws of motion do not yet make science. Newton's greatness lies, first, in his claim that his laws of motion are universally valid and, second, that he had shown something of that universality. I mean his proof that the motion of the moon is governed by the same acceleration as is the fall of an apple or stone to earth. This coupling of the earth and of the moon was a bold step into the universe of things. It revealed in a single stroke the very essence of science, which is the universal applicability of its laws. This is what is meant by the phrase that all science is cosmology, that is, all science is about the cosmos or the universe. This is why every really fundamental law of physics reveals something all-encompassing about the universe; this is why almost all truly great physicists write pages, at times entire chapters, and on rare occasions, entire books which are equivalent to a cosmology either in outline or fully developed.

There are several pages in Newton's writings which are equivalent to a cosmology. A few of those pages appeared in Newton's time, another few about thirty years after his death, and still another few very important and revealing pages only about twenty or so years ago. All those pages show two things: First, Newton's preference was for a universe which was finite and spherical, floating in an infinite space filled with the ether which he did not hold to be matter in the ordinary sense. That such was Newton's preference can easily be gathered from the *Spectator,* a magazine whose editor, Addison, was a good acquaintance of Newton. In the July 9, 1714 issue of the *Spectator,* Addison in fact wrote that according to Newton and reason, the world is finite in an infinite space. This phrase was then taken over by Voltaire in his book on Newton's physics, a book which saw over 25 editions prior to the nineteenth century.[8]

The other thing to remark about Newton's cosmology is that he bungled about the scientific merit of a truly infinite material universe in which stars could be found to infinity in any direction. I said bungled because he was told about a proof which convincingly showed that such a universe entailed a scientific contradiction. Newton rejected the proof perhaps because it was formulated not by a scientist, but by a classical scholar, Richard Bentley, who was also Master of Trinity College, Newton's own college, and a rather overbearing clergyman to boot. However that may be, the proof of Bentley was given an exact formulation almost two hundred years later.[9] According to that formulation, the gravitational potential in an infinite universe of homogeneously distributed stars is infinite at any point. Such a universe cannot exist physically.

The origin and whole history of the so-called Newtonian universe shows something of man's science in two different senses. One is the greatness of man's mind as evidenced by his science. Newton's third law, which is the basis of his law of gravitation, proved exceedingly powerful. It enabled subsequent scientists, such as Euler, Herschel, and Laplace, to explain most peculiar features of the motion of planets and of distant double stars. In other words, the science of Newtonian gravitation was truly a science because it allowed man to reach far into the cosmos. But Newtonian gravitation could not give a scientific account of the universe, inasmuch as the universe was taken for a so-called infinite Newtonian universe. That such a universe was not rejected categorically by Newton and that in the nineteenth century it became generally believed in is the other sense of Newtonian science being but man's science. For all its greatness, the scientific mind is not infallible. In its reasonings it repeatedly became the victim of foibles, biases, prejudices, and even of sheer blindness to the obvious.

For us, late twentieth-century men, Newtonian science is a thing of the past. Everybody knows that Newton has been superseded by Einstein, but very few people know the true reason for this. The usual reason given is that Einstein showed everything to be relative. Nothing could be further from the truth. Einstein's theory of General Relativity is the most absolutist theory ever proposed in the history of science. In fact, the entire success of Einstein's theory is that it is absolutist. According to it, the value of the speed of light is independent of any reference systems and therefore has a value which is absolutely valid. According to the same theory, all inertial and accelerated reference systems are absolutely equivalent. Being a great scientist, Einstein also worked out a cosmology. Since he knew that the three-dimensional Newtonian universe was an impossibility, he had to turn to a four-dimensional framework. There are several forms of a four-dimensional space-time manifold, such as a cylindrical space or hyperbolical space, which are compatible with an infinite mass. But these solutions seemed to Einstein to be too peculiar, and therefore to contradict the principle of simplicity. So he took a four-dimensional manifold in which the motion of material particles can only be circular. As a consequence of this he had to regard the finite and material universe as spherical. Within a month, we are still in 1917, another scientist, de Sitter, found that Einstein's spherical universe was unstable. At the slightest disturbance in it, that is, at the slightest motion of any of its parts, be they galaxies, stars or atoms, such a universe had to expand. Einstein was not at all happy with this finding, but this is another story.

We are now at the theoretical origin of what is today called the expansion of the universe. In the 1920s, the rate of expansion was predicted and soon verified by the recessional red shift observed in the spectrum of most galaxies. If, however, the universe is expanding, there has to be a time in the past when it was very small, perhaps as small as an atom.

To speak of the early universe as an atom is very appropriate in the atomic age. The discovery of atoms and of the atomic structure of all the chemical elements led to speculations about the genesis of those elements. Around 1950 a rather promising theory was formulated about the condition in which electrons and protons could unite into hydrogen, hydrogen into deuterium and tritium, the steps toward helium. The gist of that theory was a hypothetical early state of the universe in which the universe consisted only of photons, electrons, protons, and neutrons. Such a universe was in a rapid expansion and dropped through a very specific temperature and pressure range. Most importantly, such a universe had to leave behind a very specific radiation, which was in fact detected in 1963.

Since then, many other advances have been made in scientific cosmology, the hottest field of research in science today. All these findings are expressive of two all-important facts. The first is that man's science is so marvelously powerful a thing as to give man the ability to have a real, that is, scientifically reliable grasp of the universe. The second is that the view given by science about the universe is a very special view. In that view, the universe appears to be a most peculiar, most specific entity. Being very specific, the universe is not different from any other thing. All things are terribly specific. Precisely because they are very specific, they reveal, indeed they suggest with a brute force, that they could be different from what they are. In other words, specificity always reveals the non-necessary character of a thing or anything. This is precisely what is revealed by modern science about the universe as a most specific entity. Now if the universe is not necessary, that is, is not necessarily what it is, then it is contingent. If, however, it is contingent, its actual shape and its very existence are dependent on a choice which transcends the entire universe. That choice or power can only be the creative omnipotence of God. Such is the chain of events of reasonings which show that man's science is not only a view of the universe but also a view of creation and that ultimately we have to begin with God. Both history and logic show that God, the Christian God, is needed in order to let man have science, and if that science is truly a science or cosmology, man's view of the universe becomes a view of creation.

Such an outcome, as one would expect, is most repulsive to secular humanists. They are as numerous among scientists in general and cosmologists in particular as they are in any other professional group. In fact, they should seem all the more numerous because secular publishers (including university presses) are much more willing to publish their writings than writings done in the vein, for instance, of this lecture. The pattern is also "secular" in the sense of long-standing. Thirty years ago all the publicity, including the very important marketing of inexpensive paperbacks, was given to the proponents of the so-called steady-state universe. The chief aim of that theory was to take out of cosmology the metaphysical sting which was brought into it by the expanding universe. Since that expansion forcefully showed the time-conditioned contingent character of the universe, the steady-state-universe theorists, some of them professed atheists, postulated that the average density of matter in the universe, which decreases by the expansion, is compensated by the appearance, out-of-nothing and without a Creator, of new hydrogen atoms in the space left empty by the receding galaxies.

Of course, they did their best to give a scientific rationale to that antimetaphysical, antirational, and antiscientific extravaganza. They pointed at a discrepancy, now completely resolved, of the age of stars and the age of the universe. The very fact that within a few years the discrepancy was resolved shows how minor a problem it really was and how extravagant it was to propose for its solution a most extraordinary process, namely, the steady creation, without a Creator, of hydrogen atoms out of nothing. The solution, extravagant even from the purely philosophical viewpoint, was defective also from the strictly scientific viewpoint for two reasons. First, no such radiation was detected. Most importantly, it did not follow at all scientifically that even if there had been observed an extra amount of 21 cm radiation characteristic of H atoms, the nothing could not be assigned as the immediate antecedent of that radiation. The nothing is never an object of scientific, that is, partly empirical, inference. Yet for all such outstanding defects in the steady-state theory, it had been touted for two decades as one of the three most respectable cosmological models.

The two other models were the model of a single-expansion and the oscillating model. The latter has been turned into another smokescreen against the view of the universe as God's creation. Like the steady-state theory, the oscillating model, too, had very serious scientific problems. But in the so-called higher popularizations of that model, those problems have been systematically ignored for obviously secularist or materialist reasons. In the oscillating universe, one world-age, or expansion-contraction cycle, would be followed by another in endless sequence. Once that sequence is taken to be really endless, then it is readily taken for a proof of the eternity of the world, which is the very opposite of a principal aspect of the Christian dogma of creation. According to that dogma, the world was not only created but also created in time; that is, the past time-span of the existence of the world is strictly finite. There is another conflict between the Christian notion of a created universe and the oscillating model. A created universe embodies purpose, whereas a universe oscillating forever stands for the very opposite. It stands in fact for an eternal treadmill in which worlds and civilizations would follow one another and repeat one another in an endless sequence.

Time allows but a very brief mention of other cosmological models serving a distinctly secularist, agnostic, and materialistic purpose. One of them is called the multiworld model in which there are as many universes as there are observers. How one observer can communicate with another observer, that is, get out of his own world into another world, is not explained in that theory. Another such model is the model of an accidental universe. Its chief promoter, P. Davies, a British scientist, has just come out, not surprisingly, with a book[10] in which science is pitted against Christian religion.

That nothing happens by accident is, of course, a chief tenet of Christian religion, according to which not even a sparrow falls to the ground, or a hair is bent on our head, without our Heavenly Father willing it. That nothing happens by accident—that is, by sheer chance, that is, really without a cause—is also a chief tenet of science about the material universe. For if anything were truly accidental, there could be no consistency, and without consistency there could be no laws, not even statistical laws, because even they imply one or two parameters which imply consistency. In fact, the best and latest scientific discoveries or laws about the universe show us a universe which is the embodiment of the highest degree of consistency, both in space and in time. Indeed, everything is so consistently interconnected in the universe as modern science reveals it to us that an account of the extreme specificity of the primeval condition of the universe permits the inference that only in such a universe could man arise, a being even more specific or peculiar than the universe itself. While the universe does not know itself, man knows both himself and the universe. More importantly, he can see beyond the universe both the first and the ultimate which is God and have thus a view of creation. All this and much more should come to mind in speaking of God and man's science.

[1]H. Power, *Experimental Philosophy in Three Books: Containing New Experiments, Microscopical, Mercurial, Magnetical* (London: John Martin and James Allestry, 1664), pp. 191-2.

[2]J. Priestley, *An Essay on the First Principles of Government* (2 ed.; London, 1771), pp. 4-5.

[3]J. Bronowski, *Science and Human Values* (New York: Harper and Row, 1959), p. 90.

[4]H. Melville, *Moby Dick* (New York: The Modern Library, 1926), p. 185.

[5]*Planets and Planetarians: A History of Theories of the Origin of Planetary Systems* (New York: John Wiley, Edinburgh: Scottish Academic Press, 1978), p. 188.

[6]In fact his scorn was so thorough that he did not dignify the idea to a comment. See *On the Heavens*, Bk 3, ch. 1. (298b).

[7]This is a paraphrase in a condensed form of his statement. For its actual wording, see my *Science and Creation: From Eternal Cycles to an Oscillating Universe* (Edinburgh: Scottish Academic Press, 1974, 2d enlarged paperback edition, 1986), p. 233.

[8]*Elemens de la philosophie de Newton,* first published in 1738.

[9]The full story is told in my *The Paradox of Olbers' Paradox* (New York: Herder and Herder, 1969), pp. 60-66.

[10]*God and the New Physics* (New York: Simon and Schuster, 1983).

5

Brain, Mind, and Computers

Originally, my book *Brain, Mind and Computers,*[1] was supposed to be a chapter with the title, "Physics and Psychology," in another book of mine, *The Relevance of Physics.*[2] I must therefore say something about *The Relevance* to help you understand the real aim of *Brain, Mind and Computers. The Relevance* grew out of an experience which I had in 1951 as a young professor of systematic theology. In that year the lectures had to be on the essence, existence and attributes of God. It was then that the idea seized me that I should work out a watertight and overpowering proof of the existence of God based on modern physics and astronomy.

Address given at the invitation of the American Scientific Affiliation at its Convention in August 1970, and first published in *Journal of the American Scientific Affiliation,* 24 (March 1972), pp. 12-17. Reprinted with permission.

In retrospect this was brashness itself, but perhaps natural for a scholar still in his twenties. I must say, however, that I went about the business rather methodically. Providence too helped. In late 1953 I had to give up teaching owing to a surgical mishap which deprived me for years of the effective use of my vocal chords. It did not take too long to decide what to do with all the time on my hands. Since I already had a B.S., I entered graduate school in the fall of 1954. My hopes were that by the time I had my Ph.D. in physics I would have the proof in my hands.

I had my Ph.D. four years later, but not the scientific proof of the existence of God. Luckily enough, my vocal chords were not yet good enough for teaching. This meant ample time for further studies. During my graduate-student years it became evident to me that the question of a scientific proof of the existence of God had a very important history to it. As a result, I spent the years 1958-60 reading history and philosophy of physics at Stanford and Berkeley. It was there and then that I received the answer to my problem. For reasons inherent in the method of physical science, no watertight proof of the existence of God can be built on its data and conclusions. But this also meant that no refutation of the existence of God could be built on physics either.

This was my first glance in depth on the limitations of exact science and of its method. I also soon began to realize that I learned something which had tremendous bearing on the whole context of modern scientific culture. It was not difficult to see that the major ills and woes of our modern society come from an undue emphasis on the scientific or quantitative method. In all this there was no basically new insight. Others said it long before me, but one aspect of the problem was still to be spelled out in detail. This special aspect consisted in giving a detailed documentation of the limitations of physics through the very words of its best practitioners. To present the limitations of physics convincingly, it had to be done by physicists themselves and by physicists of all ages.

This is what *The Relevance of Physics* is about. It is a multidimensional analysis of the history of physics through the reflection of physicists on their own aims, hopes, accomplishments, and failures. By multidimensional analysis I mean that the book retraces the history of physics through eight different angles. Four of these relate to the frustrated hopes of reducing other areas of studies to a branch of physics. In *The Relevance* I tried to illustrate this failure with respect to biology, philosophy, ethics, and theology. Originally I also planned in that section of the book one more chapter that has grown into a separate book with the title *Brain, Mind and Computers*. In it I did not aim at producing a resounding proof of brain-mind dualism. I merely tried to show that when it comes to the problem of brain-mind interaction the positions known as physicalism, reductionism and behaviorism, fall very short of their high-flying claims.

In other words, if I have made any contribution to the question of the brain-mind relationship, and to the defense of dualism, it was a negative one. What I tried to do was to clean the air, to dissipate some heavy fog, to unmask a very systematic and very successful publicity campaign which tries to create the illusion that every notable investigator of the topic has turned his back on dualism.

Whether I succeeded is unimportant. But we must recognize that in every major field of human endeavor, proofs and demonstrations have a restricted role. Much depends also on creating or dissipating a mental or cultural atmosphere. To take an example, nobody has ever proved that the universe was a clockwork mechanism, but for two centuries everybody came to believe it. How did this happen? Any student of cultural history knows it or should know it. It came about by a combination of wishful thinking and of a systematic publicity campaign. Those of wishful thinking wanted a disarmingly simple solution; those of the publicity campaign had an ax to grind. Voltaire and the encyclopedists made no secret about that.

Future history will tell how much planning has been behind the attack which the champions of twentieth-century physicalism and behaviorism waged on the world of values and on dualism in particular. Preliminary conclusions can, however, be safely drawn by those who have some insight or first hand experience into the hiring policies of many departments of psychology, sociology, and philosophy. The presence of wishful thinking should be all too evident for those who can read between the lines, or who have read, for instance, Skinner's *Walden Two*. Of course, as long as theological and philosophical values were the target of that attack, the academe and the media kept applauding. There was no particular concern shown either when man's mind became equated with a feedback mechanism. Things, however, suddenly went sour when a new generation began to implement a basic tenet of their elementary, high-school and college education. The tenet is that ethical values are merely patterns that can and must keep changing. Consequently, all that is needed for the justification of a new morality or new social philosophy is that a sufficient number of individuals should act it out. The reasoning is that if you have a certain number of people behaving in a specific manner, you have a pattern which, however distasteful or destructive, should be acceptable, because it is a pattern.

There is an inner logic in everything, or in a more colloquial form, one has to pay the piper one day. Nowadays, modern society is doing just that, but I wonder if its own havoc will bring it to its senses. At least, I do not see any sign that a serious reconsideration of false and destructive premises would already be under way. Twenty-five years ago history had witnessed the conclusion of a great crusade fought for human rights, for the inalienable rights of any individual whatever his color and social status. Today, expressions that evoke the absolute dignity and inalienable rights of the individual, are frowned upon in much of the academe as conceptual dinosaurs.

Modern secular and technological society still has to come to terms with an unavoidable reconsideration. It still must admit that there is no escaping from the labyrinth of pattern-philosophy except by recognizing that there is something eternal and spiritual in man which should be given unconditional respect. Herein lies the existential background of the ultimate explanation of the presence of consciousness and thoughts in man. As I said before, the fashionable and prevailing presumption is that mind and soul are only names and are of concern only for backward theologians and clergymen.

This was rather bluntly put two years ago by Mortimer Adler in his book, *The Difference of Man and the Difference it Makes.*[3] There he stated that the defense of an immaterial principle in man, call it soul or mind, is today a matter of concern only for Roman Catholics and Orthodox Jews. His failure to mention Protestants should be rather revealing. At any rate, I am most pleased to be among scientists who are uncompromising Christians as well, who refuse to sell out to pattern-philosophy and to a sophisticated godlessness that lure away many Christians.

I also have to tell you that few things can shock me more than when I am told by fellow Roman Catholic theologians, mostly younger ones, that we should not be concerned with the defense of dualism. It is outmoded, they say, and we can very well do without it. Well, I once asked one of these whether he would still exist after his body had been duly cremated and his ashes scattered into the nearby river? Then and only then did he realize the obvious, namely, that Christian existence is inconceivable without the acceptance of dualism.

A reacceptance of dualism by society is the only road toward social health. Vindication of dualism means, of course, far more for us believing Christians. It means for us the securing of rational grounds without which faith cannot survive in any thinking man. Vindication of dualism also means for us a basically favorable climate in which one could speak more confidently about the Magna Carta of Christianity, the resurrection of Christ and our eventual resurrection on the last day.

The problem has a very deep relevance for each of us personally. Moreover, a thorough acquaintance with the problem can help a great deal in strengthening Christians, especially the younger ones, and increasing their number. I said "great deal" and frankly I am somewhat uneasy about it. I should have rather said "great deal, yes and no."

A "great deal" is a quantitative expression. It refers to measurements and measurements are always so many comparisons along a scale. A good grasp of the "Brain, Mind and Computer" problem should mean a great deal in a far deeper or philosophical sense. But I doubt that good philosophy alone can produce many convinced adepts for dualism. If dualism is still around and strong, it is largely because there are still Christians around, and Christians are generated not so much by lengthy arguments as by the immediate, instinctive grasp of the incomparable greatness of Christ.

That Beethoven's *Ninth Symphony* or Rembrandt's *Nightwatch* are incomparable masterpieces, are propositions that must be grasped instinctively. By instinctive I do not mean mystical or mysterious. What I have in mind was once very forcefully expressed by the Nobel-laureate physicist, and a great Christian, A. H. Compton. As he discussed in a lecture at Yale the claim that the laws of physics left no room for the freedom of the will, he raised his little finger, bent it and said that if the laws of physics ever should come to contradict his conviction that he can move his little finger at will then all the laws of physics should be revised and reformulated.[4]

Of course, most people would say that they know that they can move their little finger at will, and that they are conscious of that. But very few are those who are able to see the immensity of such obvious experiences. Technical discussions about "Brain, Mind and Computers" can help a great deal to deflate modern biases against dualism. Such discussions can clear the atmosphere but would not necessarily prompt one to an enthusiastic appreciation of the clean air, much as he or she may suffer from its pollution.

So much for some background factors that detrmine the value and effectiveness of those air-clearing arguments. The rest of this paper should deal with the arguments themselves. The arguments are in a sense negative. They probe on four fronts the physicalist claim that with the advent of electronic computers one has on hand a physical model on which the physicalist explanation of mind can safely be based. But a physicalist explanation of mind also presupposes that the human brain is really analogous to some specifically known mechanism, and preferably to the electronic computer. Again, a physicalist explanation of mind presupposes the successful analysis and classification of all psychological processes along a quantitative framework. Finally, it is the burden of the physicalist explanation to show that human reasoning corresponds to the combination of atomistic concepts, which in turn are accurate images of sense perceptions.

It is these four major claims that are placed under close scrutiny in the four chapters of *Brain, Mind and Computers*. Of the contents of the first chapter, entitled, "Computers and Physics," I would here recall only one point. It is about the endlessly repeated claim of many present-day computer engineers and writers on computers that computers do really think. They indeed succeeded in building up a consensus, an atmosphere in which it has become an infallible sign of progressive thinking to attribute at least some rudimentary thinking to computers. To unmask the fallacy of this consensus the historical approach seemed to be rather appropriate.

Computers, it is generally believed, are the products of our own age. Actually, they have a very long history. They have been in the making for the past three hundred years ever since Pascal constructed the first adding machine. The next genius to work on computers was Leibniz. Another mathematical genius, Charles Babbage, built in the 1820s the first modern digital computers, and the first analog computer was designed in the 1870s by Lord Kelvin and by his brother, Professor James Kelvin. The twentieth century merely witnessed the electrification and electronization of those machines in the hands of Vannevar Bush at MIT and Aiken at Harvard. If there was in our century a truly creative addition to computer theory it was the work of John von Neumann. It concerned mainly the generalization of memory storage and of combinatory procedures.

All these creators of computers, so distant from one another in time, temperament, and background, had at least one thing in common. They all took pains to emphasize that computers do not think in any sense of the word. You can find the detailed documentation of this in the first chapter of my book. To bring together that documentation was a rather straightforward task. All I had to do was to dig up the material which was at most hinted at, but usually passed over in silence in all books on "thinking machines." Frankly, why that silence? The art of burning books, of annihilating records, of removing them from easy circulation, or of keeping a methodic silence about them is more with us than ever. It certainly does not indicate scholarship or objectivity or unconditional love of truth. But how would you expect the recognition from physicalists, allegedly respectful only of facts, that all the great creative contributors to computers had a view diametrically opposite to the physicalist claim about computers?

Physicalists, I am sorry to say, are more concerned about creating an atmosphere favorable to them than about the careful, balanced presentation of facts. A very good illustration of this is the way in which Babbage is handled in modern computer literature. Take, for instance, the best modern monograph on Babbage, *Charles Babbage and His Calculating Engines,* written by Philip and Emily Morrison.[5] There, in a short footnote, you find mentioned that Babbage based a proof of the possibility of miracles on the theory of digital computers. Well, actually he wrote a whole book on this which was published as *The Ninth Bridgewater Treatise,*[6] a famous series of apologetical works dealing with problems of natural theology. Babbage was a devout Episcopalian, of which no mention is made in the Morrisons' monograph. To crown the comedy, if not conspiracy, there is an excerpt from *The Ninth Bridgewater Treatise* in the work by the Morrisons, but the excerpt is a mere Appendix in the *Treatise.* It has little if anything to do with the train of thought which represented an integral and an important part in Babbage's intellectual convictions, namely, his religious and philosophical belief.

One may, of course, argue that Babbage was mistaken in basing a scientific proof of the possibility of miracles on computer theory. But this is purely a secondary matter. The important point is that no one can gain an objective picture about Babbage's theory and philosophy of computers without a careful study of *The Ninth Bridgewater Treatise,* a very fine theological work. But giving an adequate account of that work would also reveal in one stroke that the most creative contributor to calculating machines was also a most articulate advocate of brain-mind dualism. It is of these and similar facts that the physicalists do not like to remind their readers or their audiences.

Physicalists do not like to dwell either on the long series of rebuffs administered to them by brain research. Special emphasis should here be put on the expression "long series," as intellectual debates often bog down in the gossip of the moment. How often do we hear stated that such and such a discovery led us to the threshold of a major breakthrough and yet somehow that magic threshold is never crossed. A sobering monograph could, for instance, be written on the role of wishful thinking in the evaluation of recent biomolecular research into the secret of life. But even more sobering should be a detailed illustration of the fact that recent failures to produce life *in vitro* are merely the last phase of at least a century-long process. This is not to suggest that a dualist should be alarmed if self-reproducing units would be formed in test tubes. The step from the non-living to the living is enormous. But it should dwarf in comparison with the gap that separates the living from what is living and self-conscious. So far there is no physicalist explanation for the former, and of this physicalists should constantly be reminded. The burden of producing quantitative, experimental proofs is on him and not on the dualist. Physicalists like to appear ten-feet high. Actually they are stooped under the gigantic burden of producing two proofs, of which not even the far easier is in sight yet.

The incomparably more difficult of the two is the still awaited physicalist account of memory and consciousness. Here again, the disparity could hardly be greater between the physicalist claims and the profound mysteriousness that envelopes the two areas. In the second chapter of my book, entitled "Computers and the

Brain," I dwelt at length on the enormous complexity of human memory, and of its dogged resistance to any classification neat enough for the purposes of physicalists. But in addition, there remains the problem of identifying memory units, memory storing, and memory retrieval processes in the brain. Headlines in the *New York Times* and in *Scientific American* notwithstanding, ignorance on these points is complete. The same holds true about consciousness. There is no indication whatever that a physiological explanation of thinking and consciousness is anywhere near.

Sir Charles Sherrington, the foremost student of brain in this century, took indeed the view that four hundred years of research would still be needed to have that physiological explanation. Well, four hundred years is an awful lot of time and prophecies of this type demand a great deal of faith. Sir Charles himself wrote and spoke during much of his career in a style that could give no real comfort to physicalists. Being a great scientist, he did not sweep under the rug the enormous difficulties which a physiological explanation of human thinking had to face. But he looked askance at the notion of an immortal, immaterial principle of human cogitation as a violation of causal reasoning. While recognizing that "mind, for anything perception can compass, goes in our spatial world more ghostly than a ghost," he also insisted in the same breath that

> With the insertion into the human individual of an immortal soul, . . . a trespass is committed. The very concomitance of the two concepts, which seems a basal condition of our knowledge of them, is thrown aside as if forgotten. Such amplification of the one concept may be legitimate for a revealed religion. Its evidence then rests on the ground we do not enter upon here. But as an assertion on the plane of natural knowledge it is an irrational blow at the solidarity of the individual; it seems aimed against that very harmony which unites the concepts as sister-concepts. It severs them and drives off one of them, lonely enough, on a flight into the rainbow's end.[7]

This statement, made in 1940, was probably his most publicized utterance on the matter, but not his last one. Twelve years later, he asked to his home Sir John Eccles whom he considered his intellectual heir. I have the privilege to know some details of that conversation from Professor Eccles himself. Sherrington spoke a great deal about the mystery of brain-mind interaction and concluded: "For me now the only reality is the human soul." What follows are the words of Professor Eccles, a leader in brain research and a Nobel-laureate. "I did not break in to ask if this statement was an act of faith expressing a religious conviction, though I thought he so implied. Five days later he was dead."[8]

The soul to which Sherrington gave his vote refers to a clearly metaphysical or theological reality. The original Greek name for soul, *psyche,* has of course no metaphysical connotation when used to convey a major preoccupation of our time, the study of psyche, or psychology. This change in semantics can easily be understood if one takes a quick look at the origin of modern psychology. Modern psychology was born in the wake of the first triumphs of Newtonian or mechanistic physics. Exact beginnings in intellectual history are difficult to define but Locke is as good a choice as any to represent the start of modern psychology. That start was made in the hope that a physics of the soul could be written. Such was at least the perspective in which Voltaire and Hume saw Locke's chief merit. A hundred years later, during the early nineteenth century, textbooks of psychology often carried titles, "Intellectual Physics," "Mind Physics," and the like. That the eighteenth- and nineteenth-century associationist psychologists looked at physics as their idol, should be well known. The start of psychophysics with Fechner was also motivated by the hope that the data of psychology lend themselves to a systematization exactly similar to the laws of physics.

Fechner, most of the early associationists, and Locke, were still dualists. For them the existence of a soul in a metaphysical sense was a tenet which they refused to doubt. The first major modern psychologist who combined physicalism in psychology with materialistic monism was Sigmund Freud. As he knew very little physics, he boldly drew up in 1895 the plan of a "Project for Scientific Psychology." By this he meant the total and rigorous reduction of psychology to physics. Within a year he gave up working on the plan but not the hope. His system based on the libido was still a physicalist account of psychology though without physics and its terminology. Freudian terminology was in fact so "unscientific" (opposite to quantitative and physical) that it served as a chief target of the behaviorists. Watson, for one, derided the "demonological terminology of the Freudians," while Freud described behaviorism as a theory "naive enough to boast that it has put the whole problem of psychology out of court."

This bitter conflict anticipated the frustrations of twentieth-century physicalist psychology. On the one hand, there is the deep seated antagonism between psychoanalysts and behaviorists. The former claim that introspection and empathy are basic tools of research, but for behaviorists introspection is an anathema. In the camp of psychoanalysis the clashes are very sharp between the followers of Jung and Freud. Equally uncompromising is the opposition in the behaviorist camp between the Watson-Skinner school and the Gestaltists. Tellingly, the bone of contention is always physics, or rather the measure of carrying physics into psychology. Jung parted with Freud because he saw in Freud's physicalism an abdication of human personality, of its strivings and its goal-directed attitude. The Gestaltists in turn accused Watson and his school of their failure to make use in psychology of the conceptual wealth developed by modern physics.

However that may be, one thing should be certain for any un-biased student of twentieth-century psychology: it is not a science in the sense physics is a science. The data and the subject matter of psychology are as complex as ever, and have such strange features that their handling by the methods and concepts of physics is simply impossible. This is a lesson which a dualist cannot afford to forget. It is also a lesson of which a physicalist should be constantly reminded. For if man is truly a servo-mechanism and nothing else, then why is it that the great realm of man's psyche just cannot be pigeonholed into the categories of physicalist psychology?

Such a question does not cut much ice with most cultivators and interpreters of psychology. The reason for this is their philo-sophical shallowness. Gone are the days when a giant of psychol-ogy, like William James, no friend of dualism, could still have a clear perception about the anguish of monists, and about their true predicament: "The monists," he wrote, "writhe like worms on the hook to escape pluralistic or at least a dualistic language, but they cannot escape it."[9] Gone are the days of straightforward recogni-tion of the basic truth that no one can make a silk purse out of a sow's ear. The most relevant truth about physicalist psychology is still the statement made by Priestley, one of the founders of asso-ciationist psychology: "I see clearly and acknowledge readily, that matter and motion however subtly divided, or reasoned upon, yield nothing more than matter and motion still."[10] Much of the confusion in today's psychology comes from the fact that physicalists can be so forgetful of such an elementary truth.

Whether they are forgetful can only be known by inference. All one knows is that they do not talk or write about these things. Physicalists are fond of pointing out that all that man can observe are material, physical signs. However that may be, physicalists talk and write profusely and by this very fact they unwittingly trap themselves. Language and its written symbolism are the very rebuttal of physicalism. True, we know about thoughts and concepts only through spoken or written words, but it is also well known that concepts are not strictly codified in words. There is always some overlap, some undefinable margin of uncertainty, the like of which does not and cannot occur with machine components. Wittgenstein learned that through his frustrating failure to find atomistic concepts, from which the rest of thought could be mechanically built up. His failure was rather inexpensive as compared with the failure of those who tried to do something similar with languages. What I have in mind is the highly subsidized program of machine translation. After two decades and after millions of dollars, it has now been largely shelved. Yet, machine translation is only the most elementary part of the vast program aimed at a quantitative systematization of language.

This reference to "quantitative" should serve as an opportunity to clear up one possible misunderstanding. Perhaps I gave the impression that I conceded to the physicalist whatever there was quantitative in human thought and experience. Far from it. I merely tried to emphasize that physicalists have not even reached first base unless they have succeeded with the quantitative systematization of brain research, of psychology and of conceptual analysis. As far as the record shows they do not seem to have any chance in this respect. But suppose they do. Should then a dualist throw up his hands? Not at all. He has not yet used his most effective weapon, which really strikes the physicalist in his presumed stronghold, the realm of the quantitative, and especially the realm of quantitative proofs. These latter rest on our ability to count and to do arithmetic in a consistent way. As consistency presupposes laws, counting too makes sense only if it is done according to some laws of arithmetic. Depending on the extensiveness of the arithmetic one uses, its laws too form a more or less extensive set. This set also must have its proof of consistency or else 2 and 2 will not always and necessarily make 4 and the whole enterprise will collapse.

In 1930, Gödel proved that no sufficiently broad set of laws of arithmetic can have its proof of consistency within itself. To have the proof, one must reach out for assumptions lying outside the set and to prove the consistency of these assumptions, one must rely on still further assumptions. This means that to prove the consistency of quantitative science one must rely on considerations which the prevailing jargon calls metaquantitative or metamathematical. In older times, when there was still more courage to call a spade and spade, one would have said not metamathematical but metaphysical. I do not wish to argue about words. The explanation of man in terms of machines breaks down if one admits at least the realm of the metamathematical. Steps that are metamathematical or metaquantitative, cannot have by definition quantitative symbolization which as machine parts could be built into a computer.

The last remark should be a warning about an often heard interpretation of Gödel's theorem with reference to the mind-computer problem. The mind, so goes the typical saying, can therefore do something that the machine cannot do, namely to formulate Gödel's theorem and therefore the mind is still superior to machines. Implicit here is the admission that machines can do some or a great many things that the mind can do, such as addition, multiplication, extracting square roots, performing numerical integration and even proving some theorems of geometry. Herein lies the worst fallacy of the whole modern discussion about computers as artificial intelligence. Machines do not add, they do not calculate, they do not integrate any more than a gutter does not *add* or integrate by being the channel for millions of raindrops. In an electronic computer not raindrops but electronic impulses are channelled along strictly predetermined routes. In the process no addition is performed. It takes a mind, always a mind, to abstract meaning from each step through which the machine is directed by its specific man-built mechanism.

The ultimate proof of this has little or nothing to do with expertise in computer science. The ultimate proof rests on having a mind sensitive enough for the enormous magnitude of such basic human experiences as one's ability to move one's little finger at will and one's conviction of having proved something. The process of proving need not take the form of an esoteric theorem in integral equations. It may be as simple as Pythagoras' theorem which until recently was was called *pons asinorum,* or the bridge for donkeys or dunces. It certainly saved some poor students as a last-resort question, but it also doomed, legend has it, the Pythagorean who discovered it. The Pythagoreans were in a sense the first physicalists. They claimed that everything was composed of unit lengths. But the hypotenuse of a right-angled triangle with unit sides is not another unit of integers, but the square-root of two, an irrational number.

It is the privilege and marvel of the mind to find rhyme and reason even in what may appear irrational. It is the privilege of the human mind to take for real what became known as imaginary numbers. Only the human mind can imagine, that is, perceive meaning under the layer of disconnected sense data. Only the human mind can grasp facts and also muster intellectual respect for them. In this attitude of respect, which is definitely not machine-like, is comprised the whole dignity of man. Perception of truth is only part of the story: man also must respect facts and truths to survive and to make progress. No one put this more impressively than T. H. Huxley, Darwin's champion and a sharp antagonist of dualists: "Sit down before fact as a little child, follow humbly wherever and whatever abysses nature leads, or you shall learn nothing."[11] Since this is my favorite quotation which I have been carrying in my breastpocket for years, I should say something about it. It is from a letter of Huxley to an Episcopalian minister, Kingsley, who in a long letter tried to comfort Huxley and raise his eyes to things eternal following the death of Huxley's seven-year-old son. Huxley's reply was polite but defiant. He urged Kingsley to have full respect for the facts of nature, which in Huxley's view excluded soul, God, and eternity.

If facts are only the facts of nature, then perhaps Huxley was right. But there are also the facts of human experience and the facts of history. Nothing shows better their paramount importance than the fact that the facts of human experience and history cannot be repeated. Unlike the facts of nature, they are unique. Without respect for these facts, there can be no true respect for facts of any kind, including the facts of nature.

I wonder if Huxley ever sat down before one fact in particular, the fact of the child from Bethlehem and with the open receptive eyes of a child. Such eyes are symbols of the unconditional respect which Huxley advocated for the lifeless facts of nature. Clearly, somewhere, there was some bias, some oversight. This is all the more regrettable as Kingsley's letter to Huxley made it sufficiently clear, that dualism rests ultimately on respect for facts, for all facts without any restriction, *and* on one's willingness to be led by them even if the journey is bound to that eternity which is promised to any and all ready to become "like little children."

[1]New York: Herder and Herder, 1969. Second enlarged paperback edition, South Bend, IN: Gateway Editions, 1978.

[2]Chicago: University of Chicago Press, 1966. Second printing 1969.

[3]New York: Holt, Rinehart and Winston, 1967, p. 285.

[4]A. H. Compton, *The Freedom of Man* (New Haven: Yale University Press, 1934), p. 26.

[5]New York: Dover, 1961.

[6]Within two years (1837-38), it went through two editions.

[7]*Man on His Nature* (1940; 2d edition, Cambridge: Cambridge University Press, 1951), p. 255.

[8]J. C. Eccles, *Facing Reality* (New York: Springer Verlag, 1970), p. 174.

[9]W. James, *A Pluralistic Universe* (New York: Longmans, Green and Co., 1909), p. 201.

[10]J. Priestley, *Hartley's Theory of the Human Mind on the Principles of the Association of Ideas with Essays Relating to the Subject of It* (London, 1775), p. xxii.

[11]The letter was written on September 23, 1860. See L. Huxley, *The Life and Letters of Thomas Henry Huxley* (London: Macmillan, 1900), vol. I, p. 219.

6

The Role of Physics in Psychology:
The Prospects in Retrospect

It was about a hundred years ago that history witnessed the birth of psychology as a science based on systematic experiments. The date of birth is usually given by historians of psychology as 1860, the year when T. Fechner published his *Elemente der Psychophysik*. It is, of course, somewhat arbitrary to fix so accurately the birth of a particular branch of science. In all its branches, science is a gradual and continuous process and this is also true of the origin of most aspects of the scientific enterprise. Yet, disagree as we may about the year 1860 as the year of birth of modern psychology, there can be no dispute about the true character of the star under

Lecture given at the invitation of the Department of Psychology, University of Chicago, March 10, 1967.

which the birth took place. As the title of Fechner's book indicates, that star was the star of physics.

This is not to say that prior to the emergence of experimental psychology, physics had no fascination for the investigators of human thinking and volitions. For all their differences, the great philosophical psychologists of the seventeenth and eighteenth centuries had one thing in common: the apparent perfection of the physics of the day was the model they wanted to imitate. French Cartesians, British empiricists, German idealists, and sundry associationists all looked at physics as their guiding star. Thus Voltaire saw the key of Locke's contribution in the very fact that, as he put it, Locke everywhere relies "on the torch of physics."[1]

It was hardly a usual torch. Its light, instead of diminishing with time, kept increasing in brilliance. And so did everyone's admiration for it, students of psychology not excepted. A case in point was Herbart, a pioneer in educational psychology, in whose words "the regular order in the human mind is wholly similar to that in the starry sky."[2] For Herbart the mind was a realm of spotless clarity that could be molded, educated along the lines of pure reason. He did not suspect that what he saw of the mind was but the brilliant peak of a huge iceberg the great mass of which, the subconscious, was floating in dark and murky waters. The discovery was made by Freud, and he had to struggle to have his great insight accepted as a working hypothesis at least. Opponents, critics, and Freud's own reflections brought about many a significant change in the original concept of the subconscious. On one crucial point there was not, however, any wavering on Freud's part. He never parted with his belief in physicalism, which in his case meant that all phenomena of the psyche are to be understood in the same way as the energies which are at work in the physical universe.

Originally Freud tried to achieve nothing less than to furnish mankind with a psychology worthy of being called a branch of natural science. The aim of such a psychology was, as Freud put it, "to represent physical processes as quantitatively determined states of specifiable material particles and so to make them plain and void of contradictions." The passage which is from the introductory paragraph of Freud's forty-page-long "Project for a Scientific Psychology" dating from 1895,[3] might have been taken from the writings of Watson, the founder of behaviorism. Though poles apart, the Freudian and the behavioristic formulations of psychology had this much in common: both viewed the psyche as a mechanism obeying laws as exact and as deterministic as the laws of physics. In both cases the aim was similar: the cure and control of man conceived as a wholly deterministic system. At times this aim was stated with shocking directness: "In short, the cry of the behaviorist is, 'Give me the baby and my world to bring it up in, and I'll make it crawl and walk; I'll make it climb and use its hands in constructing buildings of stone or wood; I'll make it a thief, a gunman, or a dope fiend! The possibility of shaping in any direction is endless."[4] In so speaking Watson merely borrowed from the physicists. Two thousand years before Watson, Archimedes had already used the phrase, in the well-known version: "Give me a stable point and I will move the earth." In Descartes' version the phrase went as follows: "Give me matter and motion and I will construct the universe." In our century it was one of its leading physicists, Eddington, who wrote: "Give me a world in which there are relations and I construct matter and motion."[5] Such a performance would certainly imply the derivation of the laws of physics.

Undoubtedly, a principal aim of physics is to gain control over the phenomena of nature. Behaviorism is no different. Or to quote Watson again, "The interest of the behaviorist is more than the interest of a spectator; he wants to control man's reactions as physical scientists want to control and manipulate other natural phenomena."[6] At the basis of such a program there is the conviction that human thought, feeling, and action can be given a meaningful interpretation only in terms of physics. Or as K. S. Lashley put it: "To me the essence of behaviorism is the belief that the study of man will reveal nothing except what is adequately describable in the concepts of mechanics and chemistry." These words of Lashley date from 1923.[7] Two years later there followed the most radical appeal for physicalism in psychology, A. P. Weiss' *Theoretical Basis of Human Behavior*. It is a work replete with references to proton-electron interactions that according to Weiss are ultimately the only meaningful accounts of psychological phenomena.

Great as the temporary hold of behaviorism was in psychology, just as great in the long run was the opposition to it. The principal leaders of that opposition were the Gestaltists. The two camps, however, were not implacable enemies in every respect. Both had the same unreserved admiration for physics. Just as behaviorism rested its case with physics, so did the Gestaltists. What should come first to mind in this regard is the principle of psychological isomorphism which in Koehler's formulation states: "Experienced order in space is always structurally identical with a functional order in the distribution of underlying brain processes."[8] It should also be recalled that Koehler, although a leader of Gestaltists, praised unreservedly the resolve of behaviorists to achieve in psychology the exactness of physics. For him the fine emulation of physics was the "creative force of behaviorism."[9]

It should not therefore be surprising that Koehler traced the basic shortcomings of behaviorism to the insufficient familiarity of behaviorists with physics. In this connection Koehler emphasized two points: First, in trying to imitate physics, behaviorism ignored the historical development of physics; second, behaviorism seemed to be wholly forgetful of recent developments in physics. As to the first point, the history of physics, Koehler insisted that early classical physics was largely based on qualitative considerations. Consequently, psychology, being a young science, should not be ashamed of making ample use of qualitative considerations. The point, I hope, is clear. According to Koehler, whatever physics did and does ought to be good not only for physics but should also be exclusively good for other sciences as well. More of that claim later. Let us rather return to Koehler's second criticism of behaviorism, its neglect of recent developments in physics. Had behaviorists paid more attention to modern physics, they would have been saved from the pitfall of atomistic mechanism for which only parts exist but not wholeness. Koehler, however, noted that modern physics had provided ample evidence that Nature is based on units clearly displaying the features of wholeness. In this regard he referred to the modern concept of atoms where the combination of the nucleus and the surrounding electrons results in something more than the mere sum of the parts.

Another concept of modern physics that seemed to lend support to the primacy of wholeness was the concept of field. As early as 1920 Koehler tried to capitalize on it in a study concerned with the perception of stationary and moving geometrical forms. The true emergence of Field Theory in psychology had, however, to wait for someone with considerable training in modern mathematics and physics, Kurt Lewin. His work is important as it possibly represents the most resolute and detailed effort to recast traditional psychological discourse in terms of field physics and mathematics, especially topology. As such, Lewin's efforts may throw a unique light on the question of the applicability of mathematical physics in psychology.

The results have not been worth the effort. Mathematical notation, vector diagrams, integral signs may impress the mathematically uninitiated, but will not necessarily cut much ice with mathematical physicists. They know the truth of what Eddington, one of the greatest theoretical physicists of our century, wrote about mathematical formulas: "It is easy to introduce mathematical notation: the difficulty is to turn it to useful account."[10] Thus to take a particular case, one may boldly put on the blackboard that $B = f(L) = f(P,E)$. In plain English this is equivalent to saying that Behavior is a function of Life-Space which in turn is the function of the combination of Personality and Environment. In physics notations of this type are extremely frequent and indispensable. Making the same notations just as frequently in psychology does not, however, guarantee either their usefulness or indispensability. To begin with, in physics a formula like the foregoing makes sense only if the exact characteristics of the function $f(P,E)$ can be specified. In other words, one should know whether P and E are to be added or multiplied, or handled in any of a great number of ways. It is most doubtful that even that minimum of mathematical exactness can be achieved when dealing with such concepts as Personality and Environment.

It is even more important to note that there were times when there was no room in physics for formulas like the one above, including the inverse square law, or the formula $s = \frac{1}{2}gt^2$ indicating the distance covered by a freely falling body, to mention only a few and familiar cases. For two thousand years, from Aristotle to Galileo, physics was discussed in an organismic framework in which there was no room left for mathematics. It was believed that the fall of stones was due to an innate tendency present in them to move downward. In a similar way, the upward motion of fire was assigned to an irresistible striving in it to seek out higher levels. What could be easier for man to "understand" than a striving similar to his own strivings and volitions? Yet this explanation, so neatly tailored to man's subjective experience, left physics in a hopeless blind alley.

To make a meaningful advance, physics had to strike out on an entirely new path; it had to turn its back on everything subjective, such as volitions, and even the so-called secondary qualities such as color and flavor. Physics, in order to become physical science had to cease to be about *physis,* or nature, which in its original connotation means the totality of existence, both subjective and objective, the inner world as well as the external world. In the so-called objective world of physics there was only room for matter and motion. On the other hand, in such a world mathematical formulas could be applied with apparently no limitation and with an extraordinary effectiveness. In the history of physics this drastic change of method took place within the first half of the seventeenth century. Psychologically it was nothing short of a catharsis or perhaps a traumatic experience. As I put it in *The Relevance of Physics:* "To foresee the behavior of things, man had to depersonalize his study of the physical universe. It was as if one were to consider the beautiful display on the stage of nature a poetic disguise and look for the ultimate reality in the ugly, soulless mesh of ropes, pulleys, and levers found backstage."[11]

That drastic change in the outlook of physicists was not, however, complete in Galileo's and Newton's generation. It is a change still going on. Physicists are still busy pruning their vocabulary of such organismic concepts as force, resistance, and the like. And if they still use such words, they do so out of sheer linguistic expediency and are eager to make it clear that their concept of force has nothing to do with the experience of force taking place in a living organism. Today, physics has reached the stage of being almost identical with abstract geometry. In fact, the more abstract the geometry is, the better it seems to serve the physicist.

Being familiar with that forbidding abstractness I wonder whether psychology can ever follow physics into its abstract realm of non-Euclidean geometry, and *n*-dimensional space-time continua. Psychologists advocating the reduction of psychology to physics seem to have but a hazy view of what physics is about. No wonder that they failed to notice the grave implications of what they advocated. At any rate, past efforts to reshape psychology along the lines of physics remained stalled at the very periphery of what constitutes the subject matter of psychology. Moreover, the results were in not a few cases simply trivial.

In connection with Fechner's work no less a psychologist than William James formulated the devastating evaluation: "Fechner's book was the starting point of a new department of literature of which in the humble opinion of the present writer the proper psychological outcome is just nothing.''[12] This indictment is all the more noteworthy as in his youthful years Fechner was thoroughly familiar with what went on in physics. Most other psychologists, eager to reduce psychology to physics, fell far behind him in this elementary prerequisite to achieve their aim. Thus Freud openly admitted the scarcity of his knowledge of physics and, while he kept his faith in physicalism, he rapidly scrapped his ambitious program of working out an exact psychology.

As for the various behaviorists, if they had anything in common it was their shocking unfamiliarity with physics though they had hardly written a page without making reference to it. Watson, for instance, seemed to be wholly oblivious to the fact that in his time physics had already left behind its classical stage and also parted with that ironclad determinism which formed the backbone of behavioristic psychology. All this should remind us of the elementary truth that no reputable architect ever plans a building of brick or steel unless the properties of steel and brick are carefully kept in mind. Otherwise the edifice will either crumble or not even go beyond the stage of preliminary bragging.

In our case it was the behaviorists who did much of the bragging about physics. The psychologist who really tried to go beyond bragging and actually built a psychology based on physics was Kurt Lewin. It was not physics' fault that the edifice built by him could not support itself. To begin with, physics in a proper sense never entered Lewin's constructions in psychology. Not that his writings lacked diagrams, vectors, a long array of sundry mathematical symbols, and an endless list of terms borrowed from modern physics. The real trouble was that in introducing those terms, Lewin gave them a meaning wholly different from their customary acceptance in physics. In modern physics, force is a property of space, or to be specific, it is the geodesic which the free particle follows in traversing space. Lewin's concept of force is, however, basically anthropomorphic, a feature that had been banished from physics long ago. Again, the concept of space as used by Lewin and the concept of space in modern physics are wholly different concepts. The psysicist's concept of space is a mathematical construct, whereas Lewin's so-called hodological space still awaits its mathematization, if this is possible at all. Again, while energy considerations play a fundamental role in physics, physics is innocent of what Lewin called *causal* energies. The same discrepancy is evident when one compares Lewin's concept of field and the notion of field as understood in modern physics. Again, Lewin spoke a great deal about topology, but no mathematician specializing in topology would recognize Lewin's topology as that well-known branch of mathematics. Worse, Lewin, by distorting basic concepts of physics, brought in through the back door long discredited notions of Aristotelian physics into his psychological field theory, based allegedly on modern physics. For this is what Lewin was doing when he insisted that theoretical science utilizes in its formation of laws "the total situation in all its full concrete individuality."[13]

However, it cannot be emphasized enough that this "full, concrete individuality" is of no concern whatever for physics. When Goethe, Schelling, Hegel, and the *Naturphilosophes* tried to prove the contrary early in the nineteenth century, they merely succeeded in making a laughing stock of themselves in the eyes of every physicist. Concrete individuality at the same time is of utmost importance for psychology. To deal with that concreteness, psychology has to avail itself of conceptual tools rather different from those that physics can provide. Consequently when the psychologist borrows the concepts of physics he is faced with an inevitable dilemma. He may choose to abandon the rich individual concreteness of psychological data; or he may furtively transform the meaning of the conceptual tools of physics in order to make them somewhat suited for the requirements of the subject matter of psychology. Obviously, neither procedure can be recommended from the viewpoint of scientific method. He cannot do the first, that is, discard the subjective experience, as such a step would lead to a drastic curtailment of psychology. He should not do the second, that is, divest the concepts of physics of their basic meaning, as such a step would fly in the face of scientific logic. Furthermore, if he keeps the terms of physics within their original meaning, he is once more led to a severe narrowing of the range of psychological investigations.

The latter point is worth exploring in some concrete manner, in reference, for instance, to the phenomenon known as rumor-mongering, or gossiping. Assuming that the laws of physics are supreme, one may conclude that the "thinning out" of rumors with distance is similar to the weakening of the gravitational field with distance. To a surprising degree this is borne out from experience. For instance, let leaflets carrying sensational news be dropped from an airplane over a given locality. Then, after a certain period of time, let investigators be sent to interrogate people in places at different distances from the "source of rumor." The findings will show that the number of people who heard the news is proportional to the source of strength (the number of leaflets dropped) divided by the square of the distance of the particular place from the source, that is, the point where the leaflets were dropped.

On the face of it the triumph of the physicalist psychologist could not be more complete. Yet, it is a hollow triumph in the case of every physicalist psychologist who remains consistent and applies but the laws of physics in his investigation of rumors and gossiping. The inverse square law, however impressive in its precision, tells him nothing more about the topic and will leave him in complete ignorance about the exciting subjective reality of rumor-mongering. Moreover, the inverse square law would not tell him that there is a difference between gravity and rumors, grave as these may be.

Physicists, of course, have long since been aware of the fact that even the most effective formula of physics is but an empty shell, and that only the subjective human experience can fill it with meaning. The inverse square law applies equally well to gravity and electricity, and by the same token is equally indifferent whether referred to gravity or to electricity, or to the flow of heat in a uniform medium. Yet gravity, electricity, and heat are not the same; intelligent human discourse will simply break down both in physics and outside physics if that difference is taken lightly or simply ignored.

This means that even in physics formulas are not enough, notwithstanding the fact that of all fields of inquiry, that of physics is possibly the most narrow. It is a field strictly limited to the quantitative aspects of the physical world. Conscious of that limitation, physicists view with misgivings the efforts of physicalists who try to discuss in quantitative terms the non-quantitative aspects of physical reality. At times physicists air their apprehension on this score in a humorous vein, at other times they voice most serious warnings. The poem, "Mathematician in Love," written by a prominent nineteenth-century physicist, William J. M. Rankine,[14] is undoubtedly bursting with humor that conveys with graphic evidence the inanity of reducing psychology to physics. The first and last three of its eight stanzas should readily bring home that inanity:

A mathematician fell madly in love
  With a lady, young, handsome, and charming;
By angles and ratios harmonic he strove
Her curves and proportions all faultless to prove,
  As he scrawled hieroglyphics alarming.

"Let x denote beauty,—y, manners well-bred,—
  "z, Fortune,—(this last is essential),—
"Let L stand for love"—our philosopher said,—
"Then L is a function of x, y, and z,
  "Of the kind which is known as potential."

"Now integrate L with respect to $d\,t$,
  "(t Standing for time and persuasion);
"Then, between proper limits, 'tis easy to see,
"The definite integral *Marriage* must be:—
  "(A very concise demonstration)."

Said he—"If the wandering course of the moon
  "By Algebra can be predicted,
"The female affections must yield to it soon"—
—But the lady ran off with a dashing dragoon,
  And left him amazed and afflicted.

As to the serious side, instead of bogging down in generalities, it will be more useful to concentrate on a single question, the question of man's consciousness of being able to make free decisions. As far as physics is concerned, there is no point in looking for freedom in the physical world. On that basis the physicist can calculate with astonishing accuracy and for centuries in advance the motion of celestial bodies. Overawed by the sweep of deterministic laws valid for the physical world, some philosophers began to feel very skeptical about man's ability to decide and act freely. They insisted that man's consciousness of his freedom is but a subjective impression, the validity of which can be no match for the validity of the laws of physics which recognize but strict determinism.

It is little known but philosophers and psychologists doubtful of man's freedom could never claim the support of prominent physicists. The fact (amply documented in chapter IX of my *Relevance of Physics)* is that Galileo, Newton, Euler, Laplace, Helmholtz, Maxwell, Planck, Einstein, and many other great physicists rejected time and again the contention that the laws of physics had undermined man's conviction about his own freedom. In their view those who exploited physics against the freedom of the will had simply no grasp of what physics was about. This point was phrased some thirty years ago with special vividness by Arthur Holly Compton, a leading figure of American physics before World War II and a Nobel laureate:

> It seems unfortunate that some modern philosopher has not forcibly called attention to the fact that one's ability to move his hand at will is much more directly and much more certainly known than are even the well-tested laws of Newton, and that if these laws deny one's ability to move his hand at will the preferable conclusion is that Newton's Laws require modification.[15]

On hearing this, physicalists would shake their heads in disbelief. After all, their whole philosophy is based on their belief in the absolute supremacy of the laws of physics. To that supremacy they are willing to sacrifice everything, human freedom not excepted. Or as Skinner stated: "The hypothesis that man is *not* free is essential to the study of human behavior." I would not object to Skinner's statement if it read instead:

"The hypothesis that man is *not* free is essential to the behavioristic or physicalist study of human behavior."[16] As a nonbehaviorist who believes in freedom, I would not propose to curtail the freedom of behaviorists to curtail their own horizon. If somebody wants to worship an idol let him do it. Physicalists are such worshipers. Their idol is a rather narrow concept of the method of physics and what they are doing can best be called the worship of method, or methodolatry.

Their most recent attempts to reduce psychology to physics are couched in the language of cybernetics and information theory. The method they fall back upon is operationalism and its underlying philosophy, logical positivism. It must be admitted that the chief proponents of logical positivism are at least fully aware of the drastic nature of their propositions. Carnap himself compared the impact of the eventual reduction of psychology to physics to what was achieved by Copernicus, Marx, Darwin, Nietzsche, and Freud in intellectual history. Copernicus dethroned man from his central position in the universe, Darwin reduced him to the status of an animal, Marx degraded human history to the interplay of purely material factors, Nietzsche stripped the origin of morality from its sacred halo, and Freud unveiled the ugly sources of man's most noble motivations. These historic innovations, Carnap noted, met with great emotional opposition. "Now it is proposed," he went on, "that psychology, which hitherto has been robed in majesty as the theory of spiritual events, be degraded to the status of a part of physics. Doubtless, many will consider this an offensive presumption."[17]

The only appropriate comment on this is that all those who take offense at Carnap's position are absolutely right. For his proposition is as offensive in human terms as it is presumptuous scientifically. If Carnap is right, slide rules and adding machines should be credited no less and possibly more than man for each act of computation. Moreover, man should consider electronic computers as units that think and should expect their temperature to rise when operated by a punch card technician with a peachy complexion. While poking fun at physicalist psychologists may have its effectiveness, it can also detract from the fact that they are deadly serious about reducing man to a machine and about raising machines above men. They are not at all ineffective in proselytizing. Thus a physicist at NASA proposed rather recently that man should leave to computers the exploration of other planetary systems. The advanced forms of computer thinking, it was claimed, would be better suited for intellectual discourse with the inhabitants of other planetary systems.

One should not, however, dwell long on the shuddering spectacle of a consistent application of operationalism. Space travel is still in its infancy and its long-range future is rather conjectural. It is, however, a fact, not a conjecture, that operationalism cannot cope with some basic aspects of physical science. Positivism and operationalism were rejected by a distinguished array of modern physicists, such as J. J. Thomson, Einstein, Max Born, and others. They found that operationalism just could not do justice to the intricacies of that psychological phenomenon known as the act of scientific discovery. Curiously, the same was admitted by Bridgman, a Nobel-laureate physicist and possibly the most articulate spokesman of operationalism among physicists. When pressed on occasion to define the scientific method, he quipped: "Scientific method consists in doing your damndest with your intellect."[18] Obviously, he meant that scientific thinking implies far more than the straightforward organization of data as operationalism would have us believe.

What is basically wrong with operationalism is that it assumes the human mind to be a mere rubber stamp of quantitative and empirical data. It is a position as erroneous as that of idealism which proclaimed that mind to be an absolute master over nature, an *a priori* source of all information about it. For the modern physicist human intellect is neither the rubber stamp nor the master of nature. For him the intellect is an artist who, while taking its raw material from experiments, reorganizes the data into theories that point to new, unexpected features in the universe. While the operationalist and the physicalist or reductionist psychologist looks down on the intellect, the physicist marvels at the power of reason, and his marveling does not diminish as time goes on. The series of scientific discoveries is not what operationalism would have it: an inevitable process on the intellectual assembly line. Rather, scientific discovery is a creative act, like the creation of poetry, or the production of any artistic masterpiece, music, painting, or sculpture. It is an act inaccessible to a psychology for which a run-of-the-mill type physics represents the reliable form of explanation. Freud at least was utterly honest about that. Twice he made a remark which amounts to the admission that what is the best and most inspiring and most lasting in the human psyche is beyond the reach of physicalist psychology, or in his case, psychoanalysis: "We have to admit," Freud wrote in his study of Leonardo, that "the nature of artistic attainment is psychologically inaccessible to us."[19] He repeated the same in his study of Dostoevsky: "Unfortunately, before the problem of the creative artist, analysis must lay down its arms."[20]

What prompts that surrender should be rather obvious. Great scientific breakthroughs cannot be predicted. They may come and they may not. This is not to say that man is unpredictable only when it comes to the use of his scientific abilities. The aspects of man's unpredictability are many. As any other obvious truth, this one too is within the easy reach of the man of letters. As D. H. Lawrence noted: "A horse is always true to its pattern but a man you can never rely on."[21] Physicalist psychologists prefer, however, the hard and expensive ways to obvious truths. A case in point is a computer symposium held less than a year ago at Stevens Institute of Technology. There reports were read about various attempts to predict social behavior by computers. The reports were unanimous in emphasizing that computers cannot cope with the sudden changes that are commonplace in human behavior.

Machines do not change, they only break down. Only man can change and he often does it in a most unexpected manner. In this lies a considerable part of man's uniqueness and dignity. Physics shall never touch on that, for the very reason that its interest is limited to the non-living and, even there, only to the regularities which are accessible only as probabilities as long as physicists must rely on quantum mechanics. Therein lies a limitation of the method of physics which remains a most significant practical limitation even if one does not hold with the great majority of physicists that randomness is a basic property of physical reality.

Physics has indeed built-in limitations of its own. There are two principal ways of getting a close-up view of those limitations. One is open only to the professional physicist and philosopher of science. The other is less deep an approach, but certainly as telling, if not more so. It consists in an unbiased look at the history of physics which shows not only triumphs but also failures, and above all, an uninterrupted process of revisions and drastic changes. The physics of 1967, however marvelous in many a respect, is not exempt from the law of flux, changes, and revisions. No one can tell what physics will look like fifty or a hundred years from now. Those who try to reduce psychology to physics would do well to ponder this fact. Physics, contrary to popular belief, is far from being a discipline with a permanently established conceptual framework.

Unfortunately, awareness of this is not always strong in the broader scientific circles. A hundred years ago, for instance, classical physics was believed to have approached the threshold of a final, ultimate explanation of the universe. Today, even high-school students of physics know how naive that expectation was. Characteristically enough, it was in such naive times that Fechner launched his ambitious program of grafting physics on psychology to make psychology a science. His aim could not have been more noble. He wanted to vindicate the distinct existence of a mental realm as opposed to the material. As he summed up the essence of his research: a geometric series of physical energies activating the sense will produce only an arithmetic series of mental intensities. In this difference he saw, mistakenly of course, the clinching proof of an essential difference between the mental and the physical.

Actually the trend he started in psychology made its effect felt in the opposite direction. It was not Fechner's fault, nor should psychophysics as such be blamed for it. Psychophysics is a most valuable tool in analyzing the outward manifestations of the human psyche. Yet, as any other good and valuable tool, psychophysics too can be exploited for dubious purposes. In the hands of some, it strengthened in psychology the trend toward physicalism and the underlying belief that man was but a machine. A basic feature of physicalism is its inordinate love of mathematical symbols and geometrical figures. Of such a love or infatuation poets long ago noted in general that it is hopelessly blind. In psychology the infatuation with the quantitative method produced a most serious blindness. It is a debilitating restriction of the perspective, the deliberate oversight of a large part and indeed the substantial part of the psychological reality.

The consequences are anything but heartening. The emphasis on the utilization of physics in psychology led not to the saving of man's soul, as Fechner hoped, but to its loss. By soul in this context I do not mean a metaphysical or religious entity. What I mean by soul is man's firm and solid feeling that the realm of values, purposes, and decisions is a realm of far greater importance than any other realm, scientific or otherwise. When that realm is systematically weakened, then sooner or later a crisis has to set in, the weight of which burdens all of us today. The crisis is the crisis of values in a so-called world of facts. It is a crisis that did not creep on us unawares. Men of great insight had warned us about it years ago in impassioned words. Among these men was that great American psychologist, William McDougall, who never bartered scientific integrity for easy popularity. As he warned in 1930:

> I do suggest and contend that the crude materialistic theory of human nature, the theory that man is a machine and nothing more, taught dogmatically every year to hundreds of thousands of innocent school-teachers and college students, cannot fail in the long run to contribute very considerably to the decay of morals and the increase of crime. For it is a theory utterly incompatible with any view of man as a responsible moral being and utterly incompatible with any religion that the plain man could recognize as such; a theory which

represents man as incapable of choosing between good and evil, as the purely passive sport of circumstances over which he has no control; a theory which, if it is accepted, must make all talk of self-control, of self-improvement, of purposes and ideals seem sheer nonsense, survivals from an age of naive ignorance.[22]

Subsequent developments have fully justified him. A generation later another leading psychologist, Erich Fromm, could but sadly go on record: "Theologians and philosophers have been saying for a century that God is dead, but what we confront now is the possibility that man is dead, transformed into a thing, a producer, a consumer, an idolator of other things." And in a most revealing remark he added: "Psychiatrists should concentrate on the pathology of normalcy—the drive to conform."[23] The normalcy and the conformity to which Fromm referred as symptoms of grave mental sickness are the normalcy and conformity as defined by physicalist psychology, or ultimately by physics. It should then be obvious that not only methodological or theoretical reasons militate against the reduction of psychology to physics. There is a far more serious, distinctly existentialist reason as well. A psychology fashioned along the lines of physics is not merely a mistaken intellectual exercise, in the long run it will inevitably turn into a deadly psychological poison. For that reason alone physics should have but a very restricted role in psychology. It can never be emphasized enough that physics like any other branch of science has its own built-in limitations. Full awareness of those limitations is possibly the best measure of the true intellectual stature of any scientist. For as Maxwell, one of the greatest physicists who ever lived, noted almost exactly a hundred years ago: "The greatest achievement of the scientific mind is to know the limitations of the scientific method."[24]

[1]Voltaire, *Lettres philosophiques,* ed. G. Lanson (Paris: Marcel Didier, 1964), vol. II, p. 168 (Thirteenth Letter).

[2]Herbart made this declaration in the Introduction to his famous *Lehrbuch zur Psychologie* (1816); see his *Sämtliche Werke* (Leipzig: L. Voss, 1850), vol. V, p. 20.

[3]Sigmund Freud, *The Origins of Psychoanalysis: Letters to Wilhelm Fliess, Drafts and Notes:* 1887-1902, ed. Marie Bonaparte *et al.* (New York: Basic Books, 1954), p. 355.

[4]J. B. Watson, *The Ways of Behaviorism* (New York: Harper and Brothers, 1928), pp. 35-36.

[5]A. S. Eddington, *Space, Time and Gravitation* (Cambridge: Cambridge University Press, 1929), p. 198.

[6]J. B. Watson, *Behaviorism* (New York: The People's Institute Publishing Co., 1925), p. 11.

[7]K. S. Lashley, "The Behavioristic Interpretation of Consciousness," *Psychological Review* 30 (1923), p. 244.

[8]W. Koehler, *Gestalt Psychology: An Introduction to New Concepts in Psychology* (1929; New York: New American Library, 1947), p. 39.

[9]Ibid., p. 34.

[10]A. S. Eddington, *The Philosophy of Physical Science* (New York: Macmillan, 1939), p. 138.

[11]S. L. Jaki, *The Relevance of Physics* (Chicago: University of Chicago Press, 1966), p. 51.

[12]W. James, *The Principles of Psychology* (New York: H. Holt, 1890), vol. I, p. 534.

[13]K. Lewin, *Principles of Topological Psychology,* tr. F. Heider and G. M. Heider (New York: McGraw Hill, 1936), p. 57.

[14]W. J. M. Rankine, *Songs and Fables* (Glasgow: James Maclehose, 1874), pp. 3-6.

[15]A. H. Compton, *The Freedom of Man* (New Haven: Yale University Press, 1935), p. 26.

[16]B. F. Skinner, *Science and Human Behavior* (New York: Macmillan, 1953), pp. 447-48.

[17]R. Carnap, "Psychology in Physical Language" (1932), in A. J. Ayer ed., *Logical Positivism* (Glencoe IL: The Free Press, 1959), p. 168.

[18]P. W. Bridgman, "The Prospect for Intelligence," *Yale Review* 34 (1945), p. 450.

[19]S. Freud, *Leonardo da Vinci: A Study in Psychosexuality,* tr. A. A. Brill (New York: Vintage Books, n.d.), p. 119.

[20]"Dostoevsky and Parricide" (1928), in *Sigmund Freud: Collected Papers,* ed. J. Strachey (New York: Basic Books, 1959), vol. V., p. 222.

[21]As a spokesman for the supremacy of sexual urge, D. H. Lawrence had no choice but recommend: "Be a good animal, true to your animal instincts." *The White Peacock* (London: Duckworth, 1924), p. 146.

[22]"The Psychology They Teach in New York," in W. P. King (ed.), *Behaviorism: A Battle Line* (Nashville: Cokesbury Press, 1930), pp. 33-34.

[23]Reported in *The New York Times,* April 17, 1966, p. E2, col. 3.

[24]J. C. Maxwell, "Paradoxical Philosophy" (1878), in *The Scientific Papers of James Clerk Maxwell,* ed. W. D. Niven (1890; New York: Dover, 1965), vol. II, p. 759.

7

Order in Nature and Society:
Open or Specific?

It is an old truth that the present, which is the father of the future, is also the child of the past. At any moment man, individually and collectively, is in transit from past to future, as if he were history lived and living. This is why there is a very instructive history also behind the great confrontation which today splits the globe into two camps. Liberals and regimenters (socialists) began to make history well over a century ago and some of their writings have become the kind of classics against which latter-day liberals

First published in *Order Freedom and the Polity: Critical Essays on the Open Society,* ed. G. W. Carey (Lanham, MD: University Press of America and Intercollegiate Studies Institute, 1986), pp. 91-111. Reprinted with permission.

and socialists (regimenters) measure their own originality or all too often the lack of it.

An historian of science can bring a special perspective to this great confrontation and its origins. One need only recall the resolve of the followers of J. S. Mill or Karl Marx. They all tried to appear scientific as they argued the respective measure of liberty and regimentation, then as now the chief bone of contention. J. S. Mill discoursed on political liberty on the basis of a vast study of logic and scientific method. The measure of that vastness was coextensive with the universe. He found grist for his mill of liberalism even in the evolution of solar systems and galaxies. Few paragraphs in his prolific writings give a more telling glimpse of the nature of the liberalism he preached than the one in which he spoke of remote areas of the universe where two and two do not necessarily make four.[1] This suggests that behind the aversion to constraint, so characteristic of liberalist politics and economics, there may lurk a view of the universe in which anything can happen and allegedly does happen. Such a state of affairs, it may be noted in passing, reflects a radical multiplicity, a multiverse, which is the very opposite to a thoroughgoing coordination of things and processes within a coherent framework, or to the converging of all into a unity, a uni-verse in short.

The view that anything can and will happen, that there are no strict boundaries and forms, that everything is in flux, received in Mill's time further support in Darwin's theory. Darwin loved to return to the notion of chance, to the image of an unspecified primordial cosmic soup, out of which by some strange accidents there arose, after a long chain of unpredictable turns, our present flora and fauna—an unlikely offshoot of the past and an unforeseeable matrix of the future. Not surprisingly, Herbert Spencer, who coined the phrase "struggle for survival," also articulated a cosmic philosophy based on the tenet that anything could happen. The universe of Spencer was a multiverse both in space and in time. From a hypothetically complete or *almost* complete homogeneity he tried to derive a most specific and fully coordinated state of affairs—our universe—which in turn was to dissolve itself into a nondescript homogeneity. From it there would arise another, wholly unpredictable cosmic situation.[2] As is well known, Spencer had his greatest vogue in America, where more than one captain of industry, a Rockefeller, a Carnegie, and others, saw in Darwinian science a carte blanche for an industrial struggle in which the only certain thing was that the stronger would devour the weaker.[3] So much for the background which a historian of science may provide about the scientific underpinnings of the so-called liberal outlook on life. That outlook implies the least amount of restraint in human interactions, because interaction among physical entities all across the cosmos is supposed to proceed along ever variable patterns.

No less strong was the confidence with which the opposite camp, or the spokesmen of strict social regimentation, felt their program and creed to have been steeped in science. In the preface to the second edition of *Das Kapital,* Karl Marx made it all too clear that the laws of society as derived from the tools of production were meant by him to be as exact as the laws of physics.[4] This is not to suggest that Marx knew more than a smattering of physics, although less than a hundred years ago anyone with a moderate scientific inclination could gain a fairly good grasp of physics if he applied himself seriously for a year or two. Unfortunately for Marx, his chief consultant in matters scientific, Friedrich Engels, remained woefully ignorant of physics, his prolific discourse on it notwithstanding. That not only application but also scientific frame of mind may have been in short supply in Engels' case should be clear to any unbiased reader of Engels' *Dialectics of Nature,* which became a canonical writing for party ideologues concerning the interpretation of science.[5] But the *Dialectics of Nature* leaves no doubt about Engels' conviction that Marxism was a strictly scientific theory.

This connection between science and socio-economic theory aiming at strict regimentation is no less clear in an undeservedly forgotten Marxist classic, the *Eternité par les astres,* written in 1871 in a most fearsome French prison, the island fortress of Taureau off the port town of Morlaix in Brittany.[6] Its author was none other than Louis Auguste Blanqui, Marx's chief antagonist for the leadership in the First International. Part of the antagonism may have been derived from Marx's realization of Blanqui's superiority as a speaker, thinker, and activist. It is indeed difficult not to admire the sweep with which Blanqui elaborated on strict cosmic determinism, which would produce through eternity the recurrence in an infinite number of times of exactly the same configurations, physical conflicts as well as individual and social struggle. In spite of all his sweep and consistency, Blanqui did not face up to the problem of why there should be any struggle in a fully deterministic existence, let alone the problem of why there should be a free and purposeful call for class struggle if everything was fully determined. He chose to dodge the question of freedom, a perennial source of nightmare for advocates of complete individual and social regimentation.

The consistency with which Blanqui and other regimenters of society swept under the rug the question of freedom has an additional instructiveness. It is related to the question of the use of science as viewed by social theorists, be they the advocates of unrestrained liberalism or of strict regimentation, or, to use contemporary clichés, of an open or of a closed society. Around 1870 there was unanimity concerning the strictly determined nature of physical interactions. Almost all those who supported the notion of causality in physical interaction rested their case on the strict determinacy implied in the Newtonian laws of physics. The most graphic and memorable statement of causality in all physical processes came at that time from none other than T. H. Huxley, as he reminisced on the first reactions to Darwin's theory. Huxley had particularly in mind the objection which dismissed the Darwinian mechanism of evolution as a reign of pure chance, the very opposite of what mechanism ought to be. Natural selection and Darwinism as a whole were, Huxley argued, the very opposite to the reign of chance, because they were science and science could not tolerate chance events. While the subtle hereditary changes and the interaction of organism with the environment could elude exact observation in most cases, the situation there was no different from the splashing of waves against rocky shores:

> The man of science knows that here, as everywhere, perfect order is manifested; that not a curve of the waves, not a note in the howling chorus, not a rainbow glint on a bubble which is other than a necessary consequence of the ascertained laws of nature; and that with sufficient knowledge of the conditions competent physico-mathematical skill could account for, and indeed predict every one of those "chance" events.[7]

This beautiful declaration was the embellished echo of Laplace's famous passage about a superior spirit who, being in possession of all parameters of all bodies at a given instant, could calculate and predict every future situation.[8] Laplace, it is well to recall, carefully avoided any reference to human freedom. He most likely would have revolted at the thought that his dicta on that superior spirit were the outcome of an ironclad necessity. Huxley would have protested in the same way against the inference that his and Darwin's scientific works, or any discovery made by any scientist, was a foregone conclusion, an inevitable outcome of upbringing, education, or, to mince no words, of the whirl of molecules within the brain and the brawn.

How is it then that the same deterministic Newtonian science gave rise to two very different social philosophies: one aiming a unlimited freedom, the other at the practical absence of any freedom at all? The answer to this question helps to understand not only the historical antecedents of the present-day conflict but also the true measure of science behind the actual conflict itself. The liberals—a J. S. Mill, a Spencer—had in view more than science taken in a strict technical sense. They rather entertained a picture of Western intellectual history in which science, or rather its rise in the seventeenth and eighteenth centuries, coincided with and presupposed the liberation of human reason from transcendental shackles, superstitions at worst, metaphysical dreams at best. This picture received its hallowed codification on Condorcet's *Essay on the Progress of the Human Mind*[9] and became a staple fare of education through the influence of Comte's positivism. In other words, science meant for those liberals much more than its technical contents and methodological precepts with which they were often unfamiliar. Science for them represented above all a state of mind unfettered by any presupposition, a state of mind open to all possibilities, and a mental attitude aiming at maximum behavioral freedom.

In the opposite camp, the camp of strict social regimentation, the emphasis was on the content of science, on its alleged witness that everything, including human behavior, individual and social, was strictly determined. The historical context of the rise of science was in that camp ascribed not to a new mentality but to the industrial conditions that necessarily formed the frame of mind needed for doing science. Not surprisingly, the cultivation of science within that camp had to be subject to organizational control. Long before Lenin achieved political power, he called for a sustained vigilance over science as well as scientists.[10] His call was a loud echo of the voice of social Utopians, aptly called the Prophets of Paris, of whom Fourier and especially Comte thought up astounding ways of putting science into a strait-jacket lest the cultivation of science encourage aspirations for intellectual freedom. The enslavement of science became a reality whenever the proletariat could set up its dictatorship. An ideology, which ascribed the chief cause that moulded human society to social organization, could only be hostile to Mendelian genetics, which left no room for the dream that the socialist behavior of the revolutionary generation would be inherited by subsequent generations. Lysenkoism was not the only example of party dictatorship over science. Brain research and neurology had to suffer no less serious setbacks, once the Pavlovian reflex theory was imposed in the name of dialectical materialism. The cultivation of cosmology, relativistic physics, and quantum theory also had to suffer. Tellingly enough, this dictatorship over science was relaxed only when, in the early 1950s, Soviet physicists told the Party that they could not produce the scientifically sophisticated tools needed by modern warfare unless their research was not interfered with by Party ideologues.

About the time when Lenin tried to harness science for the program of social regimentation, and free-for-all capitalism looked for support in the evolutionary science of Spencer and Darwin, there appeared Bergson's *Evolution créatrice,* a heroic effort to vindicate for human freedom a more than verbal meaning.[11] That Bergson suspected nothing of the coming of social regimentation on a vast scale, that is, the turning of Marxism into statehood, should be of no concern here, revealing as it is of the short-sightedness of a penetrating mind. As the product of a typically Western bourgeois milieu, Bergson focused on Cartesian (Newtonian) mechanism and on its Spencerian-Darwinian extension to biology. He certainly made a stir by forcefully reminding his generation of the point made long before him that no novelty can occur in a universe conceived in terms of mechanistic physics. Yet every change, even mere physical change, implies novelty and this is certainly true of biological processes, to say nothing of mental and volitional experiences. All these are taking place in time, the perennial parameter of novelty. While Bergson's emphasis on time as primary matrix could call for serious qualifications, for our purpose it should be sufficient to note its fundamental role in Bergson's philosophy, which being that of a great thinker was a philosophy of

cosmic range. It was not only about things, organisms, and persons
that Bergson stressed the fact of their endurance across time. He
emphatically noted, by using italics, that "the universe *endures.*"[12]
This cosmic endurance immersed in the flow of time was for
Bergson the reason for an endless rise of novelties in each and
every context. He went so far in emphasizing the unique character
of all such novelties as to speak of continuous creation through
which the future becomes so novel that its prediction on the basis of
the past and present is, to quote his words, "a veritable
absurdity."[13]

Bergson had, of course, to lay great store by biology, in which he
found a storehouse of refutations of ironclad mechanism. Biology
was far less in view when, twenty-five years after the publication of
the *Evolution créatrice,* he published its sequel, *Les deux sources de
la morale et de la religion.* There, in trying to vindicate the
evidence of novelty in social evolution, he made much of the notion
of an open society as opposed to a closed one. The latter was rooted
in the instinct of self-preservation, individual and tribal, the former
in altruism, which Bergson saw best exemplified in the love
preached and practiced by Christ. About the reason for the emergence of Christian love at a specific point in the historical evolution
of humanity, Bergson stayed with generalities. His ultimate appeal
was to the universe as a mysteriously living entity with a quality of
life well-nigh divine. He saw the entire universe "peopled with intentions,"[14] all of which were groping toward something divine as
they became conscious in man whose ultimate responsibility was to
"fulfill . . . the essential function of the universe which is a machine
for the making of gods."[15] Such was the grand conclusion of *Les
deux sources,* which went through seventeen editions in only three
years, an appropriate indication of the impact, very transitory to be
sure, it had made.

Bergson's universe, the foundation of his open society, was certainly open—it was, indeed, wide open to any and all novelty, including the ones that hardly fitted into his cosmic optimism tainted
with pantheism. Revealingly enough, his account of the universe
was void of specifics. Thus, one would look in vain in Bergson's two
main works for any specific norm or precept which would impose
itself on humanity in the sense which is the case with a law of
nature or, rather, with a natural law. The only sense in which
Bergson was specific was negative, namely, his courageous

criticism of such opponents of free development as dictatorial regimes. Freedom of action and of thought he certainly wanted to preserve even at the price of risking his own security. But he laid down no norms in terms of which mankind should face up to over-population, by far the greatest threat, in Bergson's opinion, to human survival.[16]

Bergson's avoidance of specifics about his open society and the rules governing it, an avoidance which is certainly of a piece with the lack of specific contours in his notion of the universe, is all the more curious because he was not unfamiliar with the startling developments in physics during the first three decades of the century. Bearing witness are the questions he posed as Einstein faced a distinguished audience at the Sorbonne on April 6, 1922.[17] Bergson may have sensed that although modern physics more than amply discredited classical physics (or rather the mechanistic materialism often taken for it), which certainly excluded novelty, the advent of a new physics was a threat in disguise to his cosmic view of an unspecified and interminable novelty or openness. For as modern physical science grew by leaps and bounds, each subsequent advance unfolded aspects of the universe which show it be not so much indefinitely open as distinctly specific. As any specific entity, the universe too is therefore definitely limited to a very finite number of future possibilities or novelties.

Modern physical science had quickly become the prey of that two-fold exploitation in the hands of liberals and regimenters which had already befallen classical or Newtonian physics. Modern, or twentiety-century physics added a new perspective, however, to the dispute between the two camps and also a new standard by which both are to be judged. This holds true also of a third way, which created no less stir than did Bergson's and which owed much to Bergson's at times rather poetical philosophizing.

The new perspective is related to quantum mechanics, or the mathematical method which deals with the enormously vast and crucial range of atomic, nuclear, and subnuclear phenomena. The word quantum, although it appeared in various meanings here and there in philosophical and scientific literature well before 1900,[18] came into its own historic role in that year with a paper which Planck presented to the Berlin Academy. In that paper Planck argued that a most fundamental type of radiation, called black-body radiation, cannot be accounted for unless one assumed that the emission of radiation took place in discrete units or quanta. During the next quarter of a century every major advance in atomic physics brought further evidence on behalf of Planck's claim. Indeed, that progress brought to the fore much more than Planck originally envisioned, although he suspected from the start the philosophical thrust of further progress in quantum theory.

In 1925 Heisenberg discovered that the calculation of energy differences between spectral lines called for a mathematical technique called matrix calculus. A strange technique indeed, which implies that on the atomic level one must work not with ordinary algebra but with a non-commutative algebra in which x multiplied by y is not necessarily equal to y multiplied by x. In other words, on the atomic and subatomic levels conjugate variables, or pairs of certain physical parameters, such as position and momentum, time and energy, obey rules with consequences anything but ordinary. The most important of these, enunciated by Heisenberg in 1927, states that the simultaneous measurement of such pairs implies an uncertainty at least as large as Planck's quantum.

Heisenberg's uncertainty principle has since become a cultural matrix. A recent example of this is an essay in *Time* following the almost fatal shootings of President Reagan and Pope John Paul II. The narrow escape of both was in the eyes of many a miracle, an act of Providence, a view which, the essayist argued, was above scientific objection because for science all events are ultimately chance occurrences.[19] But the essayist's understanding of chance, whatever else might be said of it, has no foundations in quantum mechanics. What he would find there, if he looked, is that its formulators are bogged down in an equivocation which is the result of their failure to distinguish between two propositions: one states the limited measure of man's ability to measure exactly, either in theory or in practice, a physical interaction; the other states that because exact measurement of an interaction is impossible, the interaction itself is inexact in the sense that the effect can contain more than what is contained in its cause; that is, the effect is not caused fully, and may not be caused at all. The first of these statements is purely operational, the second is radically ontological. To suggest that the first implies the second is sheer equivocation, the result of an elementary mishandling of the laws of logic.[20] It would not be tolerated in any moderately good freshman course untainted with that modal or subjective logic which Hegel grafted on to modern thought. Yet this equivocation or logical fallacy has become part and parcel of our modern scientific culture. There the notion of chance has grown, soon after Heisenberg's enunciation of the uncertainty principle, into the basic dogma of anti-ontology. In that culture the real is replaced by the unreal garbed in the cloak of chance. While for the unwary that garb means only the absence of exact measurement, for the "initiated" it is a specious cover-up for a situation in which the real becomes in the end a mere appearance, to the delight of phenomenologists, who forgot their initial resolve to make no utterance whatever about reality as such.[21] Hence the rise of the widespread belief, amounting to a climate of opinion, that anything can happen and that man therefore is not bound by anything specific such as natural law, which obviously presupposes a specific ontological order.

Such is the allegedly scientific foundation of the notion of "open society" which, in post-Bergsonian times, had Karl Popper as its chief ideologue through his *The Open Society and Its Enemies*.[22] Indeed, in arguing against universal determinism as invoked by "closed" Marxist regimes, Popper made much of quantum indeterminancy.[23] Confident that he had thereby deprived Marxism of its scientific basis, he felt free to point his finger at the Messianic or religious inspiration of Marxism. For an avowed rationalist like Popper the chief threat to his "open society," which he carefully distinguished from the one advocated by Bergson,[24] had to reside in religion. And since only one religion, Roman Catholicism, stood persistently for the rationality of religion even when implying the supernatural, a careful reader of *The Open Society and Its Enemies* could not help feeling that its real target was neither Plato, nor Hegel, nor Marx, nor Hitler, but the Catholic Church, for which Popper voiced only contempt, though with careful indirectness, by heaping scorn on the Middle Ages.[25] Such was, however, a deft and accurate strategy, as only during the Middle Ages did there arise a broadly shared conviction that existence and its norms were very specific, since the universe owed its existence to a Creator who could have brought forth an infinite number of worlds, all very specifically different from one another.[26] In that conviction, actual creation and actual cosmic specificity were two sides of one coin.

In the 1980s, when we see Western society disintegrating in more than one respect, it should seem clear that the rationalism of the Enlightenment, which liberated man from supernatural constraints, brought about a frightening kind of openness. It is the openness of a barrel casting off its hoops and losing all its contents, an openness in which all norms, even purely pragmatic and essentially biological norms, are brazenly dispensed with. Suffice it to recall the recognition of lesbian and homosexual couples as legally married units, an outcome which fills with foreboding even diehard rationalists and professional pragmatists. They cannot help but recognize both the biological indispensability of "normal" marriage and the Church as its only consistent defender.[27] It becomes more and more evident that the real enemies of open society are not societies based on absolute and even on supernatural revealed truths, but intellectual circles that have opted for chance as the ultimate. Their option is fallacious to the point of pushing to the brink that modern "open" society whose sole strength lies in its inherited capital of absolute truths and values on which it has been thriving as a parasite.

Ideas are more dangerous than weapons. The latter may or may not be used. Ideas—the history of philosophy, theology, and of political theories shows this all too well—run their courses inexorably. It was no accident that, say, Fichte's works were readily available in field libraries of German armies. The hundreds of millions of copies in which the ideas of Stalin and Mao were made available were very effective in sparking bloodthirsty purges and marches of madness. By the same token, an ideology which claims, even if on the basis of science, that anything can happen, will inevitably invite anarchy. Distinctly anarchical are several symptoms of Western society which, following the rejection of traditional constraints, have spread all over during the last thirty years.

As one would expect, spokesmen for Marxist regimes and ideologies fought tooth and nail against this scientific abolition of ontological causality in the name of quantum mechanics, or rather of its Copenhagen interpretation. It was not unexpected, either, that their own defense of causality had to be counterproductive. Being an offshoot of Hegelian dialectics, Marxist realism could never see reality for what it is. Partly because of this, the defense of causality in Marxist realms bogged down in its efforts to revindicate Newtonian determinism or, rather, the possibility of exact measurements. Freedom, of course, remains a nightmare within Marxist realms in more than one way. It is, however, no less nightmarish to find some well-meaning Western scientists arguing that the Heisenberg indeterminacy principle provides a narrow margin within which freedom can operate. Few of these scientists are so clear-headed as was Eddington, the first to propose such a defense of freedom and also the first to recognize that it was sheer nonsense.[28] It is well to recall that if the questioning of freedom is not to become a begging of the question itself, it cannot cast doubt on the freedom of raising that very question.

So much for the new perspective which twentieth-century science gave to the question of freedom. Once again, as was the case a hundred years ago, philosophical and valuational presuppositions prevailing within a society, that is, in its ideological matrix, could play a much more important role than the science available to that society.

The same may not be true with respect to another major development in twentieth-century science, which, as has been previously suggested, may play the role of a standard against which debates about the measure of freedom, or rather the openness or closedness of society, should be evaluated. This other scientific development is not yet a quarter of a century old. It was only in 1963 that a strange radiation was observed in the Bell Telephone laboratories in Holmdel, N.J. The radiation has since become famous under the name of the 2.7°K cosmic background radiation. All too often, and very wrongly, this radiation is presented in the literature, technical and popular, as something which gives the age of the universe; nay, something which puts us at the threshold of creation.[29]

The 2.7°K radiation is extremely valuable for a reason which, for better or for worse, has already been dubbed the anthropic principle.[30] In plain scientific terms the 2.7°K radiation proves two things. One is that the universe was smaller and smaller as its history is traced further and further into the past. This is an independent confirmation of the expansion of the universe which has been known for about fifty years, although some scientists kept doubting that the red shift in the spectrum of galaxies was really a proof of their recessional velocity. Further doubts on that score are hardly permissible. The other thing proved by the 2.7°K background radiation concerns theories about the formation of the elements, theories first proposed in the 1950s. According to these theories, the formation of the lightest chemical elements could take place only if about 15 billion years ago all matter in the universe was contained within a volume not larger than a planet, a volume in rapid expansion. Furthermore, all matter in that phase (lasting for much of the first three minutes of cosmic evolution) had to consist of protons, neutrons, and electrons, together with 40 million photons for each of these particles. Such a mixture had a specific pressure (and temperature) which provided a specifically needed rate of expansion against the gravitational force.

Since 1963, enormous scientific work has been done on this very early phase and on earlier and even shorter phases of the universe, with a result which invariably has the thrust of a stark philosophical message. The message is that we human beings are part of an immensely specific and coherent state of affairs, which involves the entire universe. That there is a universe may be a trivial statement, though not for those who are aware of the claim of all post-Humean and post-Kantian philosophies that the idea of the universe is merely a bastard product of the metaphysical cravings of the intellect. In this age, which has achieved for the first time in history a truly scientific grasp of the universe, the Kantian position about the universe cannot be openly maintained by "scientific" philosophers, whatever their vested interest in that position which undermines the rationality of looking at the universe as a jumping board to its Creator. The avoidance of the notion of the universe on the part of professedly "scientific" philosophers should seem therefore most revealing.

One would look in vain for a non-trivial reflection on the *reality* of the universe (the totality of consistently interacting things) in Popper's recent book, *The Open Universe,* which contains a mere page on what has been revealed by modern scientific cosmology about the universe.[31] No less characteristically, Popper did his dialetical best to make the status of the Big-Bang theory appear "very precarious," although it alone explains the 2.7°K background radiation which Popper did not find worth mentioning. As late as 1982, Popper still was resting his case on half-century-old equivocations about indeterminacy which would never give rise to permanent specificities, let alone to those very specific features which, as unveiled by modern scientific cosmology about the universe, should overpower a truly open intellect. On the contrary, modern scientific cosmology overpowers the speculative intellect by unveiling a universe with very specific features. Indeed, precisely because those features are so specific, they discourage attempts to consider them to be the mere creations of the mind. Only a most self-centered thinker would claim that the existence of ten billion and one protons for every ten billion antiprotons is necessary on a priori grounds. Yet such a specific ratio is required if 40 million photons, or units of electromagnetic radiation, should be available during the first ten-thousandth of a second for each proton, neutron, and electron, so that the cooking of the lightest chemical elements, mentioned above, may get under way.

The formation of those elements, hydrogen and helium, is the pre-condition for the subsequent formation, in the core of stars, of all the heavier elements. One of them, carbon, forms the backbone of organic chemistry and, in that sense, of human life as well. Whatever its marvelous range of properties, carbon has become a commonplace even for organic chemists. Yet even in itself carbon should be a cause for wonder because it is a most specific construct. Around no other element can the theoretical chemist build a world as variegated as around carbon. One only need recall speculations about silicon-based life, which some dreamy-eyed cosmologists present as alternative forms of life in outer space, to realize that in this regard silicon is a poor second to carbon, to say nothing of other elements of the Mendeleev table. Our admiration for carbon should know no bounds when we realize that a whole universe of very specific sub-nuclear particles and very specific forces ruling them was necessary to produce carbon. Indeed, the cosmic cooking process followed a most specific recipe, prescribing second after second every step of the process. A most crucial phase of it could have lasted for only about three short minutes some 15 billion years ago.

Such is the scientific background of the so-called anthropic principle. Since we humans, so many anthropoids, are made of carbon, it appears to many modern cosmologists that the universe was made for the sake of man, that is, for a purpose. They could have, of course, taken any element in order to reach the same conclusion. They could indeed have taken the blueness of the sky, the average size of a mountain, the average size of a star. These and many other very ordinary aspects of the universe have their explanation in a most specific coordination of all constituent parts of the universe. This coordination, startling in itself, becomes the more astonishing the further we trace its properties back in time.

When a scientist, marvelling at this extraordinary state of affairs, begins to suspect that such a specificity indicates a designer, and therefore a purpose, he merely shows himself a poor philosopher, a Johnny-come-lately kind of wisdom lover. If a scientist fails to recognize that his scientific work is a proof of purpose, his marvelling at cosmic purpose, or anthropic principle, will not produce noteworthy results. This is why so many cosmologists slide from the anthropic principle to the worst kind of anthropocentrism, the solipsism of idealist philosophy, for which only the ego exists.[32] A realist can hardly do more with idealists, be they scientists, than wish them well. One has to be on guard, however, against the perennial snare of idealism. Even the slightest cavorting with it can deprive one of the sense of reality without which any discussion about the measure of freedom will run out in trivialities, at best, or in sheer willfulness, individual and regimented, at its very rawest.

About the willfulness of regimented society little needs to be said, except (to remain with my topic) in the form of a brief reference to the suspicion under which the science of cosmology is kept by Marxist regimes. It is clearly realized in those realms that modern scientific cosmology, by presenting us with an enormously specific universe, almost becomes a first chapter in theology, a chapter on Creator and creation. Consequently, the respective measure of freedom and law in human society becomes a metaphysical issue, a prospect which can hardly be tolerated within Marxism, whether it be cruelly institutionalized or the humane kind still dreamed about by some academics in the West. This, of course, holds true also of the so-called open society which in the Western world has so many spokesmen, many of whom mean openness in a distinctly anti-theological sense. To argue with them on theological or metaphysical grounds is entirely futile. Nor can one argue against them with reference to natural law. They would answer in derision that many Christians, nay Catholics (especially among these the self-styled Thomists of the transcendental kind), are cutting their own throats with the very scalpel with which they dissect natural law. But against these champions of an open universe and against some of their unwitting allies one can effectively argue in the name of science. In science they believe, and therefore they must be open to a discourse about the vistas opened up by such a commonplace element as carbon. Carbon can indeed be turned into heaps of hot coals on the heads of spokesmen of an openness according to which, since everything is possible, everything should be tried out because all constraints are artificial, purely man-made.

The anthropic principle, or to speak less metaphysically, the very scientific carbon principle, shows exactly the opposite, namely, that very few things are possible. If one takes three or four constants—the speed of light, the radius of an atom, the charge of an electron, the mass of a proton—then one can show that the sky can only be blue, a mountain can never be higher than ten miles, and a star never one hundred times heavier or ten times lighter than our sun.[33] If one says carbon and if one knows what goes into the cosmic production of carbon (indeed the whole cosmos goes into it), one has stated a very narrow track for a carefully engineered cosmic engine which runs its course on a very specific timetable. Clearly, far from everything should be considered possible in a universe in which stars and planets would have never evolved if the total mass of the universe had differed by a mere one percent from its actual measure. The claim about the openness of the universe is a subtly disguised claim that the universe is fuzzy, that is, undetermined in its very foundations. It is on that claim about cosmic fuzziness that rests the further claim that it is unscientific to speak either of law or of freedom, let alone of an objectively proper relationship between liberty and constraint. Whatever the universe of some philosophers, the universe of science is the very opposite of that fuzziness which underlies the doctrine of the so-called open society in a so-called open universe.

The art of determining the objective proportion of constraint and liberty does not belong to science but to metaphysics, ethics, and theology. The art in question is not even the domain of that jurisprudence which readily reinterprets a constitution steeped in natural law according to the dictates of the latest Gallup poll. The relatively little and indirect contribution which science can make to that art must not, however, be belittled. Whether we like it or not, we live in an age of science. Science has become a currency which is universally accepted and looked for. The value of that currency is hardly ever questioned in a broad and systematic sense. Warnings about the limitations of its value are often intemperate. Moderate voices are not given a public hearing, let alone sufficient publicity. Truth, unfortunately, cannot compete with half-truths in newsworthiness. One need not therefore expect a sudden change in the climate of opinion, even if there developed a wider awareness about the enormous degree of lawfulness, specificity, and coherence in the universe from atoms to galaxies and beyond.

To grasp the significance of that enormous degree of specificity, which with all its exactness is embedded in reality, one should resort to philosophical tools more penetrating than phenomenology, however intuitive, can provide. The tools of the latter remain ineffective for the purpose even when wrapped in biological terms, as was the case with Bergson, or in terms of evolutionary paleontology as articulated by Teilhard de Chardin, who wanted to inject new life into the Bergsonian approach. Thus, whatever Fr. Teilhard's intentions, he only made palatable in some Catholic circles, to which his influence was largely reduced, the view that man was after all but a product of nature. Against a purely naturalistic explanation of man, so fashionable in this age of science, one can and must however stress that precisely because of scientific reasons, man cannot be less specific an entity than is the universe.

The best and most exact data in science suggest indeed that mankind, no less than the universe, has been put on an extremely narrow track. Traditionally speaking, that narrow track conjures up natural law, which cannot be defended if it cannot be shown that nature is most specifically lawful. This is not to suggest that there is much cogency in the merry galloping of, say, an Edmund Burke who, in one and the same sentence, went from the laws of commerce through the laws of nature to the laws of God.[34] The real situation is much more complex than Burke's statement would have us believe. But reality is not so complex as to be that sophisticated chaos in which anything is falsifiable except, of course, the principle of falsifiability.

To be sure, reality, as described by modern science, evidences a great deal of openness to novelty. Unlike the mechanistic universe, in which novelty was impossible, the universe as described by modern science goes through specifically successive stages, each with a predominance of features which could not come about in any of the preceding or subsequent stages.[35] In that sense our universe, a most specific universe, is a place for novelties but never in the sense which is tantamount to somersaults in logic. Science cannot justify the somersault according to which something evolves out of something which is not there. Nor does science justify the kind of mental acrobatics which assure us of the rise of life out of non-living matter and of the emergence of consciousness out of mere sensitive life. The distinctly dinosauric touch of this latter claim may suddenly appear very modern, or avant-garde, if one recalls a warning made recently from a scientifically most prestigious post. Sir Andrew Huxley, president of the Royal Society and a great-grandson of T. H. Huxley, can hardly be suspected of hostility toward a so-called evolutionary openness, the basis of claims that man can take his destiny, his measure of freedom and constraints, in his own hands. Yet Sir Andrew stated in his Presidential Address nothing less than that science offers only speculations about the origin of life, and as regards the problem of the origin of consciousness, Darwinists by and large continue sweeping it under the carpet.[36]

If, however, such is the case, nothing can stand seriously in the way of the only true openness available for man. It is the openness of his contingent being toward its very ground which is the Creator's free act. In that act, specific laws and free choice were simultaneously given to man. Today no less than before, man must have both. Otherwise he will be the slave of a communal willfulness which blocks his view of the past, ruins his present, and deprives him of any future worth looking for.

[1]For details and documentation, see my Gifford Lectures, *The Road of Science and the Ways to God* (Chicago: University of Chicago Press, 1978; third paperback edition 1986), p. 151.

[2]Spencer's cosmology received its most concise and devastating indictment from none other than H. G. Wells, who in book I, "Metaphysics," of his *First and Last Things: A Confession of Faith and Rule of Life,* definitive ed. (London: Watts & Co., 1929) wrote: "He [Spencer] believed that individuality (heterogeneity) was and is an evolutionary product from an original homogeneity, begotten by folding and multiplying and dividing and twisting it, and still fundamentally *it*" (p. 30).

[3]The standard account is *Social Darwinism in American Thought,* rev. ed. (Boston: Beacon Press, 1955).

[4]See Marx's preface to the 2d edition of *Das Kapital,* translated from the third German edition by S. Moore and E. Aveling (New York: Appleton, 1889), pp. xxx-xxxi.

[5]A fact all the more reprehensible because by 1928, when the manuscript of Engels' book was published, not only was physical science vastly beyond the physics of the 1870s and 1880s, which Engels had in view, but his analysis of it was all too often utterly amateurish.

[6]For details, see my *Science and Creation: From Eternal Cycles to an Oscillating Universe* (Edinburgh: Scottish Academic Press, 1974), pp. 314-19.

[7]Huxley's statement is from his reminiscences on the reception of Darwin's *Origin of Species;* see F. Darwin, ed., *The Life and Letters of Charles Darwin* (New York: Basic Books, 1959), vol. I, pp. 553-55.

[8]Or as Laplace put it in the introduction to his *Essai philosophique sur les probabilités* (1814), the human mind was but a feeble outline of a hypothetical intelligence "which would comprehend all the forces by which nature is animated and the respective situation of the beings who compose it—an intelligence sufficiently vast to submit these data to analysis—it would embrace in the same formula the movements of the greatest bodies of the universe and those of the lightest atom; for it, nothing would be uncertain and the future, as the past would be present to its eyes." See *A Philosophical Essay on Probabilities,* trans. F. W. Truscott and F. L. Emory (New York: Dover, 1951), p. 4.

[9]For details, see my Fremantle Lectures (Balliol College, Oxford), *The Origin of Science and the Science of Its Origin* (Chicago: Regnery-Gateway, 1978), pp. 30-31.

[10]Lenin did so in 1908 in his *Materialism and Empirio-Criticism* (New York: International Publishers, 1927), pp. 323-24.

[11]First published in 1907. Henri Bergson, *Creative Evolution,* trans. A. Mitchell (New York: Modern Library, 1944).

[12]*Creative Evolution,* p. 14.

[13]Ibid., pp. 371-76.

[14]Bergson, *The Two Sources of Morality and Religion,* trans. R. Ashley Audra and Cloudesley Brereton (Garden City, NY: Doubleday & Co., 1954), p. 163.

[15]Ibid., p. 317.

[16]Ibid., p. 290.

[17]Those questions related to the reality of simultaneity and to the validity and fundamental character of common-sense knowledge. On both accounts Einstein kept repeating, rather evasively from the philosopher's viewpoint, that he viewed those questions only from the perspective of the operationist method of the physicist. The full transcript of Bergson's long questions and Einstein's answers is the concluding part of the question-answer period that followed Einstein's lecture on relativity before the *Société française de philosophie* on April 6, 1922; see its *Bulletin* 17 (1922), pp. 91-113. That Maritain was present at that lecture is clearly shown by a passage in his *Distinguish to Unite: or The Degrees of Knowledge* (New York: Charles Scribner's Sons, 1959), p. 158, where Einstein's resolve to consider only the operationist aspect is pointedly recalled: "Listening to Mr. Einstein lecturing on simultaneity, it was very remarkable to hear him constantly

returning to the question: what does the word 'simultaneity' mean for me, a physicist?" For further details, see my "Maritain and Science," *The New Scholasticism* 58 (1984), pp. 267-92. Reprinted in my *Chance or Reality and Other Essays* (University Press of America and Intercollegiate Studies Institute, 1986).

[18]As shown by the long list of examples in *The Oxford English Dictionary*, vol. 8 (Oxford: Clarendon Press, 1933). In that list, obviously completed a few years before its printing, no reference is yet contained to the use of quantum in modern physics, a use very much established by 1920! Not mentioned in that list is a prominent use of the word quantum, namely, a long chapter "Quantum" in Hegel's *Science of Logic*, trans. W. H. Johnston and L. G. Struthers (London: George Allen & Unwin, 1929), vol. I, pp. 217-332.

[19]*Time*, 27 April 1981, p. 79.

[20]For further details, see my "Chance or Reality: Interaction in Nature versus Measurement in Physics," *Philosophia* 10-11 (1980-81), pp. 85-105; also reprinted in my *Chance or Reality and Other Essays*.

[21]That the deceptiveness of that unintended "anti-ontology" is even greater than that of its fully conscious Cartesian counterpart was forcefully recalled by Maritain in his *The Peasant of the Garonne*, trans. M. Cuddihy and E. Hughes (New York: Macmillan, 1969), pp. 124-39.

[22]First published in 1943. Karl Popper, *The Open Society and Its Enemies*, 5th ed. rev. in 2 vols. (Princeton: Princeton University Press, 1966).

[23]Ibid., vol. II, p. 85.

[24]See the long opening note to the Introduction, vol. I, pp. 202-03.

[25]See ibid., vol. II, pp. 24-25 and 303.

[26]The first to point this out was Pierre Duhem, who did it on an astonishingly vast scale in his pioneering researches on the medieval origins of modern science, especially in his Leonardo studies and his 10 vol. *Système du monde*. For details, see "Duhem, the Historian" in my *Uneasy Genius: The Life and Work of Pierre Duhem* (Dordrecht: Martinus Nijhoff, 1984; paperback reprint 1987), ch. 10.

[27]See *Time*, 13 December 1982, p. 74.

[28]See Eddington's *The Philosophy of Physical Science* (London: Macmillan, 1939), p. 182, for his repudiation of what he had stated in his *The New Pathways of Science* (Cambridge: University Press, 1935), p. 88.

[29]In that respect, there is something subtly misleading in the very title of S. Weinberg's most informative and very readable book, *The First Three Minutes: A Modern View of the Origin of the Universe* (London: André Deutsch, 1977).

[30]For an excellent semi-technical account of that principle, see B. J. Carr, "On the Origin, Evolution and Purpose of the Physical Universe," *"The Irish Astronomical Journal* 15 (1982), pp. 237-53. For a corrective of the philosophical statements made by Carr, see my article, "From Scientific

Cosmology to a Created Universe," ibid., pp. 253-62; reprinted in my *Chance of Reality.*

[31]Karl R. Popper, *The Open Universe: An Argument for Indeterminism* (Totowa, NJ: Rowman and Littefield, 1982), p. 143.

[32]I have heard solipsist views endorsed, in the presence of fairly large gatherings, by such distinguished astronomers as McCrea and Sandage. Well-known for his solipsistic proclivities was, of course, Eddington.

[33]For a not overly technical account, see F. Weisskopf, "Of Atoms, Mountains and Stars: A Study in Qualitative Physics," *Science* 187 (1975), pp. 605-12.

[34]While Burke was right in doing so, for instance, in his impeachment speeches against Warren Hastings of the East India Company, who flouted elementary honesty in his rulings (see Burke's *Works,* 1827 ed., 16:165-66), most specific laws of commerce, such as interest and depreciation rates, have little if anything to do with natural law, let alone with the laws of God.

[35]Thus, for instance, the translational, vibrational, and rotational degrees of freedom of a molecule can be activated only in a way which does not correspond to a straight ascending line (representing the continuous increase of heat input), but along phases which follow one another as ever higher plateaux. Much of the same happens in the evolution of the cosmos, where the steady drop of temperature permits the activation of similar successive plateaux, corresponding to the formation of distinctly new configurations, ranging from subatomic particles, through atoms and molecules, to galaxies, and within the latter, to stars and planets. Herein lies the source of novelty with respect to purely material entities and not in some quasi-mystical indeterminancy, which ultimately deprives of its unique status that source of specific novelty which is man's free will and creativity.

[36]See *Supplement to Royal Society News,* iss. 12, Nov. 1981, p. v.

8

Scientific Ethics and Ethical Science

The choice of this topic, ethical science and scientific ethics, was dictated by two considerations. The first has to do with the world we live in, a world based on science, or rather on the use of tools created by science. Tools can be used properly and improperly, that is, in an ethical or in an unethical manner. This choice or dilemma presses itself upon us with ever greater urgency as the tools produced by science take on an ever greater efficiency. Herein lies the root of the desire to have an ethical science, that is, a science the tools of which are used in an ethically proper manner.

To achieve that goal, namely, to secure the control of science

Lecture delivered under the auspices of the Hellenic Society for Humanistic Studies, Athens, September 26, 1973, and published as Nr 26 of its *Studies and Researches*. Second Series; Athens, 1974, pp. 39-53. Reprinted with permission.

through ethics, an agreement should be reached about ethics. In the pursuit of that agreement it has become fashionable in modern times to assume that it is possible to have a scientific ethics, that is, an ethics based on scientific considerations. The underlying idea is that since the rules of algebra and geometry are universally accepted, an ethics derived from science would also be universally accepted.

This desire to have a scientific ethics is an impossible dream. Or, to put it bluntly, man must give up his dreams about a so-called scientific ethics, if he is to have an ethical science; otherwise, he will have neither science nor ethics. At first sight, this claim is purely philosophical, made by one who is not a philosopher. But every good philosopher knows that philosophical questions have a long history and that unfolding that history is very often the best we can do. Furthermore, since the topic, scientific ethics and ethical science, has a great deal to do with science, as a historian of science I may have some competence to discuss this topic.

The exact origins of a topic, or the first formulation of a dilemma, are, in most cases, impossible to pinpoint. In our case, the situation is different. It is this difference which provides the second consideration for selecting the topic, ethical science and scientific ethics, for this lecture delivered in Greece before a distinguished gathering of Greek scholars. The date and place of the first formulation of our topic coincide with one of the most decisive moments and places in human history. The year was 399 B.C., the month Pyanopsion during which the sacred ship made its round trip from Athens to Delos and back. The place was the prison of the city-state of Athens. It was there, in the death-row of that prison, that Socrates held his last dialogue with his friends. The dialogue, as recorded by one of those friends, Plato, is known as *Phaedo*. It is still to become widely known that *Phaedo* is probably the most influential book in the history of physics.[1]

Historians of philosophy or of ethics recall *Phaedo*, if they care about it at all, as an outmoded argument on behalf of the immortality of the soul. For historians of science the immortality of the soul is simply immaterial and they never mention *Phaedo*. Novelists and reporters specializing in prison stories also failed to discover *Phaedo*, although its story should pay off rather well. Just imagine: there is a man, Socrates, about seventy, and a several-times war-hero, waiting for his execution, with the doors unlocked, the prison-guard paid off, with his wife crying, with his friends pleading to make good an easy escape; but he decides to drink the hemlock. Why is he so stubborn? Well, the poor man is convinced that he has an immortal soul. His friends try to undermine his conviction with scientific arguments. But Socrates stands his ground by taking the view that all the arguments of his friends are based, not on bad logic, but on a wrong physics.

And then he tells them about his own experience with physics, with the physics of the Ionians, of the early atomists, and of Anaxagoras. His first youthful reaction about fifty years earlier was sheer enthusiasm.[2] The solutions of that physics seemed to be dazzlingly true! That physics gave an explanation for everything on the basis that all processes in man and in nature were just changes in patterns, the recombinations of parts in space and time. But as the years went by, something happened both to Socrates and to Athens. The golden age of heroism and cultural confidence yielded to the age of shallow philosophers, the sophists. With them the pattern-philosophy ran its full logic. Most importantly, they succeeded in creating a new cultural atmosphere in which one looked only for patterns but not for norms and truth.

There lay the real root of the so-called Socratic reaction. The overriding concern of the mature Socrates was to save ethical concern in the teeth of physical science, or rather of its unjustified generalization, the pattern-philosophy. The way Socrates went about the task was utterly wrong. He suggested that true physics should be concerned not with the *how* but with the *why,* or rather with the purpose of each and every process. According to Socrates, to mention only one example, the important question about the coming to rest of moving bodies was not how fast or how slowly they came to rest, but whether it was *good* for them to do so.

The full development of that physics came in the hands of Aristotle. In Aristotelian physics all material bodies were supposed to behave as if motivated by goal-seeking tendencies. Stones fell because they allegedly sought their goal, their natural place, the center of the earth. Fire rose because the goal of its nature seemed to be high up. Needless to say, such a physics was wrong from start to end. In the many pages of Aristotelian physics there is hardly one which is tolerably correct.[3] Yet Aristotelian physics dominated thought for two thousand years. The reason for this was not its intrinsic value, but because it struck a chord with man's deep-seated longing for goals and for purposes. At the same time it could appear, in retrospect at least, sheer madness to treat stones, water, air and fire as they were animated by goals.

What about the apparently mad conviction of Socrates? Surely if atomistic patterns were the ultimate reality, his resolve to drink the hemlock made no sense. After all, he did no wrong. His death sentence was due to a political power play by the ruling party in Athens. Was it not then madness to choose to perish under a patently unjust sentence? Madness it would have been had Socrates' concern been with the court's sentence. His real concern, however, was with the sentence of his own conscience. It told him that by escaping he could create the false impression of having considered himself guilty of the charges. His conscience told him that by escaping he would lie with his very action. Lie he would not, for he considered telling a lie as something inherently wrong. For Socrates, the word inherently stood for absolutely and eternally. He believed that truth could exist only if there was an eternal and absolute truth, and he held the same about goodness, beauty, and life, or about any true value in general.

It was on this argument that he rested his convictions of the eternity of his own conscience, that is, of his own soul. Clearly, it was then better to let his body perish under an unjust sentence than to live forever with a guilty conscience. He also had a pointed remark for his friends who argued that there were only physical, atomistic, or in modern terms, biochemical patterns and nothing else. They could see him sitting on his prison bed with his legs pulled up to his chin. Were his friends consistent, they should have said that the sole reason for Socrates' sitting right there and then was a specific configuration of his muscles and bones and nothing else. But the fact was, as Socrates put it, that his muscles and bones would long ago have moved him to a distant place if they could have had their way. That was, in short, Socrates' argument about the immortality of his own soul.

It is, however, not about Socrates' or anyone else's immortality that I want to argue tonight. Socrates may have been wrong about immortality. His argument has indeed some weakness from the point of view of logic. But he was absolutely right on a point which should be of paramount importance to all interested in ethical concerns in an age of science. Socrates was absolutely right in sensing that the conceptual framework of atomistic or quantitative science, or physics in particular, had no logical room for his concern. One could resent, if one wished to do so, the existence of ethical concern as a disturbing constraint on a man's activities. But physical science was, by its very presuppositions, powerless to provide an escape from the clutches or, if you wish, fetters of the categories of the morally good and of the morally wrong. A physics, erected into a philosophy, could do only one thing with that constraint, namely, declare that it was a pseudo-problem. Socrates' friends, who tried to save him, did precisely this. They argued that on the basis of an atomistic physics any talk about one's soul was sheer self-deceit.

It may be objected that the physics of the ancient Greeks was a poor physics even in its best form. So we should not perhaps make much of the fact that a poor physics could be but a poor guide in the labyrinths of man's ethical confinement. A better physics did not improve the situation. This became evident as soon as the new physics, or the new experimental method, began to come of age. Take, for instance, Leonardo da Vinci, the flamboyant designer of machines that seemed utterly fantastic in his times. One of those machines was a submarine. We do not have its blueprints, as Leonardo destroyed them. He did so because, as he put it, such a contraption could destroy each and every seaport in the world. In Leonardo's judgment one was not to tamper or experiment with such a fearsome device.[4]

Concerning the new experimental method, it is tempting to think of Galileo dropping small and big weights from the tower of Pisa to prove the law that all bodies fall with the same acceleration. Galileo never dropped weights or even balls from his own rooftop, let alone from the tower of Pisa.[5] The experiment was done by Simon Stevin from the famous belfry of the cathedral in Bruges, Belgium. Stevin experimented profusely. Among his many works, a group fills an entire volume entitled *The Art of War*.[6] As for Galileo, he claimed in 1610 before the Venetian Senate that the telescope was his invention. Two months later he had to admit that he merely improved the techniques of some Dutch opticians. They offered their telescopes already in 1607 to the States General of the Netherlands. They thought, and not without very good reasons, that with telescopes one could conduct battles more effectively both on the ground and on the high seas.

Galileo's finest experimental discovery concerned the law of free fall. He proved that the vertical fall was a limiting case of the rolling down of balls on a plane of various inclinations. He wrote up all the details in a famous book in the years following his trial in 1633, in unintended evidence of the moral insight that evil happens to give rise to something good. In that famous book, *On the Two New Mechanical Sciences (Statics and Dynamics),* Galileo gave a glimpse of the source of his own experimental skill. He often visited, he wrote, a place where the experimental method was practiced in a superb manner. The place was the military arsenals of the Venetian Republic.[7]

All this may help to understand the concerns of Francis Bacon, Lord Chancellor of England. As a politician, he fell in disgrace, but he carved out for himself an important niche in the history and philosophy of science. His contemporaries spoke of him as the *buccinator novi temporis,* the trumpeter of the new times.[8] He certainly blew that trumpet with enthusiasm. He drew up in his *New Organon* a vast research program. Actually, it was only a search-program. Bacon thought that if enough people went after the facts of nature, within a few years everything that could be learned about nature would indeed be learned.[9]

It was an inebriating vision and Bacon wrote on occasion as if his pen was dipped not in ink but in wine. He had, however, his sober moments too, even when dreaming about his scientific utopia. The latter is known as the *New Atlantis,* a book in which Bacon described a new civilization based on the new experimental method. In that civilization, or state, everybody was well provided for through the inventions of scientists. The *New Atlantis* was a strictly regimented state, with little freedom for the individual. Apparently Bacon took the view (he may not have been a bad psychologist) that many people, if given the choice, would take the security of the welfare state rather than the hazards of freedom. So, in order to prevent abuses in his science-state, Bacon felt impelled to impose secrecy on research. The most talented scientists in *New Atlantis* worked under security restrictions, on strictly classified research.

I did not bring up this point to refresh my phrases with the flavor of modernity, although it is not useless to realize once in a while that nothing is new under the sun. The *New Atlantis* remains a classic reminder of an early example of ethical concern in an age of science. During the seventeenth and eighteenth centuries science made tremendous, mostly theoretical, breakthroughs, but little was achieved in the way of technology. But optimism often thrives better on hopeful vistas than on factual achievements. Many seventeenth and eighteenth-century reflections on science were bursting with incredible optimism. At the same time man's lot did not improve noticeably. Epidemics still raged uncontrolled, the rate of child mortality was as high as ever, and food production remained practically at that low level to which it was raised in the Middle Ages.

What seemed to improve were the factories. But the improvement was achieved by turning human beings, women and children especially, into the slaves of vast sets of often primitive machines. The leaders of the *philosophe* movement, who did not have to sweat and toil like slaves, were, of course, very pleased with the abstract sunshine of the new scientific age. They were busy drawing up a new ethics, based on scientific considerations. They did exactly the opposite of what Socrates had done who sacrificed science to save ethics. The *philosophes,* or the Encyclopedists, sacrificed ethics to secure their shallow idea of science. In Baron d'Holbach's rude formulation, offered in his *Système de la nature,* morality was equated with the smooth running of a vast machine.[10] Happiness became the sweet humming of wheels in the vast mechanism of nature in which the individual was a small gear, though more complicated than, say, a raindrop. But ultimately man was just one drop in the vast bucket of the universe and nothing more.

What sort of concern did man, the individual, deserve, once he was reduced to the status of a mere drop? Was he to be accounted for in a special way? Not at all. Those who know but elementary arithmetic may be foolish enough to count raindrops individually. But why bother with individuals in a purely mechanistic world supported by the statistical method? The latter spares one of much toil and does away with worries about the individual. Baron d'Holbach was no mathematician, but a far better-trained *philosophe,* Condorcet, was a brilliant one. It was no problem for him to draw up the scheme of a new judicial and, by implication, ethical system based on statistical, probability calculations. In that system man was denied appeal if the judgment against him corresponded to the typical procedure, or most likely outcome.[11]

Like all others, who dreamed about a scientific ethics, Condorcet did not realize that he was writing his own death sentence. His plan was to start a refreshing wind, but through the inner logic of things it rapidly turned into the horrible storm of the Terror. During the few weeks he spent in prison there were no pleas on his behalf, no schemes to rescue him. (Unlike Socrates, he certainly would have escaped if he could). All his friends and former associates were running for dear life. There were no arguments about conscience either. Conscience was no longer fashionable, largely because of the propaganda of which Condorcet was a chief promoter. And certainly there was no prospect of an eternal vindication against the madness of the Terror. The machine-philosophy which Condorcet had helped father quickly turned into a mad social machine. It took Condorcet's life with no apologies.

During the late eighteenth century there were two notable efforts to rescue man from the clutches of a soulless science. Science, of course, was not soulless, just as a machine is not soulless, for neither machine nor science are able to have souls. But science can be turned into a soulless, or rather a soul-killing, enterprise if raised into a fundamental philosophy. This is what was done by the *philosophe* movement. Goethe rose to the bait—as he found it in Baron d'Holbach's *Système de la nature* which he read at the dangerous age of twenty. No wonder that young Goethe got violent intellectual indigestion from which he failed to recover for the rest of his life. For over four decades Goethe fought tooth and nail Newtonian science. He thought he could unmask it as a farce by his own theory of colors or *Farbenlehre*. Thus Goethe, one of the greatest poets of all times, kept repeating to the end that all that he achieved in poetry was a poor second to what he achieved as a physicist.[12] In short, he made a big fool of himself and for a very simple reason which was the fatal error of his generation. By the early 1800s almost two centuries of the scientific age had already passed, but man was still not mature enough to see the crucial difference between science and a philosophy based exclusively on science.

The other effort was wasted by Rousseau. His case tells much the same story but in a different orchestration. He made a name for himself with the publication of a most ambitious work, called *Emile*. Into that work Rousseau put in a pleasant conversational style a bitter criticism of the educational philosophy of his time. That philosophy emphasized the cultivation of intellect as befitted the age of reason. Now what is reason, or reasoning? It is judicious selection of only one of many possibilities as being true. Reasoning is the recognition that one cannot eat the cake and still have it. Reasoning is the admission that whether we like it or not, there are many constraints in the physical as well as in the moral world. Of such constraints Rousseau wanted none. Against reason that reminded him of physical and moral constraints, he held high the vision of a natural state unfettered by any constraint. In his *Emile* he set forth how a new generation should be brought up by letting each child grow up under the guidance of natural instincts. Rousseau also listed various things young men should avoid. A principal among them was hard-to-learn science. To make sure that Emile would never fall prey to the lures of the scientific establishment, Rousseau described it to him in the following words: "It has become more evident than daylight that the scientific societies of Europe are public schools of lies and that there are more mistaken notions in the Academy of Sciences in Paris than in a whole tribe of American Indians."[13]

In late eighteenth-century France, American Indians, especially the Hurons, were the proverbial embodiments of wise, unspoiled savages of nature. Rousseau certainly knew of Robinson Crusoe, who found a new life among those savages in the midst of wild nature. In eighteenth-century prints Robinson Crusoe is invariably depicted as a youngish man of twenty with long hair and moustache, his body covered with patches of animal skin, and a string around his waist, who proudly sported a double-barrelled shotgun on his shoulder. Such was the famous escape from the prisonlike constraints of a so-called scientific culture into a nature which was turned into a prison by the shotgun, a product of science.

Another two hundred years had again passed in the scientific age since the theologians of the Sorbonne hastened to brand *Emile* as a most dangerous book leading to anarchy. Those theologians were motivated not only by theological considerations but also, and probably even more so, by their vested interest in the absolutist French monarchy. They condemned Rousseau partly for wrong reasons, if condemnation was needed at all. They certainly overstated their cause by making it appear that an unconditional, meek obedience to political rulers was a sacred duty for the faithful. But they were perfectly right in sizing up *Emile* as a sure road to anarchy. In this they were right, but not for specific theological reasons. They were right because of the basic facet of the human condition. That condition means that while man is free to do anything, he must not do everything he is urged by his instincts to do. Revolt as man may, ignore moral constraints as he may, those constraints reassert themselves with fearful endurance. The more man tries to shake off those constraints, the more tightly they will close in on him. Or in plain, idiomatic language, it is to invite the constraints of destructive anarchy to think that one can get away with murder.

In that idiomatic phrase murder means all kinds of misdeeds, including especially the most sophisticated kinds of crime and misdemeanor. The phrase is as old as the hills, but it has never been so timely as in these latest decades of the scientific age. The intellectual, social and educational development of the last twenty or so years has been in the direction of shaking off constraints of all kinds. The fashionable slogan nowadays from postgraduate courses in ethical philosophy down to social studies in the fifth grade is that all ethical norms are crazy taboos inherited from the darker ages and from primitive fears. The philosophical bestsellers of our times—the works of Skinner, Monod, Marcuse, to name only the most notorious ones—are at one in claiming that there are only behavioral patterns.

There are few things as tempting as to fall in with that fallacy as long as the great majority behaves in terms of old-fashioned norms. But when the fallacy strikes home? Of the innumerable cases let me recall that of a Princeton Senior, a sociology major. A year ago he told me with great persuasion and superior assurance that sociology has disproved the validity of absolute ethical norms. There are no norms, he said, only patterns of behavior. Around Christmas we met again. He told me in a tone of outrage that pilferage has reached epidemic proportion in the campus dormitories. Nothing was safe in one's room any longer. Anything valuable one owned had to be locked up in a foot locker whenever one left one's room. I took the story in my stride. I had heard similar stories about Stanford and elsewhere, and was not surprised. My calm has visibly irritated my young friend. Are you not outraged? he asked me. No, I said to him. But don't you think you should be? he asked again with indignation. Well, perhaps I should be outraged, but you certainly should not, I told him. This threw him into a frenzy. Why should I not be outraged, he asked, when they have just stolen my wristwatch and my cassette tape recorder?

I knew whom he meant by the word "they." Some of his classmates. Well, I said to him, you remember our conversation a year ago? You remember your claim that there were no ethical norms but only behavioral patterns? He did remember though not too readily. Well, I went on, if such is indeed the case, then what forbids some students from taking on the behavioral characteristics of thieves? My friend got the point. It now dawned on him that those who ridicule absolute ethical norms in the classrooms should not cry over their absence in the dormitories.

The same also holds true of those who write into legislation the various points of that sophisticated crusade against firm ethical principles. By the inner logic of things those legislators and political leaders have their hands now full with situations that are anything but laughing matters. We need only think of the prison riots at Attica, N.Y., or at Woodbridge, N.J.[14] Of the two, Attica received much wider publicity, and almost everybody claims to know what happened there. About the riot at Woodbridge, I happen to know how it really started. Some inmates began to argue whether they were going to watch a football game or a basketball game on TV. In Attica the matters were settled by bursts of shotguns; in Woodbridge there was a deal. But for all the concessions, the situation remained very tense for a while.

The reason for this is very simple. Our society prefers to think that the real grievances of prisoners are about food, clothing, visiting rights, medical care, entertainment and the like. That inmates in American prisons are far better off than in most parts of the world is largely ignored. So the efforts go on to secure more comfort for criminals and the argument is heard on occasion that prisons should be closed down since there are no such people as criminals. Criminals are merely sick people. Such is the scientific approach, some say, to the whole problem.

But this does not seem to be an effective way of preventing things from getting worse in our prisons. The real problem of modern criminals and of modern prisons is not about material conditions. The real problem is not about the manner, the *how,* in which prisons are run but about the reason, or *why* we should have prisons and why some people should be locked up there. A culture, a scientific age, which has brushed aside the question about the why as a pseudo-problem and pseudo-question, will not be able to cope with its prisons and prisoners, wherever they are in a very broad sense. For the big question for a prisoner is not *how* he is in the prison, but *why* he is there. And he will have no peace of mind until this question has been settled for him in a satisfactory way. The big question today is still the question with which Socrates grappled in his own prison. He answered the question by pouring science into the molds of ethics. The scientific age tries the very opposite by diluting ethics into the molds of quantitative science and of its superstructure, pattern-philosophy.

The Socratic solution is faulty, but the modern solution is simply self-destructive. Man can live without science; he did so for a million years. But man cannot live without ethics. The horrible turmoils and the unbearable existential stresses of a scientific culture show this all too clearly. Those stresses are caused only in part by the rapid changes of man's environment. The burden of those stresses is made particularly heavy by futile efforts that consist in trying to eliminate all constraints from man's life. There is a bold effort afoot to create man anew, to emancipate him from an existence which has much resemblance to being in a prison. Existentialist philosophy as advocated by Sartre has precisely that aim. It does away with all norms, all restrictions, and also with all continuity. It claims that only the actual moment, the atomistic units of time, do count. But if one moment is absolutely separate from any other, there can be no moral law since moral laws assume continuity in time.

It should be no surprise that for such an atomistic ethics theoretical justification has been sought in the atomistic structure of things. Instead of arguing fine points of the philosophy of atomic physics, one need rather recall the prospect of global destruction that was brought into our lives by unlocking the energy of atoms. The potential destructiveness of atomic energy is now aptly matched by the destructiveness of an existential atomistic ethics. In that ethics all actions are disjointed, all nations stand for their own sake, all patterns of behavior are on equal footing, from the logical viewpoint that is.

There are, of course, brave efforts to escape that logical dilemma by some pragmatic approach. There is, for instance, the claim that one should fall back on the majority voice, established by free elections. The process breaks down at most critical junctures. On the most critical issues minorities shall never be convinced by the majority wisdom whatever that may be. This problem will be avoided, so it is claimed, if we leave the decision to experts, especially to the so-called scientific elite. They are steeped, so the claim goes, in the objective, unbiased appraisal of facts and care only for facts. Of the many rebuttals of this wishful thinking let me refer only to a Ph.D. thesis from MIT, published last November. The title of the thesis is *Eggheads and Warheads: Scientists and the ABM*. The author, Anne H. Cahn, got her Ph.D. for writing up the obvious, namely, that the so-called scientific community showed no scientific objectivity in judging the matter. If that objectivity had really been at work, the opinions of scientists should have been distributed over a broad spectrum since there was a broad variety of possible ABM defenses. But as Mrs. Cahn's data showed, "scientists who favored one type of defense, also favored the others; and those opposed to one type, opposed all ballistic missile defenses." Such can hardly be called objectivity, but the lack of it was equally evident in the strictly technical aspects of the question. I quote Mrs. Cahn again: "Those who favored ABM found all types to be technically feasible; those opposed found none feasible."[15]

Another pragmatic attempt to escape the logical dilemma of atomistic ethics is based on references to the sacredness of life. If that life is meant to be the life of the individual, the attempt fizzles immediately when it comes to the question of abortion and euthanasia, to say nothing of the fact that in some states abortions are already outnumbering live births. If that life is meant to be the life of the whole species what forbids the elimination of some individuals, what forbids the elimination of entire groups, if by some curious criteria they are found unproductive, anti-social, or parasites in short?

Indeed, nothing forbade such large-scale eliminations. No age has witnessed mass murders in such huge measures and so repeatedly as did this scientific age of ours. And in each and every case the ethics that was submitted as a justification was one or another type of a so-called scientific ethics. Also, the tools of science were heavily used in committing those mass murders as if to illustrate the point that one could not have an ethical science once one espoused a so-called scientific ethics. Typically enough all those who revolted on seeing innocent blood flowing in heavy streams justified their stance by references to tenets like the inalienable rights of the individual. Few of them realized in this scientific age that such references were wholly unscientific.

Unscientific, I repeat, because the method of science, of exact science, and disciplines, like sociology and psychology that today try to be as exact as physics is, abdicate at the very outset any concern about the individual, the unrepeatable. The method of exact science limits itself to the observation of only those phenomena and events that are, by definition, strictly repeatable. This is why exact science is incapable of dealing with the unique flow of events in time, that is, with history, individual and social alike. This is why exact science is unable to get to the heart of the matter when it comes to the individual. Science can split the atom, although according to its name an atom is that which cannot be cut. The cutting up of the atom opened up possibilities for further cuts. Nothing of the sort can be done about the only true *atom* in the universe, the individual. By cutting it up, it can only be destroyed.

Long before modern analysis—conceptual, psychological and clinical—made its futile attempt at the individual to decompose him into parts, man had realized the uniqueness of the individual. This realization did not come through scientific studies. It was based on rather different sources and insights. Its most creative source was the biblical revelation. The ethical component of that revelation has many unique facets, of which one should be particularly relevant for this confrontation of ethical science and scientific ethics. In the Bible and in the whole Christian tradition there has always been a major emphasis on the crucial difference between knowing the good and doing it, between knowing the right and clinging to it with a stubborn elemental commitment. The agony of the prophets was as revealing in this respect as was the concern of Saint Paul to keep alive among Christians the flame of the new evangelical attitude.

By contrast, take a look at the naive optimism of Confucius. According to him, it was enough to teach man about the good. The well instructed man, so Confucius claimed, spontaneously *did* the good. Or in his inimitable words: "When things are investigated, then true knowledge is achieved; when true knowledge is achieved, then the will becomes sincere."[16] The hard facts of life and of history give a resounding lie to this carefree galloping in aphoristic wisdom. It may be objected that the truth of the ditty of Confucius presupposes a robust form of knowledge not available in his time. Well, the scientific age is also the age of information explosion. Would it then really follow that it is enough to know things in order to do the right things? The philosophy which sets the tone of modern education is based on such a belief. Why is it then that so many of our schools have become blackboard jungles and hotbeds of drug addiction? And why is it that venereal disease decimates our youth even in school districts where sex education has for years had a very high priority? Did not Saint Paul size up the real issue far better when he uttered cries of agony about the conflict between seeing the good and not doing it at the same time?

A really valuable ethics should not merely be a set of principles, but also a source for unfliching commitment to higher ideals. Philosophers of ethics, of scientific ethics, who are given to purism in method, would frown on this mixing of the practical with the theoretical, of this grafting ethical theory and ethical commitment upon one another. But they should not forget that science would not have conquered the loyalties of modern man, if it offered only knowledge but no power. The great attraction of science since the seventeenth century lay precisely in its ability to promise and deliver power to man over nature. The tremendous power wielded by science brings out more forcefully than anything else the eternal source of ethical concern. That source is the tragic difference between man's tools and man's aims. Or as Captain Ahab put it in Melville's *Moby Dick:* "All my means are sane, my motive and my object mad."[17] It is this disparity which forces upon man the realization that he has the duty to do certain things and should not do a great number of things. It is this disparity that underlies the momentous difference between the two moods. One is the indicative and this is used by science. The other is the subjunctive and is used in ethical parlance. The events of science were, are, or will be; the events of ethics should be or should have been.

Squirm as modern man may, there is no escape from the category of ought. He may consider it an old-fashioned prison, yet within its walls he shall forever remain. Those walls shall not disappear by a policy which professes them to be non-existent. Those walls shall forever pose for man the question which Socrates had to face in his own prison, the question of *why,* the question of *why* man is in the predicament in which he is; or, put in other words, *why* he is an ethical animal.

Without trying to come to terms with that fundamental and general question, there will be no satisfactory answer to such specific issues as whether to permit or not to permit the creation of humans in test tubes; or to permit or not to permit the chemical refashioning of brain processes; or to permit or not to permit the interference with one's genetic stock. All these and similar specific ethical questions created by modern scientific know-how are exceedingly important to analyze but time does not permit going into details here.

Here I tried to focus attention on one great lesson of scientific history. The lesson is that reductionism leads to self-defeating results. Socrates raised the right question but gave a wrong, reductionist answer, by reducing science to ethics. He ended up with a wholly false form of what "physical science" ought to be. In the opposite or modern process ethics is reduced to a branch of quantitative, behavioral science. The result is that we have a so-called "scientific ethics" which is no ethics at all and therefore it cannot be scientific. On its basis one can truly get away with murder of any and all kinds.

Clearly then, an ethical science is on hand only when its norms are taken from an ethics existing independently of science. Yet, although ethics and science come from two different wellsprings of the human genius, both must remain consistent with their basic presuppositions if they are to be intellectually respectable. This quality of consistency is particularly well embedded in physical science. This is why the label "scientific" is rightfully attached to a system of ethics which is consistent with its fundamental presuppositions about the *why* of human existence. When, and only when, there is a broadly shared conviction about a truly "scientific" ethics, mankind may muster enough moral strength to use science properly and enjoy thereby the blessings of a truly ethical science.

[1]Nothing on this point is hinted, for instance, in the heavily annotated and most widely used modern English translation of *Phaedo* by R. Hackforth (Cambridge: Cambridge University Press, 1955) which is available also in The Library of Liberal Arts Series.

[2]Ibid., p. 125. A very informative and meticulous reconstruction of Anaxagoras' physics is *Anaxagoras and the Birth of Physics* by D. E. Gershenson and D. A. Greenberg (New York: Blaisdell, 1964).

[3]A remark of E. T. Whittaker in his *From Euclid to Eddington: A Study of Conceptions of the External World* (Cambridge: Cambridge University Press, 1949), p. 65.

[4]See *Léonard de Vinci par lui-méme,* ed. A. Chastel (Paris: Nagel, 1952), pp. 156-57.

[5]As was shown convincingly in *Galileo and the Tower of Pisa* (Ithaca, NY: Cornell University Press, 1935) by the classical scholar, L. Cooper, who became suspicious of the hallowed story after he had found widely conflicting details in physicists' accounts of it.

[6]Volume IV in *The Principal Words of Simon Stevin* (Amsterdam: Swets, 1955-56).

[7]As stated clearly in the opening remark of that work. See translation with introduction and notes by S. Drake (Madison: University of Wisconsin Press, 1974), p. 45.

[8]They did so largely because Bacon himself described himself as a "trumpeter." See *The Works of Francis Bacon,* ed. J. Spedding *et al.* (London: Longmans, 1857-74), vol. X, p. 301.

[9]See *New Organon,* bk. 1, aph. 112, in *The Works of Francis Bacon,* vol. IV, p. 102.

[10]See new ed., London, 1775, p. 19. The work was published anonymously and outside France.

[11]The basis of Condorcet's reasoning was that society should tolerate serious errors made by judiciary tribunals at a rate that did not exceed the rate of fatal accidents suffered by passenger boats crossing the English Channel. For details, see my *The Relevance of Physics* (Chicago: University of Chicago Press, 1966), p. 378.

[12]For his astonishing evaluation of himself, four years before his death, see my essay "Goethe and the Physicists" (1969) reprinted in my *Chance or Reality and Other Essays* (Washington DC: University Press of America and Intercollegiate Studies Institute, 1986), p. 80.

[13]*Emile,* tr. B. Foxley (London: J. M. Dent, n.d.), p. 167.

[14]These two riots followed one another within two months in the Fall of 1971.

[15]See pp. 222-23 in her thesis published by the Science and Public Policy Program of the Department of Political Science and Center for International Studies of the Massachusetts Institute of Technology, Cambridge, Mass., 1971. In all likelihood a very similar conclusion would emerge from a careful analysis of the scientific sides taken in respect of the technological feasibility of SDI or Star Wars.

[16]See *The Wisdom of Confucius,* ed. and tr. Lin Yutang (New York: Modern Library, 1938), p. 140.

[17]See Modern Library edition (New York, 1926), p. 185.

9

The Physics of Impetus and the Impetus of the Koran

In two short years from now we shall be at the threshold of 1987, a year which undoubtedly will have as one of its chief events the celebration of the 300th anniversary of Newton's *Principia*. Three hundred years after its publication the *Principia* is still the most important scientific book ever published. In fact, in a sense it marked the beginning of exact science on a grand scale. There was, of course, plenty of science before Newton. Of the three laws of motion, which support the vast edifice of the *Principia*, Newton could claim only one, the third, as his own, and even that only in part. He would have credited Galileo with the law of acceleration

First published in *Modern Age* (Spring 1984), pp. 153-60. Reprinted with permission.

and, had he not been ill-disposed toward Descartes, he might have referred to him as the author of the first and second laws. Newton deserved all the credit for putting the three laws in the order in which we find them on the very first page of the *Principia*. The force law is the third, because as an equation it is an action-reaction statement and therefore presupposes the second law. As to the notion of acceleration in that same third law, it presupposes the notion of inertial rectilinear motion, which is what the first law is about.

In a sense, therefore, the whole edifice of physics and of exact science rests on the first law. By ascribing it to Descartes, Newton would not have been entirely wrong. Descartes spoke indeed of linear inertial motion. He even assumed that, hypothetically speaking, such a movement would continue into infinity. But such a movement was impossible in the universe of Descartes. There the major motions were all circular and were confined to within one stellar domain or solar system. For Galileo, too, the inertial motion was circular when it came to the celestial regions, that is, to the moon and the planets. Galileo did not speak of the motion of stars, nor did Newton for that matter. Contrary to countless statements to be found everywhere in the literature, technical and popular, for Newton the material universe was finite. Although that universe was floating in an infinite space, its material particles, stars or atoms, were not supposed to stray into infinity. In other words, when Newton said that a body would indefinitely continue its inertial motion along a straight line, he did not mean actual infinity. It was only in the nineteenth century that the inertial motion as an infinite straight line was taken in a realist sense, but not for long. All permissible paths of motion are more or less curved in the universe as interpreted in Einstein's General Theory of Relativity.

In view of this the inertial motion as formulated by Buridan and Oresme in the fourteenth century appears more modern than it would at first sight. Buridan and Oresme explicitly spoke of the inertial motion of the sphere of stars and of the planets, circular as that motion was. For both, the diurnal steady motion of the fixed stars was obvious evidence of a motion which, when once started, would go on forever if friction and resistance did not intervene. The manner in which Buridan, and later Oresme, described the beginning of motion, of any motion in the universe, is therefore of enormous importance for an understanding of the ultimate source of the physics of impetus without which there would be no Galilean physics, no Newtonian physics, not even Einsteinian physics.

Buridan's most specific statement occurs in the context of his commentary on Aristotle's cosmological work, *On the Heavens*. Aristotle, of course, insisted on the eternity of motion that was unacceptable to a Christian like Buridan. According to the Christian Creed the world was created in the beginning, or in time, which means that the past history of the universe is finite. The same creed also states that the future history of the universe is also finite. Eternity begins when an end has come to this world. It should also be noted that in 1215, or a hundred years before Buridan, the Fourth Lateran Council made it a dogma that the world was created in time and out of nothing.

All this was in Buridan's mind—and therefore we ought to keep it in mind in order to grasp the full meaning of the statement by which he separated himself from Aristotle on the eternity of the motion of stars:

> God, when He created the world, moved each of the celestial orbs as He pleased, and in moving them He impressed in them impetuses which moved them without His having to move then any more except by the method of general influence whereby He concurs as an agent in all things which take place. . . . And these impetuses which He impressed in the celestial bodies were not decreased nor corrupted afterwards, because there was no inclination of the celestial bodies for other movements. Nor was there resistance which would be corruptive or repressive of that impetus.

Buridan, who had already talked of the throw of a stone or of a javelin in terms of an impetus impressed on them by the arm, added in the same breath that in explaining motion, both celestial and terrestrial, in that fashion, he was seeking "from theological masters" as to "what they might teach me in the matter of how these things take place."

Those masters taught him indeed something of extraordinary importance for the future of science. The whole future of physics depended on making a start with the physics of impetus, given in a nutshell in the foregoing statement of Buridan. His statement was repeated almost verbatim by Oresme and reproduced all over Europe in countless manuscripts and lecture notes throughout the fifteenth century and reprinted again on a number of occasions during the sixteenth century. Rarely before or after did a statement form a more lasting and coherent tradition in matters scientific.

Buridan's impetus theory differs from Aristotle's theory of motion in that the eternity of motion is rejected by it. It also differs from Aristotle's theory concerning the source of motion. For Aristotle the source of all motion is the Prime Mover, who is not really different from the sphere of the fixed stars. Therefore, Aristotle's theory implies a cosmic *perpetuum mobile* not in the sense that in the absence of friction the motion of the fixed stars would last forever. Rather, Aristotle's universe is a *perpetuum mobile* in the sense that it cannot be not moving; in fact it cannot be non-existing. The necessary existence of the cosmos is a basic tenet in Aristotle's thinking. His Prime Mover is not a Creator, and if it were a Creator he could not fail to create. Whatever the role of the Prime Mover in the motion of the heavens, it is a necessary and eternal role. If that role is, as Aristotle would have it, the inspiring of the motion of stars through the Prime Mover's eliciting in them a desire to move, it is still an eternal and necessary role. Unlike the Christian God, or the Jewish God, or the Muslim God, who creates but is not under intrinsic constraint to create, the God or Prime Mover of Aristotle is neither a Creator nor is He free not to play his role, let alone to play any other role.

As for any medieval Christian, for Buridan, too, the Christian God is free to create. The freedom of the Creator to create was powerfully reasserted in 1277 by the bishop of Paris in a decree concerning a long series of cosmological questions. The decree, which exerted great intellectual influence, was well known to Buridan, who in line with Christian theology saw the basis of God's freedom to create in His absolute transcendence over anything He might create. If, however, God is fully transcendent to His creation, that is, to the entire universe, there is no need for Him, unlike for Aristotle's Prime Mover, to remain in "physical" contact, however-sublimated, with the universe so that its motion might go on.

This difference between Aristotle's and Buridan's concept of the beginning and continuation of cosmic motion bears heavily on their respective dicta on any motion, small and ordinary, such as the throw of a stone or of a javelin. According to Aristotle any motion on earth is accomplished in the same way in which this happens to the sphere of the fixed stars. Just as the Prime Mover must remain in contact all the time with the sphere of the fixed stars, be it by inspiring in it a desire to move so that its motion may continue, the source of the continued motion of any thing is that its mover remains in continuous contact with it. This is why Aristotle supports the theory of *peristasis* or a sort of self-perpetuating vortex mechanism in order to explain for instance the flight of a projectile, say of a javelin. Once the javelin leaves the hand it makes, according to Aristotle, the air in front of it separate, move along it and then close behind it as a moving force. Quite different is the case with Buridan's theory of the flight of a javelin or of any other projectile. According to Buridan the arm imparts a certain amount of motion or impetus to the javelin that keeps flying until it loses its entire quantity of motion, or impetus, or momentum if you wish, to the resistance of the air. In other words, just as in the case of Aristotle, where a theology (pagan, pantheist, and non-creationist) determines the physics of motion on earth, in Buridan's case too theology (Christian or strictly creationist) determines physics, but with a result as different as the two theologies are different. In the case of Aristotle theology stifled physics; in the case of Buridan theology laid the possibility for physics by inspiring the formulation of the physics of impetus.

Between Aristotle, or the Greeks of old, and Buridan, or the Latin medievals, there were, of course, the Muslims not only historically but also scientifically. Much of the Greek scientific and philosophical corpus reached the Latin West through Muslim mediation. By the time this happened, the Muslim world had for almost half a thousand years been in the possession of almost all the extant scientific and philosophical works of the ancient Greeks. In fact, the translation of those works into Arabic was done with an impetuous hunger for learning. It matched the territorial expansiveness of Muslim religion behind which stood the impetus of the Koran as its chief propellant. The ensuing process, which has been amply researched and discussed in a vast literature, has some salient characteristics. First, the acquisition of Greek learning was followed by a considerable elaboration of several of its aspects. Medicine in general and ophthalmology in particular come first to mind. Ophthalmology in term required intensive study of optics. There and also in algebra and trigonometry Muslim scholars did original work. With the optical work of Ibn al-Haitham (Alhazen) there is on hand a promising balance between experimentation and theory.

In addition to talent there was also a vast social matrix, the Muslim world, making possible easy communication over a land mass stretching from Baghdad to Cordoba with the help of a highly developed language, Arabic, a language kept alive and spread in a great measure by the daily recitation of the Koran. There were also lively exchanges with neighboring and distant cultures. The Chinese art of paper-making was quickly learned and perfected by Muslims who also noted the great usefulness for commercial purposes of the Hindu decimal system. There were, of course, some setbacks, such as the destruction of Baghdad by the Mongols in the early thirteenth century and, about the same time, the fall of Cordoba. The Crusades were not helpful either for a peaceful cultivation of the arts and sciences.

Such and similar trials and setbacks have often been taken for the cause of a tantalizing aspect of the first 600 years of Muslim history. While in the West the acquisition of Greek scientific knowledge in the late thirteenth century led within 150 years to Copernicus, within 300 years to Kepler and Galileo, and within 350 years to Newton, in the Muslim world the situation was quite different. There, after 300 years of meditation on Greek science, which takes us to the time of Avicenna (Ibn Sina), and even after twice that many years, which take us to Ibn Khaldoun, there were no signs whatever that a Copernicus, a Galileo, let alone a Newton would arise within a reasonable time. Such is a tantalizing situation because there was plenty of intellectual excellence as well as technical skill in the Muslim world. The situation is also tantalizing with respect to a possibility which did not materialize. What, one may ask, would have been the course of world history if a Galileo and a Newton had been Arabs, say, living in Cairo, between 1000 and 1200, or even as late as 1300 or 1400? Since Newtonian science was quickly followed up by a vast technological development, the same impact would very likely have been made by a Muslim Newton. This is all the more a likely conjecture because the energies of the Muslim world became activated and united by the Turks. The empire of Suleiman the Magnificent was much admired in the West for its organization, crafts, and security. It was only 200 years later that the Muslim world, insofar as it was largely a Turkish empire, became in the eyes of Western travelers the paragon of backwardness, intellectual and industrial. It is easy to guess the course of world history if at the time of the battle of Lepanto the Turkish navy had been propelled by steam engines. Two hundred years later, the Muslim world was hopelessly behind the West and still another hundred years later it lay wide open to Western colonial expansion. Such was the case to a large extent because the West had an indisputable technological superiority.

Western technology, at least in the form which gave in the eighteenth and nineteenth centuries a distinct advantage over the rest of the world, was not a fruit of manual dexterity or a result of socioeconomic pressures. The transportational, electrical, and chemical industry as it developed in the West was mostly the work of engineers well trained in the Newtonian science of motion or mechanics. It was a science because every step in it was in strict order so that the third step or law was inconceivable without the second and the second without the first. The question of why science—a robust, modern science in which one step is not only preceded by another step, but in which one step generates another in a sequence that cannot be stopped—did not arise in the Muslim world, is therefore the question of why the first law of Newton, the law of momentum or impetus, was not formulated in the Muslim world. In still other words, the foregoing question is a question about the history of the theory of impetus in the Muslim world.

That history is very late and very short. Ibn Sina (Avicenna), who died in 1037, is the only Muslim scholar who speculated about inertial motion in a way that might have issued in the formulation of the theory of impetus. What he said about a hypothetical inertial motion in a hypothetical void has been repeatedly discussed during the past fifty or so years. It is clear from those discussions that even if Buridan had been familiar with Avicenna's views on inertial motion, they would not have helped him at all. For the crucial insight in Buridan's discussion of impetus is a theological point which is completely alien to Avicenna's thinking. This is an all-important point, because, being a Muslim Avicenna could be expected to have Buridan's view on creation, which provided the latter's crucial insight. Not only is there no evidence that Avicenna believed in creation, but also there is a vast evidence that he believed in Plotinian emanationism. It is a form of pantheism, the very opposite of creationism. According to Avicenna, God necessarily and eternally produces the world, but such a God is not a Creator.

Avicenna was not alone among Muslim thinkers to hold pantheistic emanationism. He is in fact a chief figure in the camp of those great Muslim scholars who put Aristotle's pantheistic philosophy above the Koran. The story is too well known to be reviewed here, however briefly, but it is a most decisive story for the fate and fortunes of science in the Muslim world. Equally decisive for that story is the basic attitude of the opposite camp, best represented by al-Ashari and al-Ghazzali and their occasionalism. They represented a Muslim orthodoxy which rejected the notion of scientific law for fear that it would impose constraints on the infinite power of Allah, the Creator.

A Muslim orthodoxy is not necessarily *the* Muslim orthodoxy, that is, the true teaching of the Koran and in particular of the Koran's true teaching on Creator and creation. Yet, can one, for instance, confidently say that the teaching of the Koran on creation would inspire a world view germane to science? The question is all the more important because a law of science is never about a particular phenomenon, about a single occasion, but about the universal relevance of that law for all such phenomena all across the universe. In other words, all science is about the cosmos, but not about any kind of cosmos. A cosmos, a universe, is useful for science only if it is the totality of consistently interacting things. The laws of that universe are consistently valid everywhere in it and all the time. A second characteristic is that such a universe is not necessary. If the universe were necessary, be it in the form of a necessary emanationism from God, who can generate only one kind of universe, the empirical investigation of such a universe becomes meaningless. The laws of such a universe could conceivably be fathomed on an *a priori* basis, through sheer mental introspection. This is in fact what Aristotle tried to do in his *On the Heavens* and after him all the major Muslim representatives of scientific thinking.

Revealingly, that list includes even an al-Farabi, who is well known in the history of philosophy as the one who first formulated the notion of the contingency of any being other than the Creator with respect to existence. Furthermore, he did so with an explicit view to the Koran's doctrine of creation, that is, with a view to Allah's absolute power and sovereignty over all beings. Yet, that doctrine was not such as to prevent al-Farabi from saying that the starry heavens were divine and existed necessarily, which is the very opposite to being contingent with respect to existence. If, however, the heavens existed necessarily, they had to be eternal and their motion, together with all motion anywhere else in the universe, had to be eternal. In such an outlook it was impossible to do what Buridan did. Buridan, who found in the Christian dogma of creation in time and out of nothing a crucial insight for a concept of cosmic motion with an absolute beginning, could also consider any lesser motion, such as the flight of a javelin, as a motion in which the mover was so superior to the moved thing that it did not have to remain in actual contact with the moved thing.

Was it impossible to do the same for an al-Farabi or an Avicenna, or in general for Muslim thinkers, because perhaps of an ambiguity or a lack of sufficient explicitness in the Koran about creation in time and out of nothing? If such is the case then the question of the failure of Muslim scholars to formulate the proper impetus theory becomes the question of the true nature of the intellectual impetus provided by the Koran. It is a question which underlies the great ferment that has increasingly engulfed the Muslim world for the past thirty years. Those years are also the first and full exposure of the Muslim world on all levels to Western technology, which brings along an exposure to Western scientific thinking.

Not all fruits of that exposure are of course beneficial. Undue preoccupation with the quantitative, let it be scientific or technological, may atrophy man's sensitivity for qualities and values. This indeed took place in the West. The Muslim world is fully justified both in deploring the abuses of science and in trying to apply science in a humane way. But before that humane application takes place, there has to be science, that is, there have to be minds fully familiar with science. This, however, demands that there be minds fully imbued with the thinking underlying science especially if they wish to be creative in science.

The question is then whether the present-day Muslim reawakening, which is a reassertion of the role of the Koran in every facet of life, can be reconciled with the thinking demanded by science. Modern Muslim thinkers should be well aware that the problem of science versus faith or theology had once before been the crucial issue in Muslim culture. In that first confrontation, the confrontation between the Mutazalites and the Mutakallimum, no middle road was found for doing justice both to the Koran and to a science heavily conditioned by Aristotelian necessitarianism to which no Muslim corrective was forthcoming. Instead of a middle road there came extremist positions whose representatives charged one another with incoherence. Both sides seemed to have, however, one thing in common, a kind of schizophrenia. Thus the orthodox al-Ghazzali denounced the notion of scientific laws, while he also looked for them in his scientific work, whereas Averroes, who mainly cultivated science, paid plenty of lip service to orthodoxy.

Whether we shall see a repetition in the Muslim world today of what happened a thousand years ago, that is, whether in the Muslim world theologians and scientists go separate ways, remains to be seen. Certainly in today's Muslim world the chances are nil for a solution which 600 years ago was set forth by by Ibn Khaldoun, whose philosophy of history, the *Muqaddimah,* is today the most widely read Arabic work in the Western world. That solution was in substance a pragmatic avoidance of the problem. Such had to be the case with an interpretation of the history of civilization based on the claim that whenever enough people leave behind the nomadic and agricultural life and gather into cities, they will develop the crafts and the sciences. This is, of course, true only if science is taken for essentially practical skills, however refined and useful. Whatever ancient civilization we consider, we find in its great cities a variety of practical skills, but never science properly so called. And as long as, for instance, the art of measurement remained a practical skill, it was not science.

Tellingly, Ibn Khaldoun did not take geometry, helpful as it can be in measurements, for science, that is, for an intellectual enterprise cultivated for its own intrinsic beauty and merit. Instead he praised its practical usefulness, lofty as that usefulness could be, such as the moulding of the intellect along rigorous reasoning. It was such a usefulness that in Ibn Khaldoun's estimate was the purpose of the study of geometry, which in his words does for the mind what soap does for the body. Ibn Khaldoun was not sympathetic toward a cultivation of geometry for its own sake. His diffidence toward pure theories, and all theorems of Euclid are pure theories, comes through not only as he discusses theology (he obviously does not want to become involved in the age-old dispute between Mutazalites and Mutakallimum). He frowns also on speculations about general classes in the physical world, that is, what he calls secondary intelligibilia (the primary intelligibilia being purely logical definitions such as that the whole is greater than any of its parts and the like). Ibn Khaldoun, an outstanding representative of what I would call the fourteenth-century Muslim managerial upper class, is doubtful about the mind's ability to find with some certainty some such general classes, that is, as one would say today, for instance, classes of chemical elements, or classes of fundamental particles, or classes of galaxies and stars. As a top-level manager setting the course of the Muslim future, Ibn Khaldoun is a thoroughgoing pragmatist who invokes Muslim religion on behalf of his program for Muslim culture: "We must refrain from studying these things [general classes] since such restraint falls under the duty of the Muslim not to do what does not concern him. The problems of physics are of no importance for us in our religious affairs or our livelihoods. Therefore we must leave them alone." This is a tragic program indeed as far as the fate and fortunes of science in the Muslim world were concerned.

It is in connection with what became the science of science, physics, that Ibn Khaldoun's stifling pragmatism comes through most revealingly. To begin with, he is rather short on the subject with about 200 words on it. His second hundred words refer to Avicenna and Averroes as the authorities to be consulted on physics. Prior to that he gives a brief account of the topics studied in physics. The last of those topics is "the beginning of the motion of bodies—that is, the soul in the different forms in which it appears in human beings, animals and plants."

Ibn Khaldoun wrote these fateful words in 1383, in full awareness that at that time all the crafts were on a higher level in the Christian West than in the Muslim East. Nicole Oresme had just died, but his and his master's, Buridan's, epoch-making words on the beginning of motion had already begun to be copied and carried from Paris to an ever larger number of European universities. Both Buridan and Oresme introduced their discussion of the beginning of motion with a reference to souls, that is, to intelligences which in Aristotle's theory were the instrumental causes of the motions of stars and planets. To be sure, as Christians, Buridan and Oresme could have retained those intelligences as identical with angels. But they refused to make room for angels in natural science. If there was to be a science of nature, then nature had to be liberated from all remnants of animism and for a simple reason.

An anima or soul was not such if it did not have some measure of freedom of action. Now if a star or a stone had a soul, each could conceivably deviate from its predetermined path at any given moment and most unpredictably. If, however, this was possible, there could be no science which is strictly predictive about purely physical motion, even if it cannot be such about the motion of plants, animals, and human beings.

In other words, if science was to be born, nature had to be de-animized. Animism, which was always an essential feature of pan-theism, had to retreat in the measure in which the monotheistic doctrine of creation was gaining ground. Animism was no match, in the long run at least, for the impetus of the doctrine of creation when the doctrine was taken in terms of the New Testament. Its doctrine on Christ as the "only begotten Son," in whom the Father created everything, put a damper on any flirtation with the idea that any other being might be a divine begetting in terms of an emanationism which always carries an animist touch. Animism—the entire history of philosophical learnedness in the Muslim world is a witness—held its own when confronted with the impetus with which the Koran carried the doctrine of creation. In sum, the whole question of why science was not born within the Muslim milieu, or the question of why the physics of impetus was not formulated there, is in the end a theological question, which can only be answered in terms of theology, such as the true nature of the Koran's impetus. The significance of this result will not seem minor at a time when religious revival is at work in the Muslim world with a greater impetus than perhaps ever before in its history.[1]

---

[1]For the quotations from Ibn Khaldoun's *The Muqaddimah* (that is, the preface and book I of his *Universal History*), see ch. 6, available almost in full in the one-volume abridgment published by N. J. Dawood (Princeton, NJ, 1969) from F. Rosenthal's three-volume translation. For the context of Buridan's statement, see ch. 10, "The Sighting of New Horizons," in my *Science and Creation: From Eternal Cycles to an Oscillating Universe* (Edinburgh and New York, 1974; paperback reprint 1986); ch. 9, "Delay in Detour,' is entirely devoted to the theological roots of the stillbirth of science within the medieval Muslim milieu. Further material on the same can be found in ch. 1 of my Gifford Lectures (Edinburgh, 1975 and 1976), published as *The Road of Science and the Ways of God* (Chicago and Edinburgh, 1978). For references to major studies on the early history of impetus

theory see notes to ch. 9 and 10 in my *Science and Creation*. For the crucial support given by the dogma of Incarnation to the dogma of creation out of nothing within the Christian milieu, see ch. 3 of my *Cosmos and Creator* (Edinburgh, 1980; Chicago, 1981) and *The Savoir of Science,* ch. 2 (in press).

10

The Last Century of Science: Progress, Problems, and Prospects

About a hundred years ago, something very novel had taken place on the American educational scene. In Baltimore, grounds were laid for Johns Hopkins University. Unlike Harvard, Yale, Princeton, and other now famous universities, Johns Hopkins did not start as a college. It was a university, in the sense that its courses were open only to candidates for doctor's degrees. This was an entirely new idea in the United States, where doctor's degrees were first given only a hundred years ago, and where a hundred years ago graduate students, or doctoral candidates, were

Lecture delivered in September 1972 in Delphi at the Second International Symposium of the Hellenic Society for Humanistic Studies. First published in the *Proceedings* of the Symposium, Athens, 1973, pp. 248-64. Reprinted with permission.

as scarce as hen's teeth. Around 1881 H. A. Rowland, one of the first professors at Johns Hopkins and the first American to achieve international status as a physicist, received a visitor, T. C. Mendenhall, who had just completed a three-year tenure as professor of physics at the Imperial University in Tokyo. On seeing a number of graduate students in the physics laboratory Mendenhall asked Rowland: "And what will you do with them?" "Do with them?—I shall neglect them," was Rowland's unhesitating answer.[1] A hundred years later, if there is anything a professor cannot afford in an American university, it is to neglect or ignore graduate students. Today, graduate students form a large body, and have an increasingly important say in university policy-making. A professor had better not ignore them, or in a broader sense, he had better not ignore the social, cultural ambience in which he works. There is progress here, though the word progress immediately suggests a number of complications. The anecdote about Rowland is, therefore, symbolic in a broader sense, which is the burden of this paper to develop.

In Europe the change in the status of science during the last hundred years can be illustrated with a few telling data. A hundred years ago Germany was just gaining leadership in science which it was to hold for two generations. The price of taking the lead was, by modern standards, ridiculously small. In my field, physics, Germany quickly created a dozen serious chairs in physics, twice as many as those in France and in England. But whether in Germany, or France, or England, or elsewhere in Europe, requirements for a Ph.D. in physics were exceedingly low, compared with the requirements a hundred years later. A story will best illustrate the difference. A hundred years ago the famous Dutch physicist, Hendrick Lorentz, was just working for his doctor's degree in Leiden. He entered there at the age of 19 and two years later he was ready to write his dissertation. There was nothing original in it, a straight résumé of the scientific novelty of the day, Maxwell's electromagnetic equations. Yet, the jury was much impressed. Lorentz got the highest marks and was almost immediately called to teach at Leiden.

Today Maxwell is usually mentioned as one of the half dozen greatest physicists who have ever lived. But a hundred years ago the really famous physicist was William Thomson, the future Lord Kelvin. For over forty years he produced one paper a month, most of which hardly anybody reads today. He wrote thousands of pages on what did not exist, the ether, and the so-called vortex atoms, made of the ether. Kelvin was extremely popular as a speaker, but the beginning of his fame is connected with the first transatlantic cable. A hundred years ago, it was the big news, partly because when the whole length of the cable was in place, it did not work. That it finally did work was due to Kelvin. There was some originality in his contribution which concerned the properties of very long conductors. Today, it is a commonplace in textbooks of electrical engineering. A hundred years after Kelvin and the first transatlantic cable, a gigantic volume of messages flashes back and forth across the Atlantic. The messages are carried by devices about which Kelvin could have no inkling because, although he spoke much about the atomic structure of matter, he knew practically nothing about it. He was already dead when, in 1913, the systematic conquest of the world of atoms began with Bohr's historic paper. Due to that conquest, almost any message can be heard by anybody in any corner of the world with a small transistor radio.

Transistor radios are based on man's newly acquired ability to deposit various types of matter in layers that are of the width of 10^{-7} cm, or the width of about 10 atoms. A hundred years ago the resolution of the best microscopes was about 10^{-3} cm, or the width of 100,000 atoms; today, electron microscopes can see 100,000 times better and it is even possible to obtain, though indirectly, details about the nucleus which is smaller by another factor of 100,000. A little over a hundred years ago Kelvin formulated the notion of absolute zero temperature, that is, 273 degrees below freezing point. But the coldest temperature that could be produced then was about 200 degrees warmer than absolute zero. Today, there is a special branch of science, cryogenics, which studies phenomena, very strange phenomena, that occur when the temperature differs from absolute zero by one or two degrees or by the mere fraction of one degree.[2] A hundred years ago, the mercury vacuum pump was big news; the best vacuum it produced was 1/100 of the atmospheric pressure. Today, experiments are performed in vacuums a million times better, to say nothing of the almost perfect vacuum of outer space, which is now available for experimentation in orbiting laboratories.

One may indeed say that the precision of exact science increased by six to ten orders of magnitude during the last hundred years.

Compared with what happened during the previous three hundred years, this is an enormous advance. Along with these technical advances there came new conquests on the theoretical level. A hundred years ago it was obligatory to believe that every physical process derived from strictly mechanical interactions, due to mechanical force or energy. Today, all this appears a pleasant myth. Modern physics counts four apparently disconnected physical forces or fields: gravitational, electromagnetic, nuclear, and weak forces. The best minds are at work to find a unity among these four forces and the price of advance is to know ever smaller details about the smallest parts of matter. The advance has been equally impressive in the opposite direction. A hundred years ago the greatest distance that could be measured in space was of the order of a few light years, derived from the parallax of the nearest stars. Today, the distances reliably estimated by astronomers are a billion times greater, the distances of the most remote galaxies.

So much in a way of illustration about the progress made by science during the last hundred years. My examples of that progress have been chosen, for the most part, with an eye on the most elementary meaning of what progress stands for. The etymology of the word means advancing in the space-time manifold. In that respect the advance of science and of its most exact form, physics, must be admitted even by those for whom the word progress stands for something far more than a gigantic foray across space and time, into the realm of the very large and into the realm of the exceedingly small. Happily, for the sake of cultural progress, most creative physicists are in agreement that progress in the full human or humanistic matrix must mean far more than exploring and controlling the physical dimensions of space and time.

A chief reason for this agreement derives from the manner in which physics progressed during the last hundred, or rather, during the last seventy years. Instinctive thinking about progress pictures it as a steady, well-planned advance across previously unexplored areas. Such was the manner in which the progress of science was described by Bacon, by the founders of the Royal Society, by Immanuel Kant, and by the Encyclopedists. One price to be paid for that naive concept of the progress of science was the adoption of the cliché phrase that in science everything was darkness until Galileo let some balls roll down an inclined plane.[3] This Kantian and Encyclopedist phrase was duly repeated throughout the nineteenth century. It formed perhaps the only point of agreement among Herbert Spencer, the Rev. William Whewell, and Friedrich Engels, who all tried to rest their widely differing philosophies of progress on the allegedly smooth, that is, inevitable and predictable, progress of science.

The twentieth-century reading of the progress of science is slightly better than that inherited from the nineteenth century. This is not to suggest that we are more intelligent than scholars, or historians of science, were a hundred years ago. Our advantage is largely independent of our mental abilities. In the twentieth century science progressed in a way which defies a simplistic definition of progress. Or to do more justice to the facts of scientific history, one may say, that in the twentieth century science began to do in a very obvious way what it has always been doing, namely, developing, or progressing in an unpredictable manner. As a result, twentieth-century scholars have been forced to recognize that unpredictable pattern which had been largely ignored during the previous two hundred years.

That science progresses very unpredictably should be clear from the fact that its progress depends largely on the sudden emergence of geniuses. Their appearance at a particular place and time is something which has so far defied even a remotely adequate psychological and sociological explanation. Such a remark is particularly appropriate in reference to the next year that will mark the 500th anniversary of Copernicus' birth. Thousands before him knew about the heliocentric theory of Aristarchus. But its spark ignited into a torch of flame only in the mind of an obscure Pole, and in a university town, Cracow, which until then had not produced anything extraordinary. During the next fifty years thousands of scholars learned of the Copernican theory. But nothing happened until there came along, defying all probability calculus, the enormously strange mind and personality of Kepler. Without his laws, one of which was the result of two errors that almost miraculously canceled one another, Newton might not have come up with his epoch-making development of a central force obeying the inverse square law.

But let us move into the realm of modern science. There had been countless scientists who studied and measured the speed of light by the time a young boy in Munich reached the age of fifteen. His name was Albert Einstein. He was a strange boy. He hardly spoke until the age of seven. Eight years later he was seized with the question whether it was possible to travel as fast as the speed of light. That strange youthful preoccupation played a seminal part, as he himself stated, in turning him into the kind of physicist he became.[4] Or conversely, without that youthful vagary of mind, twentieth-century physics would not have become what it actually did become. Or let us recall the strange meeting of a young Polish student, Maria Sklodowska, in Paris, with an equally strange French physicist, Pierre Curie. Anyone familiar with her biography should realize that the chances were inconceivably small that their paths should have ever crossed. Yet, without that meeting of theirs many things in twentieth-century science would have taken place much later and perhaps in a very different form.[5] Examples of this kind could be listed for hours on end, though no array of evidence of this kind would tell anything to one who is convinced that science is the inevitable, let alone a smoothly inevitable, product of socio-economic conditions and circumstances or the necessary unfolding of its potentialities.

This unpredictability of scientific advance can readily be seen also from the invariable failure of predicting the future of discoveries even within a limited field and for a short period of time. Perhaps a few modern examples would not be out of place. One is an article by the famous American astronomer, Harlow Shapley, written in 1950, which included guesses about the advances astronomy was to make during the second half of the twentieth century.[6] The article was hardly fifteen years old when it was already very clear that none of the advances, which Shapley predicted, came to materialize, and a great many advances and discoveries were made about which Shapley's article contained not a hint (orbiting telescopes, quasars, etc.). The same point could equally well be illustrated by what happened in elementary particle physics. A few of the new particles were predicted, but many more turned up unexpectedly, and played havoc with well established theories. In short, discoveries, crucially new discoveries, are being made which are wholly unforeseen, and things are accomplished which only a few years earlier had been declared to be simply impossible.

The latter point bears a little illustration. In 1951 Vannevar Bush, the great organizer of American scientific technology, flatly declared that intercontinental ballistic missiles were impossible to make.[7] In 1933 Lord Rutherford, the chief architect of nuclear physics, spoke of the industrial utilization of nuclear energy as being equivalent to talking moonshine.[8] Much less known is the case of Sir George Darwin, the son of Charles Darwin, and possibly the foremost expert on celestial dynamics around the turn of the century. In 1909, he discussed the new theory which Chamberlin and Moulton in Chicago had submitted on the evolution of planetary systems. The theory is known as the planetesimal theory because it pictured the formation of planets from the meeting or collision of many small planets, or planetesimals. Darwin could easily point out that the meeting of two bodies in space, even if moving in close and similar orbits, was a most unlikely event. And to illustrate the extremely small probability, he referred to the incredibly fine marksmanship needed to hit Mars from the earth with a bullet. It will be, he said, 10,000 years before scientists would solve that problem.[9] He was wrong by almost three orders of magnitude. Instead of 10,000 years, 50 years were enough.

Playing the prophet is a risky business, but is especially so in science, and in modern science in particular. Why in modern science in particular? A chief reason for this lies in the relation between mathematics and modern science, or physics. I said *modern* science, with an emphasis. During the centuries of classical physics, mathematics played largely the role of a humble maidservant. Most mathematicians were physicists and the new pages of mathematics were written in the measure in which new problems in physics needed an exact treatment and solution.[10] But around the middle of the nineteenth century the humble maidservant declared independence. She was from there on to have her own thoughts, select her own problems, pursue her own course of research, regardless of the needs of physicists. The new development went largely unnoticed even by physicists until about the 1930s. Then Born and Heisenberg found to their great astonishment that the mathematics needed by quantum mechanics had been developed many years earlier by mathematicians, that is, by those emancipated mathematicians who began to work on problems of mathematics which at that time seemed to have no connection whatever with physics and the physical world. The best known examples are group theory, the well-behaving equations, and matrix calculus. Oddly enough, more than half a century after they had been first formulated, they were found to fit marvelously the workings of nature on its atomic level. There are of course many other examples of that puzzling fact, which Wigner so aptly called about ten years ago, the "unreasonable effectiveness of mathematics in physics."[11]

The word "unreasonable" could not have been better chosen. For it is beyond reasonable explanation that one out of so many mathematical formalisms should fit a broad range of physical phenomena, and lead to the prediction of until then unsuspected phenomena. Mathematics itself provides no criteria in this respect. It cannot tell us why some of its theorems are immensely more effective physically than many others. Gone are the days when Hilbert, Poincaré and others could still dream about an ultimate system of mathematics, assigning to all particular theorems a special place in the hierarchy of more and more fundamental theorems. Ever since Gödel formulated his famous theorem in 1930, it has become an open secret that mathematics is not a clear-cut, self-consistent pyramid of a finite number of propositions.[12] In other words, mathematics is not going to provide for physics a logically and neatly arranged ladder for unfolding deeper and deeper layers of the physical reality. This is why we may speak of the "unreasonable" role of mathematics in physics, a role very similar to the almost haphazard process which is the emergence of a genius, or the coming about of a stroke of a genius. As a result, physics, or exact science, is a very unpredictable enterprise. Its road of advance is anything but smooth. In fact, it is a road full of bumps, the impact of which is bound to dislocate an increasingly larger number of joints and with an ever heavier impact. This is very important to remember when we focus on science as a factor of cultural progress. Science makes for progress, but for a very bumpy one. The question which then offers itself, but which is not the purpose of my paper to investigate, is about how many big bumps can be had if the advance is still to be called progress and not something else.

I have spoken of the dislocation of "an increasingly larger number of joints and with an ever heavier impact." As to the number of bumps, they are proportional to the number of new major discoveries and these keep growing larger in number as time goes on. The new data about the physical world are being collected at a rate which seems to grow exponentially. From its first effective or viable birth in the late Middle Ages, science has been feeding on its own findings. But this feedback process, which until the twentieth century could appear as a healthy, organic growth, seems to turn

into a runaway mechanism. The great increase in research laboratories is only partly responsible for this. The real culprit seems to
be the "unreasonable effectiveness" of mathematics. It is enough
here to recall the famous formula $E = mc^2$. Who guessed its real
contents when first printed in 1904?[13] When a year later Einstein
gave a more fundamental derivation of it, it was still a mathematical formula and nothing else. Many of our present-day agonies
derive from the fact that the formula implies so much, and in a
literally devastating sense.

When these implications began to be seen, it became also clear
that we were largely unprepared to deal with them, or even with
smaller challenges. And yet, these challenges keep popping up at
the most unexpected moments. They certainly secure excitement
to the scientific enterprise, but they also make a steadily growing
tension more acute. It arises from the difference between tools and
goals. Science, as is well known, has an astonishing capacity to produce tools. This had been hopefully noted already in the seventeenth century, at the very rise of modern science. But it was only
with the coming of the steam, gasoline, and electric engines that
the problem of what to do with the tools has become a crucial one.
The conflict between labor and capital, as it developed during the
second half of the nineteenth century, was rooted in the manner in
which the problem of the relation between tools and goals had been
ignored.

Among those who ignored this question were the scientists themselves, who by their theoretical and experimental work created
those very tools. During World War I scientists on both sides were
eager participants in a propaganda warfare without hardly ever
asking the question of whether it was ethical to invent, to design,
and to produce tools of massive destruction.[14] The sole point I want
to make here is a matter of historical illustration. What should be
illustrated is the fact that most men of science did not feel it necessary to ask questions about the ethical dimensions of their research
and discoveries. Of course, this ivory tower attitude was violently
shattered with the coming of atomic weapons as the concluding
phase of World War II.

It should tell a great deal about the tragic aspect of the human
condition that more than a quarter of a century after the first
atomic bomb, the overwhelming portion of atomic fuel, that is,
purified uranium and plutonium, is in the form of bombs or set

aside for bombs. Because of the unreasonable effectiveness of science, and because of the unreasonable ineffectiveness of man, mankind is now sitting on the top of a global powder keg, while the supply of ordinary fuel is running out. Unless, indeed, the swords, to quote Isaiah, will be literally turned into ploughshares, mankind will progress, if this is progress, towards disastrous shortages of energy. Except for a most extraordinary turn of events, piles and mountains of atomic fuel will not be used to generate electricity and to desalinate ocean water,[15] although it is an open secret that not only coal and oil, but fresh water too, is a commodity available only in limited quantities.

The effectiveness of science and of scientific technology should seem indeed unreasonable. Thirty years ago the best computers were gigantic, unwieldy units that needed large buildings for their housing. Today, computers can be as small as larger typewriters were yesterday. Although very small, their capacity for storage has increased by many orders of magnitude.[16] Will their use be a blessing for mankind or a curse? Will they liberate man, or help destroy his freedom and privacy? Because computers are so small, they were largely responsible for the opening of manned space travel. But most rockets are still launched for other purposes. Everybody agrees that this should be otherwise. And one may even question the number of rockets that should be launched at all. It is common knowledge that the troposphere can absorb only so much jet fuel, and the stratosphere can take only so much missile fuel before they get irreversibly polluted and turn the atmosphere into a deadly, global greenhouse. Everybody agrees, and yet there is no willingness that would match the measure of agreement. Everybody agrees that technology and ecology may be on a head-on collision course. But, again, there is a painful disparity between agreement, intellectual, that is, and willingness or resolve to cope with the problem.[17] Everybody agrees that rare animal species should be protected, but whales, for instance, are now becoming an almost extinct species. There is general agreement on that, which is even ratified in an international treaty. But then, two or three nations ignore the treaty and the general scientific or ecological reasoning. They only care about the fact that whales are great producers of special oil and fat, and that infrared photography has made them easily identifiable objects from airplanes. So the hunt merrily goes on and the whales turn into a whale of a problem to anyone who cares about cultural progress with an eye on science, or scientific technology.

The disparity between knowledge and will puts us at the doorstep of the third source of challenges and problems created by science, and especially modern science, for cultural progress. This third source is the problem of interaction between science and society. In a nutshell the problem is the measure in which society may or should respond to science, and the measure in which science may or should serve society. The problem is not new. At the first recognition of this problem a very characteristic solution was proposed in the *New Atlantis* of Bacon in the first decades of the seventeenth century. It represented a total subordination of society to science in the form of a regimented state ruled by a small body of scientists. Typically enough, these scientist-rulers did some of their research in utmost secrecy. They also had the supreme power of decision on the activities of each and every subordinate. Two hundred years later, around 1800, something similar was proposed by Henri Saint-Simon. He also suggested that mankind should worship in temples built and dedicated in honor of Sir Isaac Newton.[18]

The total, if not totalitarian, response of society to science was advocated by many others in a way which usually gives itself away by its crudeness. Of the sophisticated advocacies of the same idea, one deserves to be mentioned in particular, and for two reasons. First, because it was proposed recently; second, because its message was uncritically swallowed in academic circles. What I have in mind is C. P. Snow's famous Rede Lecture of 1959, better known as *The Two Cultures and the Scientific Revolution*. From the viewpoint of composition it is certainly a masterpiece. It shows Lord Snow at his literary best. He dazzles his reader with gem-like phrases and fascinating little stories. They seem to serve one principal purpose, namely, to disarm the reader's critical sense. For unless one's mind is dazzled, how can one accept a reasoning which runs like this: Among educated men, scientists know more about culture than non-scientists or literary people. Among scientists, practical scientists or engineers are more attuned to culture than are theoretical scientists. As a third step, Lord Snow claimed that among engineers the so-called inventive engineers, who usually work individually, if not individualistically, are less sensitive to culture than engineers who work in teams on the technologization of society. And finally, Lord Snow suggested that the capitalist West should take a leaf or two from the program of the Soviet Union, because it trains far more engineers than do France, Germany, England, and the United States taken together. Six years later, in 1965, in a lecture given in Washington, Lord Snow remarked that the Soviet Union is far more successful politically, because not a few of its leaders were originally trained as engineers, and, therefore, they think more systematically and more scientifically.[19]

In raising these matters it is not politics that I want to emphasize. My sole purpose is to illustrate the trend which thinks that culture and progress should be entrusted to engineers, and specifically to one type of engineer. One of the troubles with this trend is that it does not even understand what it purports to explain, the so-called social roots of science. Lord Snow himself unwittingly admitted this as he commented on the very effective use of science in industry during the late 1800s in Germany. As Lord Snow put it, the spectacular rise of German industrial organization around 1880 or so, made for him "no social sense."[20] The trouble with that remark is that if the meaning of making sense is restricted to the meaning of "making social sense," then many important things are not going to make sense. Among these things is science itself.

Although science heavily depends on interaction among scientists, the cultivation of science cannot be regimented or entrusted to so-called scientific cadres or brigades. Wherever, or whenever this is done, the poor, self-defeating results speak for themselves. The soul of science is discovery, invention, coming from the spark of the individual genius, and its productivity is wholly different from that of carefully engineered production lines. Again, the dependence of science on this or that social ambience looks very small when compared with the driving force of that mysterious urge to know more about the workings of nature. Would it make sense, social or common sense, to derive Planck's all-consuming curiosity about black-body radiation from the social structure of the First Reich? Would it make any sense to derive Rutherford's struggle with radioactivity from the twilight of the British empire? Would it make any sense to connect Landau's theoretical work on superconductivity with any theoretical or practical facet of Marxism, or to derive Einstein's and Heisenberg's insights from the decay of the Weimar Republic? To try to do so would make no social sense. It would make no sense at all.[21]

For all its interconnection with society and culture, the scientific enterprise shows a baffling independence of its social matrix, and of social conditions and structures in general. If there is anything specific and really essential which science requires from society and culture, it is non-interference with the mysterious process of discovery. As a small but tangible support of this claim, let me refer to a very recent book which I have just been asked by the editor of *Isis* to review in its next issue.[22] The book, *Science as a Cultural Process,* was written by Maurice N. Richter, professor of sociology at New York State University at Albany. The book, in the words of its author, "is an attempt to analyze science as a social phenomenon." Or again, in the words of the author, the purpose of the book is "to contribute to the clarification of the sociological meaning of science." The clarification consists in the admission that the scientific enterprise cannot be fitted in any of the conceptual categories sociology works with.

It is certainly no small thing to hear it from a prominent sociologist that science, both historically and actually, is a unique social phenomenon. Historically, science is most unique. It came to an aborted birth in seven great cultures: Chinese, Hindu, Maya, Egyptian, Babylonian, Greek and Arabic. Science came to a viable birth only once, in late Medieval Europe, between the thirteenth and sixteenth centuries.[23] Actually, science is still unique; science, as Richter states, is not merely a profession, or merely an occupation, or merely a method. As a social form, it is not like a family or a state. From the cognitive viewpoint, science is also rather peculiar. Therein lies among other things the persistent tension between the so-called humanistic studies and scientific investigations. This manifold uniqueness of science, as Richter states, "has a crucial implication: it means that science cannot, by definition, have its course of development determined by society. . . . In the long run, society can encourage science or inhibit it, but not shape its course, or even predict its course on a long-range basis with reasonable confidence."[24]

This lack of one-to-one correspondence between social existence and scientific endeavor should tell a great deal about the complications which science presents to the cultural progress of society. This tension between science and society is worth exploring a little further. Let me go back once more to Richter's book. He suggests that if sociology is ever to cope with the phenomenon of science, it should be in the direction of looking at science as a "cultural process." Unfortunately, he leaves the term "cultural process" in its customary vagueness. Worse, according to him, the concepts of "culture" and "cultural change" do not entail goal-directedness and functionality. Such is a strange reasoning and it provides only an additional though unwitting proof that sociology is indeed at a loss to cope with the phenomenon of science. My chief quarrel is not with Richter's vagueness about the concepts of culture and progress. What is really amiss in Richter's reasoning concerns the alleged absence of goal-directedness in cultural development. I think it is very easy to show that the great spokesmen of a particular culture were very much goal-directed. There was a distinct goal, or ideal, which the men of the Middle Ages or of the Renaissance tried to implement. There was a distinct goal which inspired the leaders of the Enlightenment, and there is a very distinct goal-directedness in twentieth-century cultural aspirations.[25]

At any rate, the scientific enterprise is very much goal-directed. Its goal is an ever simpler and an ever more universal explanation of nature. To realize that goal, science had to renounce the Aristotelian or Socratic search for goals. Modern sociology in order to become an "exact science" tries to do the same thing. The trouble is that the subject matter of sociology and of science are very different. Unlike physical nature, society is a matrix of conscious efforts, and conscious efforts are always made for goals. This is a most elementary common-sense experience which can only be expressed in common-sense language. This goal-directedness of the human experience is such an elementary datum that any meaningful attempt made at refuting it betrays itself by its very goal-directedness. And herein lies the fourth principal source of problems and challenges which science creates for culture. It is the challenge of the difference between mere succession of events and chain of events subordinated to a goal. It is also the challenge of the difference between the abstract mathematical formulas of physics and their explanatory use which, if it is to be satisfactory, must be cast into common-sense parlance.

In view of the almost esoteric abstractness of modern mathematical physics, this challenge is very great. A hundred years ago Faraday already complained to Maxwell about the "obscurity" of mathematical formulas in Maxwell's electromagnetic theory.[26] Since Faraday knew little more than elementary algebra, his complaint may be somewhat suspect. But there can be no suspicion about the crucial contribution which Faraday's common-sense ideas about electromagnetic fields made to Maxwell's theory. Fifty years later Rutherford, another giant in physics with little familiarity with higher mathematics, used to endorse common sense with the remark: "A good physical theory can be explained to a barmaid."[27] Apparently, barmaids are unusual persons in more than one way. At any rate, one of the big breakthroughs in atomic physics came around 1911 when alpha particles were found to be reflected by almost 180 degrees from very thin gold foils. This meant that atoms were incredibly empty structures, with all their positive charge condensed in a center, the diameter of which was 10,000 times smaller than the diameter of the electron orbits around it. The dynamic aspects of the recoil of alpha particles could still be put in relatively simple form that lent itself to the graphic phrase into which Rutherford put the startling fact of recoil: "It is," he said, "as if cannon balls had been stopped and shot back by a thin paper." But about the same time, in the 1910s, Einstein was already employing a personal mathematician, who cast his revolutionary though still common-sense ideas into an esoteric four-dimensional geometry. Quite recently, Heisenberg described the whole problem in words which deserve to be quoted in full: "The physicist may be satisfied when he has the mathematical scheme and knows how to use it for the interpretation of the experiments. But he has to speak about his results also to non-physicists who will not be satisfied unless some explanation is given in plain language. Even for the physicist the description in plain language will be the criterion of the degree of understanding that has been reached."[29]

The tension between exact science, highly mathematical, and common sense, which needs but rudimentary mathematics, is the basic aspect of the tension between science and society, technology and culture. Since the rise of science, but especially during the last hundred years, there have been many evidences of a one-sided approach toward resolving this problem. One of these is to turn man into a machine, on the ground that man has reliable knowledge only about quantities. Hume claimed this, Voltaire too, and another figure of the Enlightenment, Baron d'Holbach, authored the famous phrase: "all errors of man are errors in physics."[30] The other one-sided approach is primitive romanticism, ready to discard machines, and busy creating suspicion about the value of science. The classic originators of this approach were the Luddites and Jean-Jacques Rousseau. The latter, in his *Emile,* or philosophy of education, took pains to dissuade his young charge from studying the sciences. And, to discredit men of science, Rousseau told Emile: "It has become more evident than daylight that the scientific societies of Europe are public schools of lies and that there are more mistaken notions [entertained] in the Academy of Sciences in Paris than in a whole tribe of American Indians."[31]

One of the reasons for these two extremist attitudes toward science as a cultural force is rather easy to pinpoint. Science, physical science, that is, had until the advent of the twentieth century a certain monolithic appearance from the conceptual viewpoint. Descartes could plausibly claim that everything derived from extension. For Newtonian science, every process was mechanical, depending on physical contact between bodies. During the late nineteenth century, the concept of energy created about science a monolithic appearance that was looked upon as something to be carefully cultivated. A good example of this is the story of theories of light prior to 1900. Although evidence both for the corpuscular and for the wave theory had been available, classical physicists by and large preferred a monolithic solution. Thus, during the seventeenth and eighteenth centuries, the corpuscular theory ruled supreme, whereas during the nineteenth century references were endless to the final victory of the wave theory. The victory existed only in the minds of those desirous to have a monolithic solution on the conceptual level.

The twentieth century has greatly changed all this. One of the hallmarks of modern physics is the so-called principle of complementarity, which states, for instance, that all particles, not only light, have wave properties, and all waves would in certain circumstances act as if they were particles. In other words, modern physics rests on the conviction that a successful explanation of physical reality demands a pluralistic conceptual apparatus even on the purely quantitative level. Other examples of that situation are provided by the set of the so-called conjugate variables. The set is composed of such conceptual pairs as energy and time, position and momentum, both linear and angular, moment of inertia and angular velocity. In a given physical situation it is impossible to know *something* about one, without knowing *something* about the other. But a perfectly accurate knowledge of one would entail a complete ignorance about the other.[32]

From the cultural viewpoint this new pluralistic conceptual framework of exact science is of great significance. It should help reinforce the conviction that many various ingredients are needed to make a healthy culture capable of progressing and growing. Science is far from sufficient to provide all that is necessary for making that kind of culture. In fact, science itself is under various kinds of challenges that disqualify it from an exclusive cultural leadership. Because of its high degree of unpredictability, science often does not act as a stabilizing factor in culture; science does not contain the criteria of the proper use of the fantastic tools it creates and will keep creating; science as a social phenomenon shows a baffling uniqueness which should discourage attempts to reshape in its terms all other cultural aspirations. All those other aspirations— arts, politics, letters, religion—depend on common-sense wisdom, judgments, and appraisals, which science itself needs as an ultimate vehicle of its explanations.

To unpredictability, to social independence, and to dependence on common-sense judgments both with respect to interpretation and to utilization, there should be added the pluralistic conceptual matrix as the fourth major feature of science, especially of modern science. Such a list of four major features of science may be conspicuous by the absence there to any reference to the so-called operational status of scientific knowledge and theories. My reason for slighting the much vaunted operational interpretation of science can be stated briefly. One may give the definition of the operational method with Bridgman as "doing one's damnedest with one's intellect."[33] Such a definition, with which I fully agree, distinguishes the operational method only from intellectual laziness and renders any argumentation about it unnecessary. Or one may define the operational method, as is usually done, as an ever more convenient reshuffling of mathematical functions which tell us nothing about reality. Such a definition tells us little more than nothing about science itself as it actually does exist, is practiced, and is carried out. On the other hand, the four features which I have listed are about science as it actually does exist, is practiced and implemented.

Last but not least, a growing awareness of those four features should entitle us to some modest optimism. On the basis of such an awareness one may hope to find a broad and common basis in which a *Gleichschaltung* of culture by science might be effectively forestalled. I said "modest optimism" because the danger of that *Gleichschaltung* is always present, ever since it was first spotted by Socrates. True, he overreacted to the atomism of Leucippus and to the mechanistic physics of Anaxagoras. In their atomistic and mechanistic physics, there was no room whatever for purpose, goal, and values. To vindicate purpose, Socrates declared in *Phœdo* that everything, even the fall of stones, had to be for a purpose. The result was the historic sidetracking of physical science by Aristotle. But one thing cannot be denied to Socrates. He saw that there were problems, very serious problems, about human culture vis-à-vis science. While Professor Rowland at Johns Hopkins ignored his problem, the graduate students, Socrates refused to ignore the broad problems of his own ambience. By making this Second International Symposium possible, the Hellenic Society for Humanistic Studies and its President, Prof. Vourveris, followed in that great Socratic tradition of awareness of cultural problems. Socrates kept saying, and this was the essence of his famous method, that all solutions depended on one's awareness that there were questions to be answered. My lecture was not meant to provide answers but only to point out directions in which the answers are indicated by the problems themselves.

[1]As recalled by Mendenhall himself in his commemorative address delivered in Baltimore, October 26, 1901. See *The Physical Papers of Henry Augustus Rowland* (Baltimore: The Johns Hopkins Press, 1902), p. 16.
[2]The importance of cryogenics has become front page news ever since the discovery in late 1987 that superconductivity can occur at temperatures higher than the boiling point of liquid nitrogen.
[3]Typically, the phrase first appeared in the Preface which Kant penned to the second edition of his *Critique of Pure Reason* where his misuse of science in connection with the four antinomies foreshadowed the shocking misinterpretation of science that fills the hundreds of pages of his last writing, the *Opus postumum*. For details, see my introduction to my translation, with notes, of Kant's youthful cosmogonical work, *Universal Natural History and Theory of the Heavens* (Edinburgh: Scottish Academic Press, 1981).
[4]See his Autobiographical Notes in P. A. Schilpp (ed.), *Albert Einstein: Philosopher-Scientist* (1949; New York: Harper and Brothers, 1959), p. 53.
[5]It should be enough to think of the strange encounter of Pierre Curie and Marie Sklodowska and their subsequent resolve to devote themselves to a

project (most unpromising under the circumstances) to produce radium from pitchblende.

[6]"Astronomy," *Scientific American,* September 1950, pp. 24-26. One of the possible major future discoveries Shapley listed would have been the finding that the Milky Way was a composite of several galaxies. . . .

[7]It is recorded in the Memoirs of Harry S. Truman, *1945: Year of Decisions* (1955; New York: New American Library, 1965, p. 21), that with a reference to his expertise in explosives Bush assured him that the atomic bomb would never go off!

[8]Rutherford did so in his address to the British Association in September 1933. See report in *Nature* 132 (1933), pp. 432-33.

[9]G. H. Darwin, "A Theory of the Evolution of the Solar System," *Internationale Wochenschrift für Wissenschaft, Kunst und Technik* (Berlin), 3 (1909), col. 930.

[10]For details, see my *The Relevance of Physics* (Chicago: University of Chicago Press, 1966), pp. 115-16.

[11]E. P. Wigner, "The Unreasonable Effectiveness of Mathematics in the Natural Sciences," *Communications on Pure and Applied Mathematics* 13 (1960), pp. 1-14.

[12]For details, see my *The Relevance of Physics,* pp. 127-29.

[13]Actually, F. Hasenöhrl was preceded by Poincaré (1900) and J. J. Thomson (1881), as documented in E. Whittaker's great classic, *A History of the Theories of Aether and Electricity. Volume II: The Modern Theories* (1953; New York: Harper and Brothers, 1960), pp. 51-52.

[14]A notable exception was Pierre Duhem, who died suddenly in September 1916, before he could implement his plan to follow up his *La Science allemande* (1915) with a book that would have had for its theme the use of science for purposes of war as a "sin against the Holy Spirit." See my *Uneasy Genius: The Life and Work of Pierre Duhem* (1984; 2d paperback edition, Dordrecht: Martinus Nijhoff, 1986), p. 215.

[15]In spite of the fact that, as P. E. Hodgson argued convincingly in his *Our Nuclear Future?* (Belfast: Christian Journals Ltd., 1983), reliance on nuclear energy is at present the only feasible answer to the inevitable depletion of oil reserves.

[16]And so did their speed. The one installed on March 9, 1987, at Ames Research Center in Mountain View, California, to support NASA projects, can perform, at top speed, 1.72 billion computations a second. See *New York Times,* March 10, 1987, p. C3.

[17]An unabashed admission of this is the conclusion of K. Lorenz in his *Civilized Man's Eight Deadly Sins,* tr. M. K. Wilson (New York: Harcourt Brace Jovanovich, 1974), who considers nuclear armament a problem easier to cope with than the weakening of emotions through over-indulgence.

[18]Saint-Simon did so in his tract, *Lettres d'un inhabitant de Génève à ses contemporains* (1803), which also contains the project for a world government headed by mathematicians.

[19]C. P. Snow, "Government, Science, and Public Policy," *Science* 151 (1966), p. 651.

[20]C. P. Snow, *The Two Cultures and a Second Look* (Cambridge: Cambridge University Press, 1969), p. 24.

[21]Such a "senseless" effort is L. S. Feuer's *The Scientific Intellectual: The Psychological and Sociological Origins of Modern Science* (New York: Basic Books, 1963).

[22]For the review, see *Isis* 64 (1973), p. 544.

[23]As amply documented in my *Science and Creation: From Eternal Cycles to an Oscillating Universe* (1974; 2d enlarged paperback edition, Edinburgh: Scottish Academic Press, 1986).

[24]M. N. Richter, *Science as a Cultural Process* (Cambridge, MA: Schenkman Publishing Co., 1972), p. 127.

[25]In that respect the goal-directed activities of dictatorial regimes differed only in organizational character from the avid pursuit of very specific goals by various socio-economic groups in democratic countries.

[26]See B. Jones, *The Life and Letters of Faraday* (Philadelphia: 1870), vol. II, pp. 392-93.

[27]Reported by Sir Cyril Hinshelwood in his presidential address to the British Association, "Science and Scientists," *Nature* 207 (1965), p. 1058.

[28]See his lecture, "Forty Years of Physics" (1936), reprinted in J. Needham and W. Pagel (eds.), *Background to Modern Science* (New York: Macmillan, 1938), pp. 67-68.

[29]W. Heisenberg, *Physics and Philosophy* (New York: Harper Torchbooks, 1962), p. 168.

[30]D'Holbach's remark in his *Système de la nature* (London, 1775), p. 19, was emphatically repeated by Condorcet in his plan for the reorganization of French education.

[31]*Emile,* tr. B. Foxley (London: J. M. Dent, n.d.), p. 167.

[32]The defect of knowledge relates, of course, only to measuring with perfect accuracy any of the conjugate parameters, and not, as all too often stated, to a knowledge whose object is ontological causality. For details, see the first essay in my *Chance or Reality and Other Essays* (Lanham, MD: University Press of America, 1986).

[33]P. W. Bridgman, "The Prospect for Intelligence," *Yale Review* 34 (1945), p. 450.

11

Science and Censorship: Hélène Duhem and the Publication of the *Système du monde*

There was a time when voluminous books and indeed multi-volume works were not a rarity. Only about a hundred years ago did some, especially scientific, journals begin to insist on parsimony with words. Scholarly criticism too has become more keen on facts and documentation as distinct from mere interpretation, let alone surreptitious rhetoric. The recent skyrocketing of the cost of printing has also forced editors and publishers to be more and more demanding about conciseness. Even well-endowed university

Paper read at the meeting of the History of Science Society at Ludiauq University, November 1984. First published in *The Intercollegiate Review* (Winter 1985-86), pp. 41-49. Reprinted with permission.

presses have become unreceptive to typescripts running to two volumes; those running to three, let alone four volumes, are usually dismissed out of hand. Works of five, to say nothing of seven or ten volumes, belong more and more to a perhaps not too distant but increasingly legendary past.

More than three decades have gone by since 1954 when the printing presses produced the last or tenth volume of Toynbee's *A Study of History,* whose first volume was published in 1934. Such a vast enterprise may be interrupted by the author's health or death or conceivably by other causes. Among these there can be an ideological opposition ready to seize on various pretexts, such as changes of socio-political circumstances, to stifle a great intellectual venture. Such opposition does not wish to be written about and certainly not frequently or at length.

Still, in all likelihood, enormously much would have been written during the last three decades if the manuscript of the last five volumes of Toynbee's magnum opus were still looking for a typesetter. There would have been endless probings into possible sinistrous forces at play behind the scenes. And what if the printing of Churchill's *History of World War II* had come to an end with the third volume? And what if large batches of manuscripts written in the hands of a Freud, a Jung, a Sartre, or a Bertrand Russell, all ready for printing, were still not feeding the intellectually hungry but rather the slimy mould in a cellar, an attic, or a warehouse? Investigative scholars would have a field day with no diminishing returns in sight.

To the remark that since nothing of that sort has happened, at least not in the recent history of Western democracies, and therefore the subject should be dropped so that parsimony with words may be observed, the answer is simple. Such a thing did happen and to a ten-volume work which is easily the most original, creative, and potentially epoch-making achievement for the interpretation of Western cultural history. The work in question is *Le système du monde: les doctrines cosmologiques de Platon à Copernic.* Its author is Pierre Duhem (1861-1916), one of the most brilliant students ever to attend that topmost of French schools, the Ecole Normale Supérieure (1882-85), who spent the last twenty-two years of his life as professor of theoretical physics at the University of Bordeaux.[1] The first five volumes—each more than 500 pages—of that work were published in five successive years, 1913-1917. Although another five volumes were ready in manuscript when Duhem suddenly died, they were not published until four decades later (1954-59).

The very fact that the second half of a most meticulously documented scholarly history of science, especially of astronomy, physics, and their philosophical background, was published after such a lapse of time is a proof of its value. Indeed its value should seem extraordinary to anyone mindful of the speed with which research becomes dated nowadays. A five-year delay is already ominous; to be behind the latest by ten years is well-nigh catastrophic. A delay of forty years should seem equivalent to plain mummifying. Yet, when in 1954 the sixth volume was published, A. Koyré, a leading historian of science, and not at all sympathetic to Duhem's perspectives, wrote that the *Système du monde* is incredibly rich in data and texts which cannot be found anywhere else in print. Implied in this was not only the acknowledgement that Duhem's research was pioneering in the strictest sense, but also that scholarship had failed to a large extent to catch up with Duhem in the forty years subsequent to his death.

The delay, in itself grave, should, in view of Duhem's scholarship, seem shocking if not simply scandalous. No probing whatever into that delay took place, in France or elsewhere, prior to the recent publication of my book, a half-a-million-word monograph on Duhem's life and on his entire work[2] as a theoretical physicist, philosopher of science, and historian of medieval science, indeed the pioneering discoverer of science in the so-called Dark Ages. My probing was largely conjectural and brief, although, as it turned out, on the right track: once Duhem was no longer alive, powerful ideological opposition—academic and political—to his findings about the Middle Ages was successful in discouraging the publisher to go on with the project.

The present paper is a renewed probing into that opposition, but on the basis of a vast correspondence kept by Hélène Duhem (1891-1974), Duhem's only child.[3] The correspondence is proof—often month by month, at times week by week—of a struggle which she carried on for thirty years in the face of an opposition whose insuperability was proportional to its resolve and ability to remain invisible.

What opened some doors for me was, so it seems, the courage with which, through a portrayal of Duhem's struggles, the Christian contribution to the intellectual formation of the Western world is defended in my book. But this is precisely what makes the question about the absence of probings into that delay even more perplexing. After all, there have been in France some Catholic scholars—philosophers, physicists, and historians—for whom Catholicism was their intellectual lifeblood and not merely a label, something to be downplayed in order to gain the esteem of "purely scholarly" circles. They could not plead ignorance about the enormous potential support which Duhem's work presented to their interest in the Christian foundations of Western civilization. They could have certainly gained the confidence of Hélène, a conservative, politically as well as religiously, and drawn on her storehouse of documents and vivid memories. Once the publication of the *Système* had been completed in 1959, the story of the delay could have been pieced together, with her guidance, into a monumental tapestry, to be unveiled at an opportune moment. That tapestry, a metaphor for a thorough documentation and unsparing narrative, would have conjured up with its somber hues some behind-the-scenes figures doing their best to repress superior scholarship. Such a tactic is a censorship more destructive than the banning of books. The latter, which is often decried as a crime against mankind second only to apartheid and camps of extermination, assures global publicity, while the former may secure complete oblivion.

The purpose of this probing is not a postmortem aimed at certain Catholic scholars in France (and elsewhere), though some of them are still alive and vigorous. Nor is the purpose a calling to the carpet of those whose creed is essentially a program of fair play, pure scholarship, respect for intellectual merit, a universal promotion of progress—in short, a cultural creed professedly free of ideology. Some of them, in the field of the history of science, could not, of course, be unaware of what went on in regard to Duhem's manuscripts. Perhaps on seeing the evidence laid out here they will be less vocal in their rather selective indignation. The purpose is to awaken through a story, full of cloaks and daggers, the readers—broadly conservative—of this journal to the importance of science for the conservation of all that is noble, beautiful, dignified, and transcendental in human life and civilization.

Conservatives are apt to aim, at best, at benevolent neutrality about science, a neutrality all too often excusing one of ignorance, if not of plain selfishness. The latter at least can be dynamic. But conservatism can be a static defense of a mere status quo for which there is no place in a world of science. Science has been since its rise in the West an increasingly potent source of novelty. For the past fifty years novelties that in a few years can transform hallowed lifestyles, eliminate jobs by the millions and coldly impose new ones, are bursting through science on mankind at a maddeningly accelerated rate. Partly because the rate is so maddening, the urge to conserve the old style is also rising with an elemental force. To try to conserve the old style is often sheer futility. Values alone can be conserved; but are they not the ones most threatened by a runaway science and technology? Is not science, if not a Frankenstein, a soulless game of man's insatiable and irresponsible curiosity? Was not science born in that great rift of modern Western culture, the decades around the French Revolution? From there instinctive association can readily carry conservatives to Edmund Burke's impassioned indictment of the Jacobins and the rest: "The age of chivalry is gone. That of sophisters, economists, and calculators, has succeeded; and the glory of Europe is extinguished forever."[4]

Is not science therefore the result of Western man's brave turning his back to the Creed in order to be his own master especially through science? Was not this tacitly admitted even by Bergson, so much at odds with the tyranny of mechanism in biology, in psychology, and in philosophy? It is sobering to think that he endorsed the cliché, produced by the leaders of the Enlightenment in terms of that turnabout, when he wrote in 1907 in his *Evolution créatrice* that science descended upon the earth on the inclined plane of Galileo.[5]

Bergson, alert and sensitive as he was to anything new in biology and psychology, should have known better. He worked in Paris, where, as befitting the City of Light, rumors about intellectual novelties are transmitted almost with the speed of light. For three years prior to the publication of his *Evolution créatrice,* two French scholarly journals had been carrying lengthy reports which should have at least created some misgivings about Galileo's inclined plane as the secular equivalent of Jacob's ladder. In fact, no one was more surprised than the author of those articles, Pierre Duhem, by then recognized as a leading theoretician of thermodynamics. As a Catholic, he certainly did not view the Middle Ages as the epitome of darkness, but he did not expect to find there science of any significance. He shared the general belief that in tracing scientific history one was to jump well over a thousand years from Archimedes or Ptolemy to Galileo. Thus in a series of articles, which Duhem began in 1903 on the origin of the science of statics, Archimedes was at first followed by Stevin and Cardanus, immediate predecessors of Galileo. But in reading Cardanus, Duhem found a cryptic reference to a certain Jordanus, a name noticed during the previous ten or so years by several historians of science who, unlike Duhem, had not cared to track down that elusive figure whom Cardanus seemed to credit with an important scientific insight.

The task, involving a search for half-a-millennium-old medieval manuscripts and the deciphering of their quasi-cryptic scripts, would have been shunned by all theoretical physicists and by most historians of science who at that time were still few and far between. Duhem's heroic effort paid a most unexpected dividend. He found that in speaking of the laws of balance Jordanus, who turned out to have flourished around 1320, enunciated the law of virtual velocities which is the cornerstone of general dynamics.

The rest is an epic of Duhem's pioneering and heroic exploration of the science of the Middle Ages as an age of primary importance for the understanding of the rise of science. A pioneering epic it was, as Duhem could not rely on printed sources: even the better works on science history, such as a three-volume work by Whewell published in the 1840s, offered but a few trivial pages on what happened between Archimedes and Galileo. Duhem certainly could not count on "peer support," that is, on academic consensus and expectation. Soon he had the not necessarily enviable distinction of towering above all his peers, a circumstance all too often sparking jealousy and in his case deep resentment. But he was undaunted. In the twelve years between 1904 and his sudden death in 1916 at the age of 56 he not only continued his prodigious series of publications in theoretical physics, but filled 120 large-size notebooks, each 200 pages long, with excerpts from medieval manuscripts which he had to beg from other French libraries. He had no microfilm, no xerox machines, no dictaphones, not even ball point pens at his disposal. Above all, he had no research assistants of any sort. Worse, he often had to hold firm his trembling right hand with his left.

His were, however, the priceless assets of steely resolve, a brilliant mind, and a facility for writing. Most of his first drafts could directly be sent to the printer. And he sent them in gigantic volumes on medieval science which until then was believed to be non-existent by the scholarly consensus. By 1906 there appeared the 600 pages of *Les origines de la statique* and the first volume of his famed studies on Leonardo whom he soon perceived as a main channel of medieval science for Galileo. By 1909, when he published the second volume of his Leonardo studies, he was already writing the *Système du monde*. By 1913, when he published the third volume of his studies on Leonardo, he had already discovered Buridan and Oresme as the original formulators of the equivalent of Newton's first law of motion.

Meanwhile, the manuscripts of the *Système du monde* had grown so vast that he was able to offer the famed scientific publisher in Paris, A. Hermann, a contract which was eagerly accepted. Hermann, then in his seventies, had great admiration for Duhem ever since he published in 1887 Duhem's *Le potentiel thermodynamique,* now in the Microprint Landmarks of Science series. Two years earlier, the manuscript of that work had been presented by Duhem, a second-year university student, as a doctoral dissertation to the Sorbonne, which rejected it. The reason for this was the inability of Marcelin Berthelot, an excellent experimental chemist and a chief pundit of the secularist ideology of the Third Republic, to see his own favorite scientific theory, the principle of maximum work, demolished by one who was not even a "beginner." Owing to Berthelot's influence the Ministry of Public Instruction gave teaching posts to Duhem only in provincial universities, although his excellence should have secured for him a prominent chair in Paris.

The contract between Duhem and A. Hermann was certainly unique on the part of an already world famous scholar.[6] He obligated himself to deliver to the publisher in mid-1913, and in each of the next nine years, a manuscript equivalent to about 500 large octavo printed pages. Compared with this the obligation assumed by the publisher to bring out one volume each year seems far easier. The publisher was to put on sale 700 copies of each volume. Duhem was to receive no royalties for the first 400 copies of any volume sold. Beyond that number he was to receive a royalty of 40 percent of the sales. The first volume appeared in late 1913, shortly before he was elected as one of the first six non-resident members of the Académie des Sciences. The second volume was published in 1914, the third in 1915, the fourth in 1916 shortly before Duhem's death on September 14. By then he was reading the proofs of the fifth volume which appeared in late 1917. The publisher was in fact so interested in the work that even in the most difficult wartime circumstances he secured the best paper for printing, of which he repeatedly and with obvious satisfaction informed the author.

Duhem left behind a batch of manuscripts which was quickly identified as the continuation of the *Système du monde*. His daughter Hélène, then 25 and his sole survivor, deposited the manuscripts with the Académie des Sciences, where her father had several trusted friends, among them Darboux, its perpetual secretary, who, however, died soon afterwards. The Académie in turn set up a committee to evaluate the publishability of the manuscripts.[7] The verdict, tendered by mid-1917, was unqualifiedly positive. As a result, the manuscript of what later became the sixth volume, was handed over to Hermann and Cie. That volume was not published until 1954.

There could have been a justifiable delay of at most five years, the immediate post-World War I years, which particularly echoed the perennial complaint of publishers about "hard times." But those publishers even then kept producing books, including large scholarly ones, by the score. This was true of Hermann and Cie., which admitted in 1926 to Hélène the fact that the first volume had completely sold out. (By the mid-1930s the same was true of the other four volumes as well.) Clearly, Hermann and Cie. was not losing on the venture, even if it had regularly and promptly paid Hélène the royalties due for copies above the first four hundred. Meanwhile the company's directorship was abandoned by Adolphe Hermann, already in his eighties. By 1930, M. Freymann, the husband of one of Adolphe's three granddaughters, was in charge and played over the next thirty years the role of Hélène's direct antagonist. He never tired of referring to bad economic conditions as the cause of postponing publication.

The indirect and more important antagonist of Hélène, and the real cause of the almost four-decade delay, should be looked for in a symptom of which a telling part is the traditional slighting of Duhem by those in the profession known as historians of science.[8] Younger members of that profession are largely unaware that the slighting in question is almost a hallowed pattern. One such young scholar admitted his utter surprise when faced with a point made in my paper, "Damned with Faint Praise, or the Fate of Pierre

Duhem," which I presented at the Boston Colloquia for the Philosophy of Science on March 13, 1979.[9] The point related to an article which George Sarton, founding editor of *Isis*, the leading history of science quarterly, published in *Scribner's Magazine* in 1919 on Leonardo the scientist. In that article Sarton presented himself as a pioneering student of Leonardo the scientist, and completely ignored Duhem's three truly pioneering volumes on the same subject. About the same time Sarton stopped reviewing in *Isis* the *Système du monde* whose first volume dealing with Plato and Aristotle he had greeted there with great applause. But as an unabashedly prominent Freemason and the son of a virulently anticlerical Freemason in Belgium, Sarton clearly perceived that volumes 3, 4, and 5 had anticipated enough of the thrust of the rest of the *Système du monde*. Such a work, a supreme threat to the strictly secularist interpretation of Western intellectual history (so dear to Freemasonic circles where science owes its origin to the de-Christianization of the West), had to be made ineffective by silence, the most innocent looking among the means of censorship.

In 1938, Sarton let *Isis* carry a notoriously virulent attack on the intellectual honesty of Duhem's scholarship. True, he also provided space in *Isis* about the same time for a call on behalf of an international subscription to promote the publication of the remainder of the *Système du monde*. In that call he seconded the elderly Mme. Paul Tannery, a good friend of Duhem and the widow of a famed historian of ancient Greek mathematics and astronomy. Sarton knew, of course, that because of his Catholicism Tannery was deprived by the circles led by Berthelot of the chair especially established for the history of science in the Collège de France.[10] The injustice precipitated Tannery's death in 1905; his widow found much consolation and support in the letters written to her by Duhem, who also wrote the leading obituary on Tannery.

That Sarton could not be sincere in his support of that call became evident in his five-volume bibliographical history of science prior to 1400[11] in which most of Duhem's publications are not mentioned with the explicitness that was called for by Sarton's method. Then came in 1948 Sarton's series of lectures at the Collège de France on the role of tradition in science, a theme most powerfully articulated by Duhem. Sarton invited[12] to his lectures the noted French church historian, Albert Dufourcq, a colleague and friend of Duhem between 1901 and 1913 at the University of Bordeaux and a most valuable protector and advisor of Hélène until his death in 1952. To Dufourcq's astonishment, Sarton failed to refer to Duhem in his lectures. In their subsequent private conversation Sarton spoke of the manuscript (which he in all likelihood never saw) of the *Système du monde* as "undoubtedly" a series of disconnected jottings, a fact fully reported by Dufourcq in his letter of May 27, to Hélène.

By then Hélène and Dufourcq knew about the explicit resistance on the part of prominent French academics—either radical leftists or radical secularists—against the publication in full of the *Système du monde*. Their chief source of information was Abel Rey, director of the Institut pour Science et Technologie at the Sorbonne, whose doctoral dissertation (1905) included a chapter, not altogether sympathetic, on Duhem's philosophy of science. Yet Rey was one of those rare scholars who in spite of ideological differences was willing to recognize intellectual and scholarly excellence. Hélène's correspondence shows that Rey did much between 1935 and 1939 to rally support in French academic and administrative circles to secure the publication of the *Système du monde*. Not being suspected in those circles, at that time heavily dominated by members of the Front Populaire, of Catholic sympathies, he could move about freely and gain firsthand information. An earful is conveyed in his letter of November 19, 1936, to Hélène. He spoke of his "stormy" meeting with Freymann who proposed the publication of the sixth volume in fascicles,[13] each with independent pagination, which would have made publication of a single volume all the more difficult. More importantly, continued Rey,

> to my great astonishment I have found him [Freymann] rather reticent concerning the subvention from the Ministry. He told me that M. Cavalier (who is director of the bureau for at least this year for some strange reason) was not favorable, nor was Perrin [a Nobel-laureate physicist] for political as well as for scientific hostility. I believe that he [Freymann] is afraid that subvention from the Ministry would obligate him to publish and in my belief he in fact finds useful that difficulty. But he does not admit it. . . . I am therefore pessimistic for the moment because I sense that he does not want to begin the publication of the manuscript.

Shortly afterwards Dufourcq informed Hélène that Cavalier was openly contemptuous of Duhem's scholarship.[14]

Half a year earlier, on May 30th, Rey wrote to Hélène of his "more than 50 telephone calls" to Freymann who over many years kept telling Hélène that the typesetting and printing would proceed with all possible speed. To facilitate quick publication, Hélène in 1937 consented to the modification of the original contract and settled with a ten percent royalty for all copies sold. In view of the first-rate printing facilities available to Hermann and Cie., volume 6, either in fascicles or as a unit, should have been available for sale by the end of 1938 at the latest. But as late as June 7, 1939, Freymann promised publication of volume 6 (with Hélène's preface) only by the end of the summer. Six months later volume 6 was still "being produced with all speed" as Hélène learned from Freymann's letter of Dec. 15, 1939. Such was Freymann's intolerable sop for Hélène's expression of her utmost grievance which he quoted verbatim and which puts in a nutshell that side of his true performance which he could no longer hide from Hélène: "You [Mlle. Duhem] tell me you [M. Freymann) will certainly invoke the actual circumstances. 'The fact is that, when the thing was possible, you did not act in spite of your formal promise given to me and in spite of the written commitment binding you.' "

Underlying Hélène's despair was, of course, the anxiety caused by the eruption of World War II. As one whose several relatives died in World War I or lost their possessions, she could be but deeply concerned about the fate in store for her father's priceless manuscripts. They could have easily become one of the irreparable cultural losses suffered by occupied France. The years of convenient copy-making were still decades away.

Once the war was over, the resolve behind Freymann's delaying tactics grew in proportion to the vastly increased opposition to it. The chief new figures he had to contend with included Dupouy, head after World War II of the Centre National de Recherches Scientifiques; De Broglie, perpetual secretary of the Académie des Sciences; and two elderly distinguished mathematicians, Hadamard and Cartan. The former was a close friend of Duhem since their student days at the Ecole Normale in the 1880s. Cartan, also a Jew like Hadamard, was most influential in obtaining in 1917 for Hélène a yearly pension from the "Société des Amis de la Science" following her father's death.[15]

In 1947 Dupouy made a large subvention available for Freymann who in face of the sum in question could no longer resort to a tactic which was a mainstay of his during the 1930s. Already Adolphe Hermann preferred a subvention from the Ministry which did not imply a strict obligation to publish each and every year for the next ten years.[16] Freymann certainly wanted no obligation vis-à-vis the Ministry which did not adjust in postwar years to actual purchasing power either the subvention accorded to Duhem's work in 1913 or similar grants. Hence Freymann could find excuse in the reduced value of ministerial subvention, and on that ground pressed Hélène for a rewriting of the original contract. At any rate, the vastly enlarged subvention was made available to Freymann in 1947 on the condition that within a year he would publish volume 6. A year later Dupouy in vain reminded Freymann of his promise.[17] By 1952 Freymann's footdragging made Dupouy skeptical about the entire matter to the extent of trying to secure publication through another publisher. The ensuing legal litigation would have, of course, well served Freymann's delaying tactics of which Fabius Cunctator of ancient Roman times might have been proud. On March 31, 1954, De Broglie squarely threatened Freymann with court action.

That almost immediately after Freymann's death, which came on April 2, Hermann and Cie. proceeded with all possible speed under its new director, Pierre Berès, is itself a strong indication that Freymann's standard excuses—rewriting the original contract, shortage of paper, rising typesetting costs, drastic decrease of library orders, especially from American universities—were so many cover-up attempts. The true cause of his incredible procrastination may lie in his apparent readiness to serve as a tool of powerful intellectual and academic circles who did not wish the second and culturally more decisive part of the *Système du monde* to appear in print.

No wonder. In volumes 6 and 7 Duhem presented a vastly documented study of the work of Buridan and Oresme. These two luminaries of fourteenth-century Sorbonne arrived at such scientific breakthroughs as the formulation of what later became known as Newton's first law of motion without which his second and third laws and the entire system of classical physics are inconceivable.[18] In volumes 8-10 Duhem provided ample evidence that such and similar breakthroughs (among them the definition of constantly accelerating motion), so important for the purposes of Galileo, had been handed down in ever wider circles of scholars. Most important, in those posthumous volumes Duhem emphatically stated that Buridan and Oresme broke with the debilitating Aristotelian physics of motion by reflecting on what was demanded by the Christian dogma of creation in time and out of nothing. Whereas for Aristotle, a pantheist, the universe and its motions could have no beginning, for the Christian the world, if it came out of nothing, and in time, had to have a beginning even with respect to the quantity of motion contained within it. But since the Creator was absolutely transcendental to the universe, the latter's motion could no longer be conceived, as was done by Aristotle, as a continuous participation in the divine, but as a power given to it once and for all.

What Duhem unearthed among other things from long-buried manuscripts was that supernatural revelation played a crucial liberating role in putting scientific speculation on the right track. But then the claim, so pivotal for the secularist anti-Christian interpretation of Western cultural history—that science and religion are in irreconcilable conflict—could only be deprived of its prima facie credibility. It is in this terrifying prospect for secular humanism, for which science is the redeemer of mankind, that lies the explanation of that grim and secretive censorship which has worked against Duhem (and his few allies) by two principal means: One is the prevention of major scholarly evidence in favor of Duhem's perspective to appear in print or at least to be printed by "prominent" publishing houses. The other is selective indignation in scholarly societies and their journals—allegedly devoted to universal truth regardless of race, religion, and politics.

No definition of truth can be hoped to be accepted universally in a professedly pluralistic society. But any definition of truth which permits the cavalier handling of monumental facts would certainly contradict scholarship insofar as it ought to be based on as full knowledge of facts as possible. Such a monumental fact of twentieth-century intellectual history is the kind of persecution which kept first-rate scholarship from appearing in print for almost forty years. When some British intellectuals pleaded insufficient knowledge about another persecution that went into high gear in the late 1930s in Nazi Germany, the late Arthur Koestler reminded them of their duty as intellectuals to track down and expose any trampling down of the intellectual dignity of man whenever word is received, however muted, about its taking place. The word about

Duhem's posthumous persecution could be ignored only by those in the field who did not wish to know it was happening, or perhaps deep in their hearts were happy about its happening. A number of them paraded as chief luminaries in the field just in those years when the complete *Système du monde* emerged in print and when a big conference of historians of science heard the brave but unechoed declaration of a leader among them: "Pierre Duhem is the acknowledged teacher of us all."[19]

That they could have found out the truth from a fragile woman, Hélène Duhem, who in 1936 published at her own cost a moving biography of her father with ample reference to his intellectual martyrdom,[20] only magnifies the case in an age so eager to find women heroes. Such a heroine was Hélène Duhem, without whose perseverance and faith the intellectual world might have been poorer by a monumental revision of a systematically distorted Western intellectual history. Like her father, she too was particularly fond of Pascal. She could have hardly failed to think of the gist of her long struggle, never discussed in public by scholars, on behalf of her father's monumental work, as she came across in the *Pensées* the phrase, more expressive than any accusing finger: "Silence is the greatest persecution."[21]

---

[1]For details on Duhem's life and work and other items not documented in this article, see my work quoted in the next note.

[2]*Uneasy Genius: The Life and Work of Pierre Duhem* (Boston: Martinus Nijhoff, 1984, paperback reprint 1987).

[3]The correspondence is in the possession of Mlle. M.-M. Gallet and M. N. Dufourcq, to whom I would like to express my appreciation for having made it available to me for this and further studies.

[4]*Reflections on the Revolution in France* (Pelican Books, 1968), p. 170.

[5]*Creative Evolution,* tr. A. Mitchell (New York: Modern Library, 1944), p. 364. Bergson's statement should seem all the more surprising because, as shown by a note (p. 264), he was not unaware of Duhem's work on the history of modern mechanics.

[6]The contract was signed by Duhem on June 21, 1913.

[7]Concerning publishability, any doubting Thomas may convince himself by a mere look at the manuscripts of volumes 7-10 in the Archives of the Académie des Sciences in Paris. The manuscript of volume 6 was given to the Library of the University of Bordeaux.

[8]The slighting is often indirect as, for instance, in the article "Oresme" by E. Grant in *The Encyclopedia of Philosophy* (New York: Macmillan, 1967),

5: 547-49, who fails to note that it was Duhem who put Oresme on the map of modern intellectual awareness.

[9]Although I was invited to present a paper on any topic relating to the philosophy of science, my paper was not considered for publication in any of the volumes of the Colloquia on the ground that it was not scholarly enough.

[10]The chair, occupied by Lafitte, "the positivist pope," from 1893-1903, went to Wyrouboff, a crystallographer and a worthy successor to Lafitte from at least the ideological viewpoint.

[11]*Introduction to the History of Science* (1927-1947).

[12]The invitation, which was not solicited by Dufourcq indicated Sarton's awareness (and possible apprehension) of Dufourcq's decade-long efforts on behalf of Hélène and the publication of the *Système du monde.*

[13]The fascicles would have been part of the ones (by then more than seven hundred) constituting the series, "Actualités scientifiques et industrielles."

[14]Jacques Cavalier, who was killed by a motorcyclist on March 21, 1937, was professor of physics, before he became in 1926 director of French higher education.

[15]Duhem's close and lifelong friendship with some prominent and staunchly liberal Jews is mentioned here because of the customary character-assassination in which he is written off as an ultraconservative, royalist, anti-Semite of extremist religiosity.

[16]Letters of April 11 and 17 of 1913 of A. Hermann to Pierre Duhem.

[17]As put in writing by Dupouy in his letter of July 11, 1951, to the Académie des Sciences, of which he sent a copy to Hélène. The material kept by Hélène is all the more valuable, because the more than 20-year-old documents of CNRS are usually "mis au pilon," that is, thrown in the incinerator.

[18]The enormous scholarly value of volume 7 is also attested to by the publication of much of its contents in English translation by R. Aryew under the title, *Duhem on Medieval Cosmology* (University of Chicago Press, 1986).

[19]A statement of H. Guerlac in Oxford in July 1961.

[20]*Un savant français: Pierre Duhem* (Paris: Plon, 1936). She did not succeed in publishing a documentary history of the publication of the first volume of the *Système.* Her manuscript, of about 40 pages, entitled "Comment fut publié le *Système du monde* de Pierre Duhem: fragments d'une correspondence," is one of a number of manuscript documents relating to Duhem's life and work which are being prepared for publication by Mlle. Gallet and myself.

[21]See *Pascal's Pensées,* with an introduction by T. S. Eliot (New York: E. P. Dutton, 1958), p. 270, (no. 919).

12

Monkeys and Machine-guns: Evolution, Darwinism, and Christianity

It often happens that when a Greek or Latin word is given a new lease on life in one of the major modern languages, and especially in English, the original meaning of the word may be replaced by a rather different one. This is particularly the case when a word, which was a strongly transitive verb in the classical context, is resuscitated as a generic noun in the modern diction. The word *evolution* is a case in point.

The root of that all-important modern noun is the Latin verb

First published in *Chronicles of Culture* (August 1986), pp. 15-18. Reprinted with permission.

evolvere. Whether used by historians like Tacitus and Livy or by poets like Ovid and Catullus or by philosophers like Lucretius, Seneca, and Cicero, the verb *evolvere* either meant to eject some*thing* with a rolling or coiling motion, or to cause some*thing* to flow out or roll out from somewhere, or to unwind some*thing,* or to unwrap or uncover some*thing.* In all these cases it was clearly assumed that the thing or the object of the action had already been there. Only one and uncertain case is found in classical Latin literature for the noun form *evolutio* of the verb *evolvere,* according to the testimony of the two-volume Oxford Latin-English dictionary.

The aura that has grown around the modern word *evolution* is precisely the make-believe that something, and often something very big, can ultimately come out from somewhere where it had not been beforehand, provided the steps of that process are very numerous and practically undetectable. This is not a new-fangled diagnosis of the process imaginatively called evolution. More than a hundred years have already gone by since the public was regaled with an inimitable dictum produced with an eye on Darwinism: "A logical theft is more easily committed piecemeal than wholesale. Surely it is a mean device for a philosopher to crib causation by hairsbreadths, to put it out at compound interest through all time and then disown the debt."[1]

Those evolutionists who want no part of an evolutionism steeped in the foregoing trick cannot, however, make nonexistent the frequent presentation of evolution in that deceitful sense. Furthermore, they should feel gratified when such a trick is identified and discredited right at the very start of the discussion. Clear air is a necessity not only for physical survival but also for mental balance. Once castrated of this pseudogenerative power to produce rabbits and bigger pieces, such as elephants and dinosaurs, to say nothing of such intangible jewels as the human mind, from under an empty hat, the word *evolution* should perhaps better yield to the word *development.* This word, so useful and modest—just think of John Henry Newman's masterful articulation of it—has at least the advantage of being much closer to the original meaning of *evolvere,* that is, to the unfolding of something that in essence at least had already been there.

This substitution will be violently resisted by Darwinists, for the essence of Darwinism is that there are no essences, except one essence, which is sheer matter. Liberal Christian admirers of Darwin would now recall his reference to the Creator at the end of the *Origin of Species*. They had better do their homework properly. That reference, inserted only from the second edition on, prompted Darwin to speak privately of his shame for "having truckled to public opinion."[2] The high Victorian times still wanted to have a bit of religious wrapping about rank irreligiosity. Darwin should have felt even more ashamed for having spoken in his *Autobiography* of his imperceptibly slow "evolution" from belief into mere agnosticism. As one who through much of his adult life had to dissimulate his true views lest a deeply religious and beloved wife be hurt, Darwin finally came to believe that he was not dissimulating anything. He might have been cured of his illusion about the evolution of his religious beliefs had he reread in his late years his early Notebooks. Available since the early 1970s in easily accessible edition, those Notebooks make it absolutely clear that the Darwin of the late 1830s was a crude and crusading materialist. There was no gradual evolution from the official naturalist of the *Beagle* who, as behove a good fundamentalist, had lectured shipmates with Bible in hand on the evil of swearing, to the author of those Notebooks. The transition was rather rapid, indicating a sudden and thorough disillusion which turns one's erstwhile object of love into a target of hatred to be exposed and destroyed by all possible means.

Darwin quickly isolated the notion of species as the central target of his attacks on God, supernatural, revelation, and Bible. This showed not so much his acumen as the patently indefensible character of the production on the third and fifth days of plants and animals "according to their kinds" as a divine warrant of the fixity of species. What *is* a proof of uncommon acumen is Darwin's relentless spotting of data, direct and circumstantial, in support of his evolutionary vision in which all, from the simplest organism to man, followed with inevitable necessity once the original soup of life was available. To his credit, Darwin did not make the claim made by Haeckel and others that science had ascertained the existence and qualities of the original soup. But his conviction was firm about the purely natural emergence of such a soup some billions of years ago.

However, Darwin never appreciated what at one point dawned on his most trusted ally, T. H. Huxley, that the mental spectacle of a forever-evolving life was a metaphysical vision.[3] That Herbert Spencer, who with enormous verbal skill kept portraying the evolution of the most nonhomogeneous from the most homogeneous, was for Darwin one of the greatest philosophers of all times, shows something of Darwin's blindness to elementary fallacies in reasoning. Reason commanded no encomiums on Darwin's part. His contemptuous remarks about the minds of geniuses were so many defense mechanisms against facing up to the problem of the mind, the greatest and most decisive problem to be faced by evolutionists, Darwinian or other. Not once did Darwin ponder the nature of purposeful action. Not once did he ask himself the question whether his lifelong and most purposeful commitment to the purpose of proving that there was no purpose was not a slap in his own mental face.

The only time when Darwin performed creditably in philosophical matters relating to his evolutionary ideology came when he jotted on a slip of paper, which he kept in his copy of Chambers' *Vestiges of Creation,* the warning addressed to himself: "Never say higher or lower."[4] He did not fully remember the gist of that warning, namely, that a scientific theory (as distinct from a scientific ideology) permitted no value judgments.

He never suspected the irony of his answering within the framework of "how" the questions about "why" and "for what purpose." He recognized, however, that there was something unsatisfactory with the "how" he held high, or the selective impact of environment on the fact that offspring were always, however slightly, different from their parents. That "how," supported by genetics as it may be, is still elusive. Indeed, so elusive as to have produced a unique feature in the history of science. Whereas in physics and chemistry the conversion of scientists to a new major theory becomes complete within one generation, in biology a respectable minority has maintained itself for now over four generations against the majority position represented by Darwinists.

The latest evidence of the deep dissatisfaction felt about Darwinism has come from strictly Darwinistic circles. Despair about Darwinism is the driving force behind that recent rush to the idea of punctuated evolution. In no sense an explanation, the theory of punctuated evolution is a mere verbalization demanded by the fact that the geological record almost invariably shows bursts of new forms and hardly ever a slow gradual process as demanded by classical Darwinism. The radical opposition to religion in general and to Christianity in particular on the part of the chief spokesmen of punctuated evolution is of a piece with the antireligious origins of Darwinism.

Many Christians have only themselves to blame if their reaction to Darwinism justifies Huxley's remark that "extinguished theologians lie about the cradle of every science as the strangled snakes beside that of Hercules."[5] There is no intellectual saving grace for those who oppose long geological ages and the exceedingly variegated fossil record with a swearing by the six-day creation story as a literal record of what happened. It is rarely remembered that their hapless wrestling with Scriptures and science is but the latest act in that intellectual tragedy which Luther and Calvin initiated by their lengthy commentaries on Genesis 1-3. The strictest literal interpretation of the creation story told there was upheld by both to the hilt. Present-day Lutherans and Calvinists cater only to the uninformed when, proud of the "main-line" status accorded to them by the secularist media, they hold high the "reasonableness" of their tradition against the "unreasonability" of fundamentalist Protestants.

A hermeneutics which sets limits to the literal interpretation must come to terms with the fact that the Scriptures were born within the Church and not the other way around, and that therefore only a Church with an infallible magisterium can guarantee the inerrancy of the Scriptures. This, of course, brings us to the branch of Christendom known as Roman Catholicism. The near-escape of papal infallibility from the clutches of the Galileo case[6] taught Catholics a lesson which stood them in good stead in the decades immediately following Darwin. Their resistance to Darwinism was from the start done more with an eye on plain philosophy than on scriptural or dogmatic texts. The essentially philosophical objections of St. G. J. Mivart, a Catholic biologist, to Darwin's theory represented one of the two main attacks that upset Darwin considerably. The other was the demonstration by F. Jenkin, a Scottish engineer, that the laws of statistics did not favor at all the evolutionary mechanism known as natural selection.

The mathematical analysis carried out by R. A. Fisher in the late 1920s made natural selection appear in a less unfavorable light. Of course, no mathematics could provide in the first place the reality of cobreeding individuals whose totality is the species. The reality of species has not ceased to remain a pointer to a fundamental question in philosophy, namely, the ability of the mind to see the universal in the individual and particular. It was with an eye on such a question that a philosopher of science, with obvious sympathy for Darwinism but with a rank miscomprehension of metaphysics, proposed in the early 1970s the working out of a biological metaphysics![7]

The proposal is typical of the thinking of those Darwinists who try to stake out a "humanist" position that affirms materialism with profuse accolades to human values. It is that "humanist" form of Darwinist materialism that alone should be of concern to Christians who take their stand on the eternal validity of values, among them the value of brotherly love. In that "humanist" form brotherly love is evoked through despiritualized labels such as "kin-selection" and "altruism," lest the unwary be alerted to the fact that beneath the Darwinian guise of humanness there lurks a "scientific materialism as the best myth humankind may ever have."[8]

That "humanism" ought to be unmasked at regular intervals, a task which is essentially philosophical. Only with some philosophical acumen and a great deal of common sense can one show that the reasoning of Darwinists is either contradictory, or simply a tacit assumption of basic realities they try to disprove and discredit. Among these basic realities are mind, purpose, and ethical principles. That they cannot be accounted for within Darwinist perspectives has time and again been admitted by leading Darwinists. To be sure, only a few of them did come across as candidly as did T. H. Huxley a hundred years ago when he warned against seeing a "moral flavour" in the survival of the fittest.[9] Only a few of them admitted as candidly as did Huxley's great-grandson, Sir Andrew Huxley, that no scientific clue has yet emerged for the origin of consciousness. He stated in the same breath that the origin of life is still an unsolved problem.[10] Equally unresolved is the status of the long-sought link between mankind and the realm of monkeys and apes, living and long-dead—a realm in which not a speck of dust is being left unturned by lynx-eyed investigators.

Most Darwinists have done their best to create the illusion that there is no major fault with Darwinism. Yet the fact is that the empirical evidence for the transformation of species under environmental pressure is still circumstantial. The measure of effectiveness that can be attributed to the same mechanism diminishes in the measure in which one considers the transition between ever-larger biological groups, from genera through families, orders, classes, to phyla and kingdoms.

None of these remarks should be construed as a rejection of the chief merit of Darwinism, which in fact assures its genuine scientific status. By ignoring all considerations of design and purpose as being possibly at work in living organisms, Darwinists cultivate biology as a science which deals only with empirical data and their correlations in the space-time continuum.

Unfortunately, the chief glory of Darwinistic biology has also become its chief delusion. The methodical elimination of questions about the reality of design and purpose has been taken by many Darwinists as a proof that design and purpose do not exist. The miscomprehension about the limitations of the scientific method also plagues many Christians who expect science to deliver proofs of design and purpose. They fail to see that such proofs can only come from that philosophy which they all too often consider an enemy of faith. Once they lose their hold on philosophy they can at best come up with poetry in prose, as illustrated by Teilhard de Chardin's flights of fancy.

Father Teilhard could do far worse. In the trenches of World War I, where he served as a stretcher bearer, he wrote glowing encomiums on the war as an unsurpassed means of promoting the heroic qualities of the race.[11] It could not be unknown to him that several members of the German General Staff had some years earlier published books in which their war plans were justified on the same Darwinist grounds. Nor could the two volumes of Darwin's letters published in 1890 be unknown to young Father Teilhard, a prominent supporter of the Piltdown man and other Darwinist causes. Those volumes contained the evidence that Darwin believed that evolution justified the Russians promoting the higher race by smashing the Turkish armies.

It is not known what Father Teilhard's reactions were to Shaw's preface to his *Heartbreak House,* published in the wake of World War I. In that war, machine guns (produced and marketed with sales-pitches reminiscent of Darwinist mottos) performed time and again as effectively in a few hours' time as did the bombs that fell on Nagasaki and Hiroshima in a second or two.[12] In that preface Shaw pinpointed "Anglosaxon" Darwinism as a chief ideological source of Prussian militarism: "We taught Prussia this religion; and Prussia bettered our instructions so effectively that we presently found ourselves confronted with the necessity of destroying Prussia to prevent Prussia from destroying us. And that has just ended in each destroying the other to an extent doubtfully reparable in our time."[13]

Of course, most Darwinists try to find refuge in circumlocutions or in sullen silence when reminded of the true nature of their ideology. In doing so they merely imitate Darwin, who from the comfort of his gentry residence largely ignored Marx when the latter reminded him that class struggle and the struggle for life had much in common. The "humanization" of Darwinism is a far greater threat to human well-being—intellectual, ethical, and spiritual— than are outspoken endorsements of war by prominent Darwinists such as Sir Arthur Keith. His praises of the pruning effects of wars, which coincided with Stalin's and Hitler's preparations for World War II, may sober up dreamy-eyed captives to the myth of progress, biological, cultural, and ethical, defined in terms of Darwinian evolution.

Only a few among those dreamers were as candid as Aldous Huxley, who attributed the favorable reception given Darwinism to the liberation through it from absolute ethical and sexual norms.[14] Only a few woke up as he did to the need to take a searching look at the word *evolution*. *Evolution* should deserve no sympathy if it serves as a proof that something can come out from where it had not been at least "in embryo." This is not to suggest that in the manner of preformationists a homunculus should be imagined inside the membrane of the human sperm or that a soul should be attributed to each and every pollen drifting through the air, because human soul or mind clearly crowns the evolutionary process. What is suggested is that evolution or rather the vast spectacle of the gradations of life which life has taken on over billions of years and through a mechanism which is at best most imperfectly understood, be recognized for what it truly is: a vision which is primarily and ultimately metaphysical.

Man is capable of such vision precisely because his nature transcends what is merely physical. Taken in that perspective, the word *evolution* should give no fear to the Christian. After all, his chief perspective, main comfort, and supreme concern ought to remain in the words: "What does profit a man if he gains the whole world but in the process he loses his soul?"—and—"Don't be afraid of those who kill the body but are not able to kill the soul"—and—"Be afraid only of the one who can relegate both body and soul to the gehenna."

Gehenna is merely the ultimate and eternal form of anarchy. This is to be kept in mind when humanist Darwinists, including most college professors, are reminded by a fellow academic of the rank inconsistency of their references to moral norms as they recommend, say, the ethical stance of civil disobedience in fighting against racial inequality. In coming to the aid of one such academic (Prof. D. Kagan), Prof. L. Pearce Williams of Cornell wrote in a letter to the *New York Times* in December 1983 of the vanishing of the moral world at the end of Victorian times.[15] He also noted that our world today is a mere consensual world, which, in view of the progressive breakdown of consensus, is rapidly heading toward anarchy.

As a historian of science, Prof. Williams could hardly fail to think of Darwin's work, which prominently figured in the assault made on the traditional moral world in precisely those times. His failure to point that out and to recall the repeated disillusionment of eminent Darwinians with Darwinism shows once more that the only thing man learns from history is that he never learns from history. But those who do not wish to take seriously the lessons of history are bound to help usher in historic disasters.

They do so by cultivating horrendous somersaults in logic whereby all things, big and small, trivial and stupendous, appear to evolve—or as the Romans of old would say, unroll—from under wrappings that seem outright pleasant. For nothing pleases nowadays more than academic respectability even if it is a cover-up for committing one big mental robbery through uncounted petty thefts —all of which are made imperceptible by phrases hollow inside their learned exterior.

[1]J. Martineau, "Nature and God" (1860), in *Essays, Reviews and Addresses* (London: Longmans, Green and Co., 1891), vol. III, p. 160.
[2]See Darwin's letter to J. D. Hooker, March 29, 1863, in F. Darwin (ed.), *The Life and Letters of Charles Darwin* (London: John Murray, 1887), vol. III, p. 18.
[3]T. H. Huxley, "Biogenesis and Abiogenesis" (1870), in *Discourses: Biological and Geological* (London: Macmillan, 1894), pp. 256-57.
[4]See F. Darwin and A. C. Seward (eds.), *More Letters of Charles Darwin* (New York: D. Appleton, 1903), vol. I, p. 360.

[5]T. H. Huxley, "The Origin of Species" (1860), in *Darwiniana. Essays* (New York: D. Appleton, 1896), p. 52.

[6]There is still no explanation why Paul V, ready to issue a peremptory condemnation of the motion of the earth, let the matter rest with a mere cardinal, Bellarmin, however prominent. See my article, "The Case for Galileo's Rehabilitation," *Fidelity* 5/4 (March 1986), pp. 37-41.

[7]Just as D. L. Hull tried to get around genuine metaphysics in his "The Metaphysics of Evolution" (*British Journal for the History of Science* 3 [1967], pp. 309-37), the various contributors to *Evolution at a Crossroads: The New Biology and the New Philosophy of Science,* edited by D. J. Depew and B. H. Weber (Cambridge, MA: The MIT Press, 1985) rely on the word hermeneutics to keep metaphysics from appearing on the scene.

[8]E. O. Wilson, *On Human Nature* (Cambridge, MA: Harvard University Press, 1978), p. 209.

[9]T. H. Huxley, "Evolution and Ethics" (1893), in *Evolution and Ethics and Other Essays* (New York: D. Appleton, 1914), p. 80.

[10]See *Supplement to Royal Society News,* Issue 12, Nov. 1891, p. v.

[11]Fr. Teilhard looked on war as the road to "The Promised Land," the title of a writing of his, from early 1919, that is available in English translation in his *Writings in Time of War,* tr. R. Hague (New York: Harper and Row, 1968), pp. 278-88.

[12]See J. Ellis, *The Social History of the Machine Gun* (New York: Pantheon Books, 1975).

[13]*Heartbreak House* (London: Constable, 1925), p. xiii.

[14]A. Huxley, *Ends and Means* (London: Chatto and Windus, 1937), pp. 267, 269 and 274.

[15]Printed in the Dec. 21, 1983 issue, p. A26, cols. 4-5.

13

The Demythologization of Science

Faith, myth, and theory constitute a vast topic[1] even if taken singly, let alone together. If they were to be treated as a topic for religion, there would still be the added problem of the many, perhaps too many, religious viewpoints which cannot be easily reconciled. This old and sad truth was keenly felt by Protestant and Catholic theologians who a year ago met in Baltimore to achieve a common interpretation of the Apostles' Creed. They failed to reach first base as they could not agree on the Creed's opening words, "I believe." The act of faith does not have exactly the same meaning in Protestant and Catholic theologies.

By not discussing the topic from the viewpoint of any of the great religions—Jewish, Christian, Muslim, and Buddhist—one does not

---

This paper, written in 1967, is published here for the first time. About its original delivery, see note 1.

thereby necessarily leave the realm of religion. Within that realm there is a religion which is often taken for something else. The dogmas of that religion are statements attributed to science, its commandments are dictates distilled from scientific fashions, its authorities are self-styled spokesmen of science, its heaven is the brave new world.[2] Often called scientism,[3] this science-religion looks upon science as the only reliable Savior and worships science with the messianic expectations of a religious faith. Science-religion was a chief ingredient of the French Enlightenment whose leaders expected to build a heavenly city on earth.[4] The prophets of Paris,[5] Condorcet, Saint-Simon, Comte, to name only a few, pinned their hopes of a new society on the science of their day which they viewed as perfection incarnate. Somewhat later it was again a mythical image of science that inspired the fathers of communism, Marx and Engels.[6] While communism has seen in a hundred years many changes, both ideological and practical, its original appraisal of science has not changed. Science, as interpreted by dialectical materialism, is supposed to bring about the Utopia of a classless society.

Concerning the strength of science-religion in our part of the world, a small detail may be more telling than long and learned volumes. Forty years ago, on May 20, 1927, a young man flew over this island, or not very far from it, and his flight made history. Charles Lindbergh had within a day become a hero though a very reticent one. Twenty years had to pass and the upheaval of World War II had to come with its nuclear twilight before he felt the urge to reveal his inner self. He did it in a now largely forgotten little book to which he gave the title: *Of Flight and Life*.[7] The booklet is a modest though revealing twentieth-century counterpart of Saint Augustine's *Confessions*. It is the account of Lindbergh's painful escape from the clutches of worshipping a false god, the god of science. "I grew up," he wrote, "as a disciple of science. To me in youth, science was more important than either man or God. The one I took for granted, the other was too intangible for me to understand. Like most of modern youth, I worshipped science. I was awed by its knowledge. Its advances had surpassed man's wildest dreams. Its benefits and powers appeared unlimited. In its learning seemed to lie the key to all mysteries of life."[8]

Science is often contrasted with theology,[9] or religion, but as Lindbergh's words indicate, scientific knowledge often ends up where theology and religion terminate, in a religious, worshiping attitude. The act of worship is obviously an act of faith. Faith in its turn is a basic ingredient in theology and religion. It may sound surprising that the same is true of science. Today, scientists in an increasing number do recognize the fact that their espousing of basic assumptions is indeed an act of faith.[10]

Faith, religious or scientific, poses a keen challenge to the inquiring mind fond of matter-of-fact knowledge. Theologians tell us that faith goes deeper than any other type of knowledge. On the scientific side, it is often asserted that only a reasoning that obeys the laws of scientific thinking can lead to objective certainty.[11] This assertion is a favorite slogan of our times and the typical twentieth-century intellectual derives obvious satisfaction from it. As a matter of fact the Middle Ages were no more engrossed in the analysis of faith than our times are with the alleged perfection of scientific method or theory. Both ages seem to have at least that much in common: the topic of theory, theological or scientific, is being talked to death.[12] This is my convenient excuse to leave it untouched today.

Having said that much of faith and theory, it remains to concentrate on myth. I will try to show that the cultivation of science can become a worshiping of science because science is full of myths. Due to their presence, science often appears to the public with a halo around its head. Much of our cultural crisis stems from that mythical grandeur accorded to science and no cure for these cultural ills shall be found unless, to put it bluntly, science be demythologized.

The myths surviving within science are much more subtle than the stories composing traditional mythologies. Actually, science proved itself a most valuable weapon against crude, superstitious myths. Thanks in part to science, man does not picture for himself the heavens as the outstretched body of a mythical deity.[13] Thunderstorms do not evoke for us the workshop of Jupiter and Vulcan, and the tail of comets is no longer viewed as the sign of imminent disasters. Concerning this last point our deliverance is of rather recent origin. It began with the publication in 1687 of Newton's *Principia* which was introduced with an ode written in Newton's honor by a colleague of his, Edmund Halley. He did not suspect at that time that his future fame would rest with his prediction, made eighteen years later, that a big comet, observed in 1607 and 1682, would return in 1758. In his encomium of Newton,

Halley took pains to note that, owing to Sir Isaac's genius,

> Now we know
> The sharply veering ways of comets, once
> A source of dread, no longer do we quail
> Beneath appearances of bearded stars.[14]

Leaving behind the realm of superstitious mythology did not, however, mean parting with myths. The father of positivism, Auguste Comte, saw in fact the whole mission of his life to lead science, and therefore thinking, to a stage of development completely free of myths. The myths, that according to Comte were still besetting science, were the myths of metaphysics.[15] While the positivist age of thinking as prophesied by Comte is still to come, positivists of all descriptions kept working strenuously on a leak-proof theory of science. I said "leakproof" with an eye on William James' remark on psychology: "a fragile structure into which the waters of metaphysical criticism leak at every joint."[16] For all the efforts of positivists and neopositivists, the conceptual structure of physical science is far from being water proof against metaphysics. Positivists did not succeed in their efforts to free science from all metaphysics which they considered as a bundle of refined myths. Their failure should be easy to understand for those who recognize with E. A. Burtt that "the only way to avoid becoming a meta-physician is to say nothing."[17] Needless to say, this is the last thing a positivist is ready to do. One must, however, admit that some positivists unwittingly called attention to the fact that Newtonian or classical physics was not only replete with metaphysical concepts but was itself the embodiment of a great myth, the myth of the machine. Mach especially was not one to mince words. In his often blunt style he spoke of the "mechanical mythology"[18] and put it in the rather unsavory class of animistic or organismic mythology.

Organismic mythology dominated the first two thousand years of the history of physics.[19] From the time of Socrates until the advent of Galileo, physics was built around the concept of organism, as exemplified in Aristotle's system of the physical world. For Aristotle the world was a huge, ever-living animal[20] and, as a result, he claimed that the most noble part of that cosmic animal, the region above the stars, had in itself the principle of perfect life, or perpetual motion. This is why the material which supposedly composed that realm was called "ether," whose etymology may have to do with the Greek equivalent of "always runs."[21] In Aristotle's physics every motion was but a participation, however remote, in the motion of the ether as a most perfect expression of life. Once, however, motion was defined as the evidence of life, it also became the evidence of purpose, of striving. Aristotle could therefore speak in the same breath of the motion of stars, of the progression of animals, of the fall of stones, and of the healing of the sick. Carrying on the Socratic tradition, Aristotle's physics has become the most palpable codification of the myth that the concept of organism was the exclusive key to understanding.

Needless to say, organismic or Aristotelian physics was a hopeless dead end. It left man totally helpless in his encounter with the realm of the non-living. To acquire mastery over that realm, physics had to demythologize itself. Helped by a late-medieval tradition anchored mainly in the writings of Oresme who spoke of the universe as a huge clockwork, Galileo and Newton were the leading figures in a process, which in the end only robbed Peter to pay Paul. In the place of organismic mythology came the mechanistic mythology, or the myth of the machine. From the mid-seventeenth century until the beginning of the twentieth century physicists pursued their work in the conviction that machine or mechanical models constituted the only trustworthy paradigm of explanation. Great figures of classical physics were unanimous in equating intelligibility with machinery, or with some specific type of it, of which the clockwork was the most celebrated owing to its popularization by Voltaire.[22]

This intelligibility in terms of a machine was believed to be exhaustive as can be seen from the mythical qualities attributed by classical physics to the supposedly ultimate vehicle of mechanical effects, the ether. For the myth of the ether did not die with organismic physics, in spite of the sharp remarks of Galileo who in his *Dialogue* heaped ridicule on the absolutely hard and yet perfectly transparent ether of the Peripatetics.[23] The ether of classical physics presented the same opportunity for intellectual credulity. From Descartes to Kelvin classical physicists spared no time and effort to figure out the inner mechanism of the ether and to find thereby the explanation of its obviously contradictory properties. The ether of classical physics had to be extremely tenuous, as the planets and stars had to travel through it at enormous speeds with no loss of momentum; at the same time the ether had also to be extremely rigid to make the rapid propagation of light possible. Classical physicists had few qualms about the simultaneous presence of these two contradictory qualities in the very same material. For them matter was the embodiment of a machinery, and machines in turn represented intelligibility itself. Such confidence in the conceptual perfection of the idea of machines was tantamount to the acceptance of a myth, the myth of the machine[24] as the paradigm of understanding.

A new age of physics could only come when the myth was recognized as such. The theory of special relativity rendered the ether unnecessary but only at the price of making mathematical formalism a sort of ultimate court of appeal in physical research. Similar was the influence of general relativity and of quantum theory. In both of them mathematics became invested with a practically unlimited heuristic value. Modern physicists are indeed amazed at the fact that mathematical theorems and techniques elaborated with no reference to physical problems a century ago, provide in countless cases the clue to the problems and findings of modern physics. This amazement of theirs is not without some mythical component. In modern physics the concept of number plays the same role as did the concept of machine in classical physics and the concept of organism in Aristotelian physics. It is a mythical role. To say with modern physicists that God is a mathematician,[25] or that the world is made ultimately of numbers, is to voice a myth, an attractive but fictitious story.

In so doing, modern physicists simply follow in the footsteps of their classical and Aristotelian predecessors all of whom were captives of the scientific myth of their times. Most present-day physicists will be rather reluctant to recognize this. Nobody likes to admit that behind a brilliant beacon of light there might be lurking the shadow of a myth. Yet, indirect references to the myth of number are not lacking in the statements made by modern physicists. Leaders of modern physics spoke warmly of the emergence in modern physics of the old Pythagorean vision of a world made of numbers. Nuclear physicists speak fondly of "magic numbers" and search eagerly for numerical relations that would provide the final clue for the system of fundamental particles.

The mentality that inspires such efforts is not without some mythical ingredient. Not only are "fundamental particles" mythical entities—the best established feature of the known fundamental particles is that none of them are fundamental—but there is also a great deal of myth in the unlimited effectiveness accorded in modern physics to the role of numbers. In today's physical science numbers are a magic road to fundamental particles. Numbers today constitute in the mind of many that mythical realm that ultimately gives rise to particles. This may sound rather far-fetched to some. But in their unlimited admiration of geometry and topology some leading present-day physicists speak of matter as something fashioned out of empty space.[26] It is rather typical that they make no effort to specify what they really mean by empty space. Their lack of attention in this respect strongly suggests that they may be under the spell of magic. For the empty space or vacuum of modern quantum electrodynamics is as much a mythical concept as was the ether of classical physics. That vacuum is the repository of a long list of recondite properties. But for all that it is still emptiness if it is a true vacuum, otherwise it is but a hollow paradox. Only minds captivated by a myth shall assert ill-defined paradoxes with easygoing credulity.

The ether and the empty space of quantum electrodynamics are paradoxical in part because of their allegedly close connection with the basic stuff of the universe. Questions about basic or ultimate aspects of the universe will always have their paradoxes especially when answers to such questions are inspired by mythical beliefs. Proud as man may be about the advances in the scientific understanding of the universe at large, such an exploration is still guided both by reason *and* by myth. We should only recall the reversals that took place in scientific history concerning the question whether the universe was finite or infinite. From Aristotle until the rise of modern science in the seventeenth century the world was believed to be finite. Obviously such had to be the case in a conceptual framework dominated by the myth that any reliable explanation rested ultimately on the idea of organism. The notion of organism implied an entity with boundaries and with a center to which all its parts were co-ordinated. Applied to the universe as a whole the concept of organism made inevitable the acceptance of a universe with boundaries and with a center to which all its parts and motions were related.

Awakening from a myth is not a pleasant experience, as shown by the reaction that accompanied the replacement of the finite universe by an infinite one. This is not the place and time to retell a well-known chapter in the intellectual history of the seventeenth century. One aspect of it deserves, however, some attention. Those, like Giordano Bruno and some Cambridge Neoplatonists, who spearheaded the cause of an infinite universe, in a sense only repeated history. They replaced one myth with another. For as can be seen from the vantage point of twentieth-century astronomy and cosmology, the infinite universe of Kant, Laplace, and Kelvin, was a myth. This will probably sound like a harsh stricture. After all not every scientific idea or view that turned out to be false should be labeled a myth. Still, the infinite universe of classical physics and astronomy shows a basic feature of every myth. Like any other myth the unquestioning belief is an infinite universe made scientists conspicuously blind to its obvious contradictions.

One of those contradictions had already been pointed out in Newton's time. In an infinite Newtonian universe, made up of an infinite number of stars, every point of the skies should appear as bright as the sun, with no difference between day and night. For twentieth-century cosmology this problem, known as Olbers' paradox,[27] is of crucial importance. Yet, grave and obvious as it is and was already three hundred years ago, it prompted but a few short discussions during the whole lifespan of the eighteenth and nineteenth centuries. In all those papers there is a conspicuous lack of sensing the gravity of the question. The authors of those papers seem indeed to be mesmerized by the concept of the infinity of the universe. It looms large before them, as a gigantic sacred cow that cannot be touched or questioned.

Such is the impact of a myth. It blocks critical sense. It diminishes alertness to new possibilities and to the inherent weakness of an apparently faultless scientific synthesis. Brilliant as was Newton's account of gravitation, it yielded impossible results when applied to an infinite universe. It should have been obvious that the total mass of an infinite number of stars should be infinite. From this it follows that at each point of the infinite space the gravitational potential too should be infinite, a conclusion patently at variance with the facts. But the myth of infinity induced the classical physicist to gloss over the problem. It was not until 1896 that an Austrian physicist, H. Seeliger, faced up to it in its true seriousness.[28] Possibly Seeliger was encouraged by the first cracks that in his time began to show on the conceptual framework of classical physics of which belief in the infinity of the universe was an integral part. That belief received a memorable phrasing only a few years earlier in Lord Kelvin's ringing declaration:

> I say finitude is incomprehensible, the infinite in the universe is comprehensible. Now apply a little logic to this. Is the negation of finitude incomprehensible? What would you think of a universe in which you could travel one, ten, or a thousand miles, or even to California, and then find it come to an end? Even if you were to go millions and millions of miles, the idea of coming to an end is incomprehensible.[29]

Only in a myth is the difference between truth and falsehood so alarmingly simple. Being the prisoner of a myth, little did Kelvin guess that he was merely paying his homage to a mythical belief. Much less could he foresee that, within a generation, scientific thinking was to make a complete turn-about, by writing the word finitude on the banner of scientific cosmology. Allegiance to the myth of infinite universe is not, however, completely gone. Witness the reluctance of many present-day scientists to admit the finitude of universe not only in space but also in time. Witness the eagerness by which the idea of a universe oscillating forever is put forward nowadays. Of course the universe may be oscillating. But a tacit espousal of the ancient pagan myth of the eternity of the universe seems to motivate the "scientific" belief that those oscillations can go on forever. Ironically, here too a most unscientific price, the slighting of the validity of the law of entropy, is part of the bargain.

In having myths of its own, science shares in the predicament of all human endeavors, such as religion, philosophy, politics, and the arts. But the vigorous flourishing of myths within science, within the scientific community, is a peculiar facet. Behind it lurks a curious, baffling aspect of the scientific movement which, unlike literature and the arts, failed to develop a school of criticism of its own.[30] True, science, especially physics, possesses in its laboratory techniques and methods an effective criterion that discredits many a false claim and incomplete finding. But this often takes a long time, even decades and centuries. In the meantime, physicists do their best to propagate and embellish the ideas and viewpoints fashionable in their day. In sum, they are building myths. It is this myth-making process that could easily be checked or kept within limits by a school of criticism working within the scientific movement. With a few exceptions, scientists reflect but little on the general philosophical and cultural roots of their favorite views. They may deplore the shortsightedness of bygone generations of scientists, yet they are curiously insensitive to their own, and needless to say, do not solicit the good services of a systematic vigilant criticism.

This lackadaisical attitude of scientists toward criticism is in part responsible for two unhealthy situations. One of them concerns the scientific community itself, the other the non-scientific public. Due to the absence of a school of criticism within science, the errors, illusions, half-truths, and wishful thinking of science are not aired vigorously within the scientific community. Consequently, many in the scientific community come under the illusion that the possession of truth is their special privilege. The sociological manifestation of that myth is the emergence of a new type of priesthood, the scientific one. Its members, like the members of the priesthood of old, are making pronouncements about everything under the sun. Like the priesthood of old, the modern scientific priesthood enjoys a built-in credibility, that most of the time goes unchallenged by other professions. What a former Secretary of State said, sums up the situation marvelously: "In this age it appears every man must have his own physicist."[31] Unfortunately enough, many physicists found it enjoyable to bask in the glory of the science-myth. In their naive belief that science is a system of unassailable verities they began to believe that familiarity with science, or the possession of the scientific spirit, makes one an oracle of wisdom. The outcome of all this was best summed up in the words of a perceptive physicist who noted how pitiful it is "to hear a physicist talking one moment with great authority and competence about nuclear physics, and then to find a moment later that he is talking with an air of equal authority about problems of international government."[32]

This dubious though very fashionable performance of many scientists could only strengthen the belief of the non-scientific public in the utopian features of science. Today, as was shown by a now classic sociological study,[33] high-school students look at scientists as supermen. Misguided as our youngsters may be, their mistaken view of the scientist clearly proves that there is something mythical about science, for supermen and giants exist only in myths. The myth is strong, persuasive, and popular. Today, as Polykarp Kusch, a Nobel-laureate physicist, noted in 1961, "the mass of men believe that the better world of tomorrow will come through science."[34] Such a belief, he added, ought to be publicly combatted. He called for a more perceptive, more temperate presentation of science. In other words, he urged that science be demythologized.

Professor Kusch is not the only physicist uneasy about the mythical image of science. In recent years several prominent colleagues of his deplored the lack of sufficient awareness of the limitations of science. Their words did not leave unscathed the scientific community itself. Scientists, as Max Born pointed out two years ago, "are aware of a higher objective certainty obtainable by their way of thinking, but they do not see the limitations of it."[35] In the same year, Vannevar Bush, the great old man of American technology, wrote: "Much is spoken today about the power of science, and rightly. It is awesome. But little is said about the inherent limitations of science, and both sides of the coin need equal scrutiny."[36]

Much the same is the message of the short but incisive book, *Man and Science,* by Professor W. Heitler,[37] one of the creators of quantum theory. It is a book dedicated to the proposition that man is far more than a machine, that man cannot derive inspiration from a purely quantitative framework of explanation. Nor did Professor Heitler mince words in tracing our cultural disasters to our preoccupation with that aspect of things and events which can be handled by science: the quantitative aspect. Exclusive concern for quantitative considerations begets the belief that everything is a machine, or a feedback mechanism, to use the expression fashionable nowadays. Such a belief, according to Heitler, is a myth, a modern superstition, far worse than superstitions of old, like the belief in witchcraft that cost many innocent lives. The mechanistic myth or superstition, to quote his words, "leads to a general spiritual and moral drying-up which can easily lead to a physical destruction. When once we have got to that stage of seeing in man merely a complex machine, what does it matter if we destroy him?"[38]

Forceful as are the statements of Heitler, Bush, Born and of others about the limitations of science, they do not represent the prevailing tone. The public is still captivated by a mythical image of science. In the perpetuation of the myth that science is the answer to everything, present-day scientists have a considerable share. As this might sound an unjust accusation, references to a few cases will not be amiss. One may take, for instance, the lecture that a few months ago concluded the thirty-seven-year-old teaching career of a Nobel-laureate physicist. In that lecture it was claimed that science is "the only valid underlying knowledge that gives guidance to the whole human adventure. Those who are not acquainted with science do not possess the basic human values that are necessary in our times." And he added, "Science is the real basis for knowing what the hell we are all about."[39]

The only truth in that statement is that we, mankind, are in a situation that should indeed evoke the image of hell. There is no need to look far to find the culprit for this hapless predicament of ours. The culprit is the myth of science, the myth that quantities, measurements, pointer needles, scales, and statistics count alone. In such a myth there is no place for values, for goals, for love, for hope, for honesty, that is, for qualities without which no human life is conceivable. The proposition that quantitative considerations alone cannot yield value judgments should be as evident as the saying that no one can get silk purses from sows' ears. Elementary as this may be, it is grandly overlooked by the devotees of the scientific myth. They will claim, as does the author of a recent article in the *Bulletin of the Atomic Scientist* that the man of science should declare far and wide his prophetic vision, and "to become, responsibly, prophets to the people, as were in earlier times oracles and priests."[40] The substance of that prophetic vision is the image of an entirely new man, designed and created by molecular biology and biophysics, a man free "not only from the external tyrannies and caprice of toil and famine and disease, but from the very internal constraints of our animal inheritance, our physical frailties, our emotional anachronisms, our intellectual limits."[41]

Compared with such a vision the most sanguine visions of the prophets of old are very pale indeed. But that pale hue should be preferable to the irresponsible vision of man as outlined by a mythical science. For if man's freedom, consciousness, love, and honesty are strictly equivalent to molecules, to be produced, changed, or abolished at the will of scientific shamans, then no logical place can remain for responsible statements, let alone for responsible scientific prophets. Responsibility makes sense only if underlying it there is a *real* possibility of free choice, or else responsibility and freedom are but illusions.

Without responsibility and freedom man too is but an illusion, and an illusory man is a dead man. It is that dead man which constitutes the ultimate product of the myth of science. Our times are actually witnessing the gradual emergence of that dead product. Its symptoms were brilliantly diagnosed by a leading psychiatrist of our time, Erich Fromm, at the meeting of the American Orthopsychiatric Association, in San Francisco, in April 1966:

> A man sits in front of a bad television program and does *not* know that he is bored; he reads of Vietcong casualties in the newspaper and does *not* recall the teachings of religion; he learns of the dangers of nuclear holocaust and does *not* feel fear; he joins the rat race of commerce, where personal worth is measured in terms of market values, and is *not* aware of his anxieties. Ulcers speak louder than the mind. Theologians and philosophers have been saying for a century that God is dead, but what we confront now is the possibility that man is dead, transformed into a thing, a producer, a consumer, an idolater of things.[42]

This frightening prospect is the direct result of a widespread error as to what science is about. Science is limited to the quantitative correlations of things. Once this limitation is ignored, science becomes a myth and a most dangerous one. In that myth the statement "science is about quantitative correlations" is replaced by the statement "there are only quantitative correlations." If this is granted, science is raised from the dignity of something to the mythical height of a thing which is supreme because it stands for all things. In this mistaken procedure consists the myth of science. In addition to being mistaken, the procedure is also deadly as it makes a dead thing out of man. Even the remote possibility of this should make the demythologization of science a foremost cultural duty of our time.

[1]The subject matter for discussions at the Fourteenth Summer Conference of the Institute on Religion in an Age of Science (IRAS), Star Island, off Portsmouth, NH, July 13-Aug. 2, 1967.

[2]It has been noted several times in recent years that the scientific community often resembles in its attitude, motivation, and claims an ecclesiastical

community or a church. A concise and incisive summary in this regard is the essay by R. E. Fitch, "The Scientist as Priest and Savior," *The Christian Century* 75 (March 26, 1958), pp. 368-70. For a lengthier discussion of the topic, see M. Polanyi, *Science, Faith and Society* (Chicago: University of Chicago Press, 1964), and H. K. Schilling, *Science and Religion: An Interpretation of Two Communities* (New York: Charles Scribner's Sons, 1962). *The New Priesthood,* the title of a book by a former nuclear physicist, Ralph E. Lapp (New York: Harper and Row, 1965), was chosen because of his realization that the paramount importance of science in today's life almost inevitably thrusts the role of priest on the scientist. Needless to say, the concept of scientific priesthood is a rather questionable one. Attention to this fact was called by prominent scientists several times in the past. On this see my *Relevance of Physics* (Chicago: University of Chicago Press, 1966), pp. 523-25.

[3]Scientism can best be described as the obstinate attitude that wants every area of human experience and reflection to be interpreted by the quantitative, experimental method of physical science. Scientism is also spoken of as physicalism, or the conviction that the method and concepts of physics provide the model for any science that aims to be "exact."

[4]On this see the classic essays of Carl L. Becker: *The Heavenly City of the Eighteenth-Century Philosophers* (New Haven: Yale University Press, 1932).

[5]The expression is also the title of an informative book by F. E. Manuel, *The Prophets of Paris* (Cambridge: Harvard University Press, 1962).

[6]On this see my *Relevance of Physics,* pp. 481-94.

[7]Charles Lindbergh, *Of Flight and Life* (New York: Charles Scribner's Sons, 1944).

[8]Ibid., pp. 49-50. On the disillusionment of various prominent men of letters with science, see my *Relevance of Physics,* pp. 496-500.

[9]The contrast was often formulated in the past as the opposition between light and darkness. For a list of works very typical in this respect, see C. C. Gillispie, *Genesis and Geology* (Cambridge: Harvard University Press, 1951), p. 257. Today the same attitude is still evident in the little asides that regularly turn up in the "cosmic speculations" of scientists who more often than not merely reveal a shocking lack of familiarity with the content of theological views they criticize.

[10]"The Role of Faith in Physics," *Zygon* 2 (1967), pp. 187-202.

[11]Today, this claim receives its most sophisticated support from K. R. Popper's apparent criticism of science.

[12]Not much light has been generated by the innumerable writings on what scientific method is about. What seems to be the most illuminating and at the same time a most trivial outcome of the endless discussions about the method of science is contained in a rather desperate utterance of P. W.

Bridgman, a chief spokesman of operationism as the allegedly last word about the scientific method: "I am not one of those who hold that there is a scientific method as such. The scientific method, as far as it is a method, is nothing more than doing one's damndest with one's mind, no holds barred." "The Prospect for Intelligence" (1945), in P. W. Bridgman, *Reflections of a Physicist* (New York: Philosophical Library, 1955), p. 535.

[13]In Egyptian mythology, the body of Nut formed the bending arch of the starry heavens, supported from below by the erect body of Shu, another deity.

[14]See *Sir Isaac Newton's Mathematical Principles of Natural Philosophy and His System of the World,* tr. F. Cajori (Berkeley: University of California Press, 1934), p. xiv.

[15]It is the usual fate of any systematic derider of metaphysics that he ends up with a system of thought governed by myths. The whole course of Comte's career is a classic illustration of this. The philosophy of positivism turned in his hands into the religion of positivism which T. H. Huxley once defined as "Catholicism minus Christianity." It embodied the extravagant myth that science can provide limitless guidance when its limitations are ignored.

[16]*Psychology* (New York: Henry Holt and Company, 1915), p. 467.

[17]*The Metaphysical Foundations of Modern Physical Science* (2nd rev. ed.; New York: The Humanities Press, 1932; Garden City, N.Y.: Doubleday, n.d.), p. 227.

[18]*The Science of Mechanics: A Critical and Historical Account of Its Development,* translated by T. J. McCormack (6th rev. ed.; La Salle, IL; Open Court, 1960), p. 559.

[19]On this, see chapter I, "The World as an Organism," in my *Relevance of Physics.*

[20]For a representative list of Aristotelian texts, see my *Relevance of Physics,* pp. 13-32.

[21]See Aristotle, *On the Heavens,* with an English translation by W. K. C. Guthrie (Cambridge: Harvard University Press, 1939), p. 25.

[22]On the clockwork as a paradigm of intelligibility in classical physics, see my *Relevance of Physics,* chapter II, passim, and pp. 288, 418, 431, and 432.

[23]*Dialogue Concerning the Two Chief World Systems,* translated, with revised notes, by Stillman Drake (Berkeley: University of California Press, 1935), p. 69.

[24]Nothing shows more forcefully the mythical character of the idea of the machine than the domination exerted by it on the mentality of the nineteenth century. As Thomas Carlyle admitted ruefully in his "Signs of the Times" (1820), "Our true Deity is Mechanism. It has subdued external Nature for us, and we think it will do all other things." *Critical and*

Miscellaneous Essays: Collected and Republished, (Boston: Dana Estes and Charles E. Lauriat, 1884), vol. I, p. 479.

25 Among modern physicists Jeans, Dirac, and others spoke in this vein. See my *Relevance of Physics,* pp. 115 and 136.

26 Particularly emphatic, and mystifying too, are the assertions of J. A. Wheeler, of Princeton University. See, for instance, his paper "Curved Empty Space-Time as the Building Material of the Physical World," in *Logic, Methodology and Philosophy of Science: Proceedings of the 1960 International Congress,* edited by E. Nagel, P. Suppes, and A. Tarski (Stanford: Stanford University Press, 1962), p. 361.

27 I discussed recent references to Olbers' paradox with emphasis on the contents of Olbers' original paper in my "Olbers', Halley's, or Whose Paradox?" *American Journal of Physics* 35 (1967), pp. 200-210.

28 "Ueber das Newtonsche Gravitationsgesetz," *Sitzungsberichte der königlichen bayerischen Akademie der Wissenschaften, Math.-phys. Classe* 26 (1896), pp. 373-400.

29 "The Wave Theory of Light" (1884), in *Popular Lectures and Addresses* (London: Macmillan, 1891-94), vol. I, pp. 314-15.

30 For a penetrating analysis of this baffling situation, see H. Dingle, "The Missing Factor in Science" (1947), in H. Dingle, *The Scientific Adventure* (London: Pittman, 1952), pp. 1-16.

31 On this remark of James F. Byrnes, see R. C. Batchelder, *The Irreversible Decision: 1939-1950* (Boston: Houghton Mifflin Company, 1962), pp. 46 and 276.

32 L. A. DuBridge, "Science and National Policy," *American Scientist* 34 (1946), p. 227.

33 Margaret Mead and Rhoda Metraux, "Image of the Scientist among High-School Students," *Science* 126 (1957), pp. 384-90.

34 See his address to Pulitzer-Prize Jurors at Columbia University, "Science Doesn't Have All the Answers," *New York Herald Tribune,* April 2, 1961, Section 2, p. 3.

35 "Recollections of Max Born. III. Reflections," *Bulletin of the Atomic Scientists* 21 (Nov. 1965), p. 5.

36 "Science Pauses," *Fortune* 71 (May 1965), p. 116.

37 W. Heitler, *Man and Science,* trans. by R. Schlapp (New York: Basic Books, 1963).

38 Ibid., p. 97.

39 I. I. Rabi as quoted in *Time,* May 26, 1967, p. 48.

40 R. Sinsheimer, "The End of the Beginning," *Bulletin of the Atomic Scientists* 23 (Feb. 1967), p. 8.

41 Ibid, p. 12.

42 *New York Times,* April 17, 1966, section E, p. 2, col. 3.

14

Science and Hope

The word *and,* insignificant in itself, may appear utterly puny when flanked on both sides by the words, science and hope, which loom large on the modern scene. Yet, to see something of the significance of that puny word one need not be a modern linguistic philosopher who writes a paper with the title "AND." Lexicographers long ago noticed that the word *and* may suggest intriguing connotations. There is, for instance, in Fowler's *Modern English Usage* under the entry *and,* a long paragraph entitled "Bastard Conjunction," or the connecting with *and* of propositions or ideas that do not call for one another. Thus, *and* in the title of this essay would be a bastard conjunction if it suggested that science and hope do not belong together and therefore should not

First published in *The Hillsdale Review* 7 (Summer 1985), pp. 3-16. Reprinted with permission.

be mentioned in the same breath. Of course, the error denoted as a bastard conjunction presupposes the possibility of the opposite, namely, a rightful tie, and it is in this sense that the word *and* is most often used. In this case the title of this essay would stand for any inquiry about the role which science has in the business of hoping, or hope has in the business of science, which is certainly a very large business.

There are still other meanings of the word *and* if Bergen and Cornelia Evans are right in their *Dictionary of Contemporary English Usage*. They tell us that one can say, for instance, "it is good *and* cold out," which is a case of intensification. In this case the title of this essay would suggest that precious as science may be, hope is even more so. One may also recall the phrase, "strawberry shortcake is yummy, *and how!*", a phrase which puts strawberry shortcake in a privileged position. If used in this sense, the word *and* would suggest nothing less than that science is the special source of hope.

There are three other meanings of *and* which are worth considering. One is the confusing of *and* with *or*. In other words, one can presumably make the error and take science for hope, or hope for science, an error not at all infrequent. Then there is the sense of contrariety which may be conveyed by that little word *and* when used with a special intonation. In this case the title of this essay would stand for the proposition: science we need, but hope even more so. And finally there is a usage of *and* about which grammarians tell us that it is strictly archaic. In the century of Shakespeare one could say, and Shakespeare did in his *Comedy of Errors,* "And you will not, Sir, I'll take to my heels," meaning: "If you will not do so, Sir, I will run away." According to this archaic or conditional usage, the title would suggest: Yes, science, indeed, provided it gives hope, or science indeed, provided we already have hope.

The century of Shakespeare, the seventeenth century, was also the century of the rise of science. It should not therefore be surprising that in that century there developed an intense debate about science, a debate pivoted around that conditional use of *and*. Moreover, already in the seventeenth century, and since then until our day, the great debates around science have been pivoted on the various shades of meanings which can be given to the phrase science and hoping, because of the shades of meaning that one can give to the word *and*. It is the history of these shades of meaning which in a sense will be surveyed in this essay. Hopefully, the survey may help to break out of that vicious circle according to which the only thing man learns from history is that he never learns from history. A careful look at the history of science and hope will then illustrate the basic truth in the old saying that history is philosophy teaching by examples.[1]

To take the seventeenth century for a starting point is all the more justified because that century witnessed the rise of science. In a sense, to be sure. The buds of the magnolia and many other planets are visible for months before they open into dazzling flowers within a few days, if not hours. So it was with the rise of science. It was slowly but visibly growing as a bud from the thirteenth century on, when suddenly it burst into full bloom in the seventeenth century and proved itself to be a plant which assures its own spectacular growth and fruitfulness. That fast and spectacular blooming of science was a very conscious process. The writings of Descartes, of Bacon, and of the various members of the Royal Society are so many witnesses in this respect. A quick look at Descartes' book called *Discourse on the Method* can convince even freshmen that the method Descartes proposed was a scientific method and that he expected the solution of all problems once that method had found universal application. Among the problems considered by Descartes was the problem of death. No sooner had Descartes published his book than he wrote to his friend Father Mersenne in Paris, that he had started working on what he called an "infallible science of medicine" to eliminate, to quote from his letter, "this bothersome business of dying."[2] Ten years later he gave up the project. His efforts taught him only one lesson, namely, that one must accept death with hopeful resignation, a lesson which he had already learned from catechism.

Bacon too saw his principal achievement in working out a method, a method of scientific discoveries. He hoped that the method would be as simple as an ordinary machine which can be operated by anyone. Once that method was on hand, there was no more need for geniuses because the method, in Bacon's words, would, "put all wits nearly on a level,"[3] and would make all discoveries a reality within a few years. The method was the *New Organon* or the New Instrument. It did not help Bacon to make discoveries; it did not even help him to see the obvious. It was as clear as a blue sky even in Bacon's day that ice or snow would delay the putrefaction of meat. But Bacon wanted to proceed "scientifically," that is, by experiments. On a cold winter morning he saw plucked chickens for sale by the roadside, he stepped out of his coach, bought several chickens and stuffed them with snow to find out how many days it would take before a chicken stuffed with snow would start decomposing. Before he had found it out, he was down with a very bad cold and was dead within a week.

Bacon called himself the trumpeter of the age of science. He sounded as a trumpet, but a trumpet is not science. Indeed it has been aptly said that no voluminous writings on science were more barren of new scientific information than were Bacon's writings. The same was true of most of his admirers—Newton was *not* one of them—in the Royal Society whose early members spoke of him as their Patron Saint. A typical case was Henry Power who published in 1664 *Experimental Philosophy in Three Books: Containing Experiments, Microscopical, Mercurial, Magnetical.* It contained nothing interesting, let alone new in the way of scientific information. The book is remembered for Power's declaration that his were the times when "Philosophy comes in with a Spring tide to lay a new Foundation more magnificent and never to be overthrown." The new philosophy was the science of mechanics, which was looked upon by many, to quote Power again, as a mighty force as impossible to keep at bay as it was "impossible to hinder the Sun from Rising, or being up, from filling the whole Horizon with light."[4]

Others, not without some good reason, looked upon the new philosophy as harbinger of an ultimate catastrophe which would envelop everything in darkness. The darkness was a life without purpose and hope. For if the ultimate truth about nature was that everything was a machine, then even human life and thinking were degraded to the level of sheer mechanism which, taken in itself, can have only sequences but no purpose. If purpose is eliminated, so is hope. Herein lay the source of a debate which raged throughout England for much of the second half of the seventeenth century. It is now remembered as the Webster-Ward debate on the principal aims of education.[5] The Webster-Ward debate anticipated much of a far better-known debate in which T. H. Huxley and Matthew Arnold were the chief protagonists two hundred years later. This debate in turn anticipated much of the clash stirred up over twenty years ago by C. P. Snow's *Two Cultures.* Webster and other supporters of mechanistic science could point out its spectacular successes, although the benefits for the individual were still very meager. Effective checking of infant mortality was still centuries away, as was a notable rise in life expectancy. In the seventeenth century, the plague known as black death could take its terrible toll almost as unimpeded as it had three hundred years earlier.[6] Most importantly, there remained the question to be answered about the purpose of life. For this question the new science of mechanics had no answer. Actually, the question itself could not even be raised within its framework. But if purpose was sidelined, so was the candle of hope extinguished. Defenders of the old humanistic learning could at least claim that within its perspective the question of hope could be kept alive. They could argue, and did argue, that even the mechanists admitted in their hearts that Aristotle was no fool when he stated that "the nature of man is not what he is born *as,* but what he is born *for.*"[7]

The situation was notably different a century after, that is, in the second half of the eighteenth century. A hundred years earlier protagonists and critics of science were for the most part devout Christians and as such imbued with hope. For what is a Christian if not a man of hope? A century later the most vocal protagonists of science as a source of hope urged that Christianity be abandoned once and for all. De la Mettrie did so at the middle point of the eighteenth century when he published his *L'homme machine,* or *Man a Machine.* Twenty years later Baron d'Holbach claimed in his *Système de la nature* that happiness was nothing more than the smooth running of the gears in that machine which is man. De la Mettrie also coined the phrase, often repeated for the rest of the century, that all errors of man were errors in physics,[8] a word which in the French form, *physique,* stood at that time also for medicine. In other words, de la Mettrie, himself a physician, seemed to suggest that by being experts in physics physicians were to liberate man from all his ills and woes, so many results of his errors. Quite a modern idea, but not altogether free of error.

The phrase of de la Mettrie, all errors of man are errors of physics, was prominently repeated in the plan for the reorganization of French education, which Condorcet wrote at the request of the new revolutionary French government.[9] Condorcet and other prophets of Paris spoke boldly about the complete reorganization of society on the basis of science. It was then that the idea of phalanster or rigid regimentation was proposed as an ideal state for man. The true state of man, or European man, was markedly different. In his famous letters on the French Revolution, Edmund Burke was not too far from the truth as he wrote: "The age of chivalry is gone. The age of sophisters, economists, and calculators has succeeded, and the glory of Europe is extinguished forever."[10]

Romanticism was an effort aimed at recovering that glory, or rather that hope and purpose. It was also an effort which showed little comprehension of science, for which great, spectacular triumphs were in store. Electric and steam industry began to change the face of Europe, shortly after Faraday, Carnot, Lord Kelvin, and others founded the new sciences of electromagnetism and thermodynamics. The explosive growth of inorganic chemistry was followed by that of organic chemistry, after Wöhler synthesized the urea in 1836, a feat which until then was believed to be impossible. Of course, there were some drawbacks. Quick industrialization resulted in a fast unplanned growth of cities which became so many breeding places of tuberculosis, the classic sickness of the nineteenth century. While tuberculosis resisted medical treatment for a long time, smallpox, the scourge of the eighteenth century, was conquered by widespread vaccination. Then came Pasteur whose work seemed to give the antidote against all infectious diseases. No wonder that science appeared once more as an answer to all men's hopes. Shortly after the middle of the nineteenth century Herbert Spencer appeared on the scene and for the next quarter of a century his books were read as Gospel truth. Six years before Darwin published his *Origin of Species,* Spencer spoke of the survival of the fittest and about the same time he formulated his famous account of science as the source of all hope:

> Thus to the question with which we set out—What knowledge is of most worth?—the uniform reply is—Science. This is the verdict on all counts. For direct self-preservation, or the maintenance of life and health, the all-important knowledge is—Science. For that indirect self-preservation which we call gaining a livelihood, the knowledge of greatest value is—Science. For that interpretation of national life, past and present, without which the citizen cannot rightly regulate his conduct, the indispensable key is—Science. Alike for the most perfect production and highest enjoyment of art in all its forms, the needful preparation is still—Science. And for the purposes of discipline—intellectual, moral, religious—the most efficient study is,

once more—Science. . . . Necessary and eternal as are its truths, all
Science concerns all mankind for all time.

In America Spencer enjoyed a tremendous vogue well into the
twentieth century, although by 1900 he was largely forgotten in his
own country. One reason for this was that fashions, including intellectual fashions, quickly go out of fashion. The other reason lay
with science itself. As the nineteenth century came to a close, it
became increasingly clear that mechanistic or classical physics was
rapidly exhausting its own potentialities. It also became clear that
science, mechanistic science, could not answer all questions. In
fact, Darwinism, as a purely mechanistic explanation of evolution
was largely abandoned, to be revived a generation later by the new
science of genetics.[12] It also became realized that the principle
known as the "survival of the fittest" depended for its truth on the
definition of "fittest" for which nobody succeeded in providing a
generally valid form. Clearly, anyone fit to survive as a fragile
ballerina was not fit to survive as a bulky butcher. Positivism, a
philosophy which claims to be exclusively scientific, also was abandoned by some of its leaders. Thus Ferdinand Brunetière, not only
a leading positivist but also the leading literary critic in France,
declared in 1895 that science was bankrupt.[13]

Brunetière spoke a bit too soon. True, science generated some
grave problems in addition to solving many. But there came unexpected experimental discoveries, almost by chance: X-rays, radioactivity, and daring new theoretical departures, relativity and
quantum theory. All these showed that science was far from being
in a state of bankruptcy. As always, there were again some
sanguine visionaries. Already in 1904, at the St. Louis World Fair,
radium was displayed as a new magic source of energy. Ten years
later the British chemist Frederick Soddy, later a Nobel laureate,
told a conference of British trade unionists about the golden age
which radioactivity was going to bring about.[14] Twenty years later,
or around 1933, Rutherford tried to put the damper on such expectations when he declared that any reference to the industrial
utilization of atomic energy was equivalent to talking moonshine.
But it took only another twenty years before the first nuclear
plants generating electricity were operational. Sometime before
that, the world at large was made aware in a most brutal way of the
fact that science is a source of despair as well as of hope. Nagasaki,
Hiroshima, the hydrogen bomb and the nuclear weapons race—all

called for an examination of scientific conscience. Was science evil in itself? There were some glib and some frantic answers offered to this question. The best answer seems to have been given by Einstein who in an interview, given in the wake of World War II, said: "It is easier to denature plutonium than it is to denature the evil spirit of man."[15]

Unfortunately, the soul-searching stopped almost before it started. There came a dozen or so years, roughly stretching from the early fifties to the mid-sixties which witnessed, in at least the more developed nations, an enormous expansion of technology and economy. In some areas the average annual income doubled in a couple of years. In the USA and Western Europe, energy and food became available in overflowing quantities, and so was clothing, thanks to the sudden rise of a new textile industry which produced fine synthetic fabric from crude oil. Television became a household word together with automobiles. Traditional children's toys were replaced by walkie-talkies. Transistor radios brought the inhabitants of jungles into a world-wide audience of the latest news. In medicine, cancer seemed to be yielding to radiation, polio was conquered, the first successful heart transplant was performed, kidney banks opened, and antibiotics reduced recovery-time from months to weeks if not days, in an increasingly large number of sicknesses.

Behind all these spectacular achievements there lay a science which had just opened and cleared up the world of the atom in a systematic way. Man's theoretical understanding of the structure of matter became so perfect and exhaustive that industry could order all sorts of new materials with fantastic properties and the goods were delivered on schedule. Technical progress was no longer a trial and error adventure, but a systematic affair which could be planned years ahead of time. The most spectacular evidence of this was man's landing on the moon. It somehow suggested that man could ask for the moon and, thanks to science, have it.

Reality was not all that rosy. The affluent society produced by science developed serious troubles. There was a widespread revolt among the youth, many of whom sought refuge from technology and science in a counterculture of psychedelic visions and drug addiction. Parallel with this came a return to astrology, or the art of reading in the stars one's destiny, an obviously desperate search for hope. Cases of mental sickness were found to be much more numerous than they were supposed to be. Antibiotics not only cured; they also gave rise to drug toxicity. Victory over bacteria revealed a far more insidious enemy, the realm of viruses. Cancer failed to be conquered and all too often efforts to contain it only brought the patients into a prolonged twilight of life. To endure it painkillers turned out to be less important than hope, the kind of remedy which no pharmacist can dispense, but which was delivered by the non-scientific hospice movement.[16]

One could perhaps still argue that science would provide solutions in most cases, once it was properly applied, but it could also be asked whether science as such could ensure its proper use or application. The record is far from encouraging. Indeed, many signs suggest that this question cannot be easily answered in the affirmative. Technology seems to be a runaway process, unexpectedly beyond our control, even beyond technological control. For three quarters of a century, technology has provided man in ever increasing numbers with internal combustion engines, of which automobiles are the most common but far from unique examples. Nobody in his right mind would deny the immense benefits man derives from having a car. Very often it literally restores hope for man, not only in the case of ambulance cars, but in a wide range of opportunities. Because of this, nobody likes to think of the number, probably as great as a quarter of a million, of those who die every year in automobile accidents, to say nothing of the much larger number of those who suffer paralyzing injuries. Still, it would be rash to say that the losses are not outweighed by the gains.

There is, however, one loss in this connection which no longer may be regained. Automobiles, jet engines, and space rockets may have already put into the atmosphere the amount of carbon dioxide which is enough to raise the average temperature of the atmosphere by two degrees Fahrenheit, a rise sufficient to ruin in the long run much of modern civilization. In other words, technology or science can easily engage man in a course of action about which one can learn only too late that it robs man of his most cherished hopes derived from science. Those aware of this would look with mixed feelings at that magnificent exhibit in the so-called spin-off center at the Space Museum at Cape Canaveral. In that center are displayed some of the byproducts of space research and space travel, about which it was so easy to say two decades ago that they were a waste of money, a quest for national vainglory, never to benefit society at large. At that spin-off center, there is displayed a painkilling device, even simpler than a heart-pacer, which, when implanted at three points of one's back, makes it possible for one to function normally even in the state of agonizing pain. A wonderful result of space medicine, and a hope for people crippled with arthritis and cancer. But one could also wish that at that spin-off center one could see displayed the antisatellite-satellites designed to wage war in space with their laser guns. They are only one of the many weapons showing the inability of technology to control the spread of war. For it is still to be proven that the technology of SDI (Strategic Defense Initiative—or Star Wars) would be an exception to that logic. This remark is not, however, offered to foster hope by reliance on a drastic arms reduction not effectively verified by on-the-spot inspection.

At any rate, technology seems to breed war. If technology had not made the production and transportation of weapons an easy affair, there would not have been more than a hundred wars since World War II, wars in the most exotic places fought by most underdeveloped people but often with the most sophisticated weaponry. Without the tools of science and technology, it would be impossible to keep over a billion Chinese, 260 million Soviet citizens, and many smaller nations under rigid dictatorial rule. Without the tools of science and technology it would not have been possible for a few gunmen known as the Red Army to terrorize Western European nations. Without the tools of science and technology relatively small nations would not be able to produce their own nuclear weapons, and have them for ready use in moments of ultimate despair, and set off thereby that global powder keg on the edge of which mankind has been sitting with more despair than hope for the past thirty years.

At this point the objection may be raised that science and technology are singled out as destructive of hope instead of pointing a finger at man, especially at man's aggressiveness, for misusing science and technology. Moreover, one could even point out that science, the science of genetics, may provide a clue for neutralizing this aggressive strain in man. Is not a breakthrough in the making, so it is claimed, in the chemical cure of various mental diseases, such as schizophrenia? Have not great strides been made in genetic engineering? Has not the bacteria *E-coli* been harnessed to produce insulin? Is not tangible progress being made from heart transplants to the implanting of artificial hearts?

Behind that objection, there are several presuppositions. First, it is assumed that aggression is a genetically determined feature in man. If such is the case, the change of some genes or perhaps of only one gene would do away with aggressiveness and, with aggressiveness gone, would also go the misuses of technology. Whether the changing of even one gene in four to five billion individuals is technologically feasible is rather doubtful, but let it be assumed for the sake of argument that science would be up to that gigantic task. After all, has not science solved in the past tasks that appeared impossible even to scientists? Was not the famous American physicist, Vannevar Bush, proved wrong when he stated seven years before the first space flight that intercontinental ballistic missiles could not be constructed?

Let it therefore be assumed that science can change before long a gene or two in each and every inhabitant of this globe. But before doing so, scientists must be sure that aggressiveness is really a genetically determined feature in man. At present not all scientists are certain concerning this point. Study of the most ancient types of human skeletons convinced Richard E. Leakey that in his very early stage man was not aggressive but rather shared his goods, and this is precisely what assured his survival.[17] But again, suppose Leakey and others are wrong and Konrad Lorenz is right and aggressiveness is a genetic feature. Still there remains one question, and this is really the big question, for which science has no answer. The question relates to aggressiveness itself and is similar to the question raised as to what is really meant by the survival of the fittest. Is man aggressive only when he robs his neighbor and when he takes up arms, or is he not also aggressive when he sets out to conquer distant lands? Is man not also aggressive when he searches for a discovery? Are not behaviorists aggressive when they insist that they should be given the opportunity to eliminate aggressiveness from man? Was that cloak-and-dagger contest, which revealed that DNA in chromosomes forms the laddersteps of a double-helix, not a form of aggression? Was not Columbus aggressive when he set sail for far away India and discovered America? Is man not aggressive when he engages in a struggle for truth and honesty? Is not man aggressive when he introduces a new style in painting, sculpting, and music? Was not Moses aggressive as he destroyed the golden calf? Did not Jesus use the whip? Did not Jesus say that the Kingdom of God takes violence and only the aggressive will seize it?

It seems indeed that saints, discoverers, and artists are aggressive no less than generals, politicians, salesmen, newsmen, or any man still kicking. Therefore any approach to aggressiveness based on genetic or medical technology, hopeful as the approach may seem, will run the risk of resorting to a double-edged sword, or in less aggressive terms, to throwing the baby out with the bathwater. By depriving man of his aggressiveness, science could put an end not only to war but to science itself and to man as far as he is a discoverer and a conqueror of truth and beauty.

A humanity deprived of its aggressiveness would resemble an anthill with little busy-bodies running contentedly about their daily chores in a peaceful but invariably similar routine. The peacefulness of ants is frightfully steady. Biologists admit that the ants have been doing the same thing for more than fifty million years. Aggressiveness is minimal, practically zero, among ants of the same species, but so is adventure. If the human species differs from ants and from all animal species, it is because man is a venturesome animal. A venture always bespeaks hope and this is no different from the great adventure that is science. Before science yielded any tangible hope, science, or rather the scientific enterprise, had to be sustained by hope. In other words, in the expression science and hope, the *and* may very well stand for its archaic or conditional meaning, namely, there will be science *if* there is already hope.

In the seventeenth century, when the word *and* still could be used in the sense of *if*, there was a bursting hope that science was truly rising and would give its yield. But as in the case of a bursting magnolia bud, the hoping was almost seeing, and therefore hardly a hope. It is in the initial stages of budding, the apparently dormant winter season, where the hope is really needed and that is just what happened historically. Such a stage was the period of three centuries before Galileo and Newton, centuries that witnessed a steady groping toward the true rise of science, or rather toward its first live birth. In those centuries, the conviction was steadily growing that a mathematical, quantitative approach to the physical world would give over it that mastery which is called science. Behind this steady conviction there could not lie science, because it was not yet in the books. But there were available certain books, the books of the Bible, which were written to give us hope.

The hope in question had for its major foundation the belief that the world was the product of a most rational and benevolent Creator. The belief was articulated in many ways, of which one biblical phrase was particularly influential for the rise of science. That phrase is from the Book of Wisdom, a book written about 170 B.C. by an inspired member of the Jewish diaspora in Alexandria, in which it is stated that the Creator arranged everything according to measure, number, and weight (Wis 11:20). Students of medieval and late medieval centuries also know that this verse of the Bible was the most often quoted biblical verse in the writings of those times.[18] All students of the Bible know that the Book of Wisdom is a celebration of hope resting on two pillars. One is the divine providence evidenced in the history of God's people, the other is the divine wisdom evidenced in the works of nature.

That hope gave rise to science and gives the basic meaning to the phrase, science *and* hope. A quick look at modern times and another quick look at very old times is enough to see further crucial aspects of this connection between science and hope. As to modern times, it should be clear that the proper use of science calls for convictions, for norms, that science cannot provide. Those norms are ethical norms and as such they presuppose a theological view of existence. Theology comes in as soon as one takes seriously the moral dignity of the human person and the inalienable rights of the human individual. Those rights and that dignity cannot be derived from chance, from necessity, from environment, from economic conditions, not even from an evolution which does not have the Creator's act for its starting point.

Bringing the Creator into the picture is not to the liking of modern times and modern thinking. Ours are no longer Christian times, that is, times in which belief in the Creator is a generally accepted belief, a climate of opinion, so to speak. Our times are also long beyond that brief phrase of modern history, the second half of the eighteenth century, the time of Voltaire, when the deists wanted to keep faith in the Creator but without the rest of biblical revelation and the Christian creed. They did not succeed. Historically, Christianity and faith in the Creator are intimately tied together, a point which can also be seen with a look at very ancient times, or ancient cultures.

A mere glance at the Great Wall of China, at the Taj Mahal, at the Pyramids, at the Acropolis, reveals that the ancient Chinese, the ancient Hindus, the ancient Egyptians, and the Greeks of old, were enormously gifted people capable of producing great cultures. Yet in all of them science experienced a birth which was only a still-birth. In all those ancient cultures there was enough talent, long enough periods of peace, plenty of material resources to permit the rise of science. But the steps, at times most fascinating steps, made in those ancient cultures toward science, invariably came to a standstill.

This fact and the cause of it are still to become the subject of broad and intensive inquiry which may contain tantalizing lessons. Obviously, we would live in a very different world, we all might perhaps speak Chinese, if science had been born in China and not in Western Europe. On the face of it, China should have been the best candidate for being the birthplace of science. The Chinese had gun-powder, magnets, and printing, and had them long before the Europeans. The Chinese had a navy as good if not better than the one which Vasco da Gama and Columbus had at their disposal. But the Chinese never sailed far from their shores. They had no interest in adventures. They wanted a stabilized society, a society of ants, with no new developments. Clearly, they had no hope that the unknown may contain something better than the known. They had no such hope, because they had no faith in a Creator, in a Lawgiver of the universe. Not having that faith, they could not muster confidence that man can ever fathom and formulate the laws of that universe.

Such was the unexpected conclusion of Joseph Needham, a Marx-ist biologist, who in the 1930s began his famous studies of Chinese scientific history.[19] His original aim was to show that cultural prog-ress was dependent on economic or biological factors alone. The stillbirth of science in China taught him the very opposite, a conclu-sion which says no less than that science presupposes faith in God if science is to be born at all and to remain a source of hope. Hope, with faith as its basis, is of course not a tangible material factor. Unlike Boston, hope is not even a place. It is strictly a state of mind. Without that state of mind, man would have never produced what is called the scientific estate. This estate will yield lasting benefits only as long as hope as a state of mind is kept alive as our most precious possession. To keep this hope alive, we need faith in God, the Father Almighty, Maker of Heaven and Earth, of all things visible and invisible. Without that faith, the *and* in the phrase "science and hope" will prove itself a misleading tie, a bastard conjunction. With that faith, which gave rise to science, science can also be kept in its right course and function as a source of blessing and of hope.

[1] A phrase of the classical author, Dionysius of Halicarnassos, was applied to the study of history by the eighteenth-century statesman, Lord Bolingbrooke.

[2] The letter was written in January 1630.

[3] *New Organon,* Bk. I, aphorism 61.

[4] London: John Martin and James Allestry, 1664, p. 192.

[5] For an informative account, with the original texts, see A. G. Debus, *Science and Education in the Seventeenth Century: The Webster-Ward Debate* (New York: American Elsevier, 1970).

[6] I have, of course, in mind the Black Death, a favorite topic with historians who try to paint the Middle Ages as dark as possible. A case in point is *A Distant Mirror: The Calamitous Fourteenth Century* by B. W. Tuchman who, though professedly a historian, does not seem to know about vast studies, that have been going on for three-quarters of a century, about the origins of science in fourteenth-century Sorbonne for which she has but few and contemptuous remarks. What she says on science (pp. 55 and 58-59) would not be tolerated by any teacher of a survey course for freshmen about medieval culture.

[7] This, of course, follows from Aristotle's more general principle that the nature of a thing is its end. *Politics* 1, 2.

[8] *Système de la nature* (London, 1775), p. 19.

[9] And also in his better known, *Sketch for a Historical Picture of the Progress of the Human Mind,* tr. S. Hampshire (New York: Noonday Press, 1955), p. 163.

[10] *Reflections on the Revolution in France* (Baltimore: Penguin Books, 1969), p. 170.

[11] "What Knowledge Is of Most Worth?" (1850), in *Education: Intellectual, Moral, and Physical* (New York: D. Appleton, 1889), pp. 93-94.

[12] As amply illustrated in P. Bowler, *The Eclipse of Darwinism: Anti-Darwinian Theories in the Decades around 1900* (Baltimore: Johns Hopkins Press, 1983).

[13] "Après une visite au Vatican," *Revue des Deux Mondes* 127 (1895), p. 98.

[14] "Physical Force—Man's Servant or His Master?" (1915), in F. Soddy, *Science and Life* (London: John Murray, 1920), p. 36. In the same breath Soddy correctly predicted the coming of atomic bombs within two or three decades.

[15]*The New York Times Magazine,* June 23, 1946, p. 42.

[16]The movement earned for its prime promoter, Cicely Saunders, the Templeton Prize for 1981.

[17]R. E. Leakey and R. Lewin, *People of the Lake: Mankind and its Beginnings* (Garden City, NY: Doubleday, 1978).

[18]As stated by a foremost medievalist, E. R. Curtis, *European Literature and the Latin Middle Ages,* tr. W. R. Trask (London: Routledge and Kegan Paul, 1953), p. 504.

[19]J. Needham, *Science and Civilization in China* (Cambridge: Cambridge University Press, 1954—), vol. II, p. 581.

Index of Names

Adams, H., 21
Addison, J., 9, 64
Adler, M., 73
Alembert, J. d', 45, 54
Alhazen, 144
Anaxagoras, 125, 138, 170
Aquinas, Thomas, 27, 51
Archimedes, 87, 178
Aristarchus, 62, 157
Aristotle, 26-7, 33, 49, 63, 89, 142-4,
    147, 150, 170, 181, 185, 201-2, 204,
    218, 228
Arnold, M., 217
Aryew, R., 187
Ashari, al-, 147
Aspect, A., 38
Augustine, Saint, 199
Averroes, 149-50
Avicenna, 145-8, 150

Babbage, C., 75-7
Bacon, F., 44-6, 61, 128, 139, 156,
    163, 216-7
Batchelder, R. C., 213
Becker, C. L., 211
Beethoven, L. van, 33, 74
Bentley, R., 9, 64
Berès, P., 184
Bergmann, P. G., 17
Bergson, H., 107-9, 111, 120, 177, 186
Berkeley, G., 6, 27
Berthelot, P. E. M., 179, 181
Blanqui, L. A., 104-5
Bohr, N., 42, 155
Bolinbrooke, Lord, 228
Bonaventure, Saint, 51
Borel, E., 16
Born, M., 22, 37, 96, 159, 208
Bowler, P., 228
Boyle, R., 45
Bridgman, P. W., 96, 169, 212
Bronowski, J., 58
Bruecke, E. W. von, 41
Brunetière, F., 220
Bruno, G., 205

Buridan, J., 62-3, 141-4, 146, 148, 150,
    179, 184-5
Burke, E., 118, 122, 177, 219
Burtt, E. A., 44, 201
Bush, V., 158, 171, 208, 224
Byrnes, J. F., 207, 213

Cahn, A. H., 135
Calvin, J., 192
Cardanus, J., 178
Carnap, R., 52, 95-6
Carlyle, T., 212
Carnegie, A., 103
Carnot, S., 219
Carr, B. J., 121
Cartan, E., 183
Catullus, 189
Cavalier, J., 182
Chamberlin, T. C., 159
Chambers, R., 191
Charlier, C. V. L., 10
Chéseaux, J. P. L. de, 10
Churchill, W., 174
Cicero, 189
Clark, R. W., 38, 54
Comte, A., 46-7, 60, 106-7, 199, 201
Condorcet, M. J., 5, 60, 106, 129-30,
    139, 172, 199, 212, 218
Confucius, 136
Copernicus, N., 95, 145, 157
Compton, A. H., 74, 95
Columbus, C., 224, 227
Cooper, L., 139
Curie, M., 158, 170
Curie, P., 158, 170
Curtis, E. R., 229

Dante, A., 33
Darboux, J.-G., 180
Darwin, C., 5, 40, 83, 95-6, 103, 105-7,
    159, 190-2, 196, 219
Darwin, G., 159
Davies, P., 68
De Broglie, L. de, 52, 183-4
Debus, A. G., 228

De la Mettrie, J. O., 218
Desaguliers, J. T., 54
Descartes, R., 25-6, 40, 45-6, 50-1, 57, 62-3, 87, 141, 168, 202, 216
Dickens, C., 4
Diderot, D., 60
Dingle, H., 213
Dionysius of Halicarnassos, 228
Dirac, P. A. M., 213
Dostoevsky, F., 97
DuBridge, L. A., 213
Dufourcq, A., 181-2, 187
Dufourcq, N., 186
Duhem, H., 173, 175-6, 180, 182-4, 186-7
Duhem, P., 24, 39, 120, 171, 174-87
Dupouy, G., 183-4, 187

Eccles, J. C., 78-9
Eddington, A. S., 51-2, 55, 87, 89, 113, 121
Ehrenfest, P., 39
Einstein, A., vii, 1-22, 32, 35-7, 43-4, 48-50, 52, 54, 62, 65, 95-6, 109, 120, 141, 157, 161, 164, 221
Ellis, J., 197
Engels, F., 104, 119, 157, 199
Euclid, 62, 149
Euler, L., 65, 94
Evans, B., 215
Evans, C., 215

Farabi, al-, 147-8
Faraday, M., 166-7, 219
Fechner, T., 79, 85, 90-1, 98-9
Feigl, H., 3, 17
Feuer, L. S., 172
Fichte, J. G., 112
Fisher, R. A., 192
Fitch, R. E., 211
Fitzgerald, F., 4, 15
Fitzgerald, G. F., 6
Fowler, H. W., 214
Frank, P., 2-4, 14
Freud, S., 79-80, 86, 91, 95-7, 174
Freymann, M., 180, 182-4
Fromm, E., 100, 210

Galileo, G., 18, 24, 62, 89-90, 94, 127-8, 140-1, 145, 156, 177-9, 184, 192, 202, 225

Gall, F. J., 47
Gallet, M.-M., 186-7
Gauss, K. F., 28
Gell-Mann, M., 17
Gershenson, D. E., 138
Ghazzali, al-, 147, 149
Gillispie, C. C., 211
Gilson, E., 40, 51, 54
Gödel, K., 12-3, 82, 160
Goethe, J. W. von, 33, 92, 130
Grabmann, M., 40
Grant, E., 186
Greenberg, D. A., 138
Guerlac, H., 187

Hackforth, R., 138
Hadamard, J. S., 183
Haeckel, E., 190
Halley, E., 9, 200
Harnack, A., 26, 43
Hartsoeker, N., 10
Hasenöhrl, F., 171
Hastings, W., 122
Hegel, G. F. W., 19, 28, 46, 51, 92, 110-1, 120
Heisenberg, W., 22, 110-1, 159, 164, 167
Heitler, W., 208
Helmholtz, H. von, 28, 94
Herbart, J. F., 86
Hermann, A., 179-80, 184, 187
Herschel, W., 65
Hilbert, D., 160
Hinshelwood, C., 172
Hitler, A., 111, 195
Hodgson, P. E., 171
Hoffmann, B., 5
Holbach, Baron, d', 129-30, 167, 218
Holmes, O. W., 51, 55
Holton, G., 3, 44, 54
Hooke, R., 45
Hooker, C. A., 42
Hooker, J. D., 196
Hull, D. L., 197
Hume, D., 27, 44, 79, 167
Huxley, Aldous, 195
Huxley, Andrew, 119, 193
Huxley, T. H., 5, 40, 83-4, 105-6, 119-20, 190, 192-3, 212, 217
Huygens, C., 44

Ibn al-Haitham, 144
Ibn Sina, *see* Avicenna
Ibn Khaldoun, 145, 149-51

Jaki, S. L., 16-7, 39-40, 42, 54-5,
  70-84, 90, 94-5, 120-2, 132-3, 139,
  151-2, 165, 170, 172, 181, 187, 211,
  213
James, W., 19, 80, 90, 201
Jeans, J., 213
Jenkin, F., 192
Jesus, 225
Jolly, P. von, 38
John Paul II, 110
Jordanus, Nemorarius, 178
Jung, C., 80, 174

Kagan, D., 196
Kant, I., 9, 11, 13, 20-1, 27-33, 38-40,
  44, 46, 49, 51, 156, 170, 205
Kaufmann, G. D., 14
Keith, A., 196
Kelvin, Lord, 10, 75, 155, 202, 205-6,
  219
Kepler, J., 47, 54, 145, 157
Kingsley, C., 83-4
Kirchoff, G., 20, 24
Koehler, W., 88
Koestler, A., 185
Kohlrausch, F., 20, 39
Koyré, A., 175
Kuhn, T. S., 39
Kundt, A., 39
Kusch, P., 208

Lafitte, P., 187
Lagrange, J. L., 24
Lambert, J. H., 9, 16
Landau, L. D., 164
Laplace, P. S., 24, 34, 40, 65, 94, 105,
  120, 205
Lapp, R. E., 211
Lashley, K. S., 87
Laue, M. von, 52
Lawrence, D. H., 97, 101
Leakey, R. E., 224
Leibniz, G. W., 23, 25-6, 51, 75
Lenin, V. I., 106-7, 120
Leonardo da Vinci, 33, 127, 179, 181
Leucippus, 170
Levi, R., 15
Lewin, K., 88-9, 91-2

Lindbergh, C., 199
Livy, 189
Locke, J., 27, 44, 79, 86
Lorentz, H., 6-7, 15, 154
Lorenz, K., 171, 224
Lotze, R. H., 20
Lucretius, 189
Luther, M., 192

Mach, E., 3, 20-1, 24, 42, 48, 50, 53,
  201
Manuel, F. E., 211
Manser, C. M., 40
Mao Tse-tung, 112
Maritain, J., 120-1
Martineau, J., 196
Marx, K., 95-6, 103-4, 111, 195, 199
Maupertius, P. L. M., 5
Maurios, A., 14
Maxwell, J. C., 6-7, 95, 100, 154, 166-7
McCrea, W. H., 122
McDougall, W., 99
Mead, M., 213
Melville, H., 137
Mendenhall, T. C., 154, 170
Mersenne, M., 216
Metraux, R., 213
Michelmore, M., 15
Michelson, A., 3
Mill, J. S., 47, 54, 103, 106
Mivart, St. George, J., 192
Morrison, E., 76
Morrison, P., 76
Moses, 224
Moulton, F. R., 159

Needham, J., 227
Newman, J. H., 189
Newton, I., 7, 9, 18, 23-4, 37, 44-6, 54,
  58, 62-3, 65, 90, 94, 140-1, 145, 157
  163, 200, 202, 205, 217, 225
Nietzsche, F., 95-6

Olbers, W., 10, 205
Oresme, N., 62, 141-2, 150, 179, 184-5,
  187, 202
Ovid, 189

Pascal, B., 186
Pasteur, L., 219
Paul, Saint, 136-7
Paul V, Pope, 197

Pemperton, H., 46, 54
Perrin, J., 182
Planck, M., vii, 13, 18-43, 48-9, 52-4, 95, 109-10, 164
Plato, 111, 124, 181
Poincaré, H., 15, 24, 160
Polanyi, M., 211
Popper, K. R., 55, 111, 114, 211
Power, H., 58, 217
Ptolemy, 178
Priestley, J., 58, 80
Pythagoras, 83

Rabeau, G., 14
Rabi, I. I., 209, 213
Rankine, W. J. M., 93
Reagan, R., 110
Reichenbach, H., 2-3, 52
Rey, A., 182-3
Richter, M. N., 165-6
Rockefeller, J. D. Jr., 103
Rousseau, J.-J., 130-1, 168
Rowland, H. A., 154, 170
Royce, J., 51
Russell, B., 174
Rutherford, E., 52, 158, 164, 167, 171, 220

Saint-Simon, H., 163, 172, 199
Sandage, A., 122
Sarton, G., 181, 187
Sartre, J.-P., 134, 174
Saunders, C., 229
Schelling, F. W. J., 28, 46, 92
Schilling, H. K., 211
Schrödinger, E., 22, 52
Schuster, C., 14
Scotus, Duns, 27, 51
Seeliger, H. von, 10, 205
Seneca, 189
Shakespeare, W., 33, 215
Shapley, H., 158, 171
Shaw, G. B., 194
Sherrington, C., 78
Sinsheimer, R., 213
Skinner, B. F., 72, 80, 95
Sklodowska, M., see Curie, M.
Snow, C. P., 163-4, 217
Socrates, 124-7, 129-30, 138, 170, 201
Soddy, F., 220, 228

Solovine, M., 11, 50
Spencer, H., 103, 106-7, 119, 157, 190, 219-20
Spiegelberg, H., 14
Spinoza, B., 25-6, 40, 57
Stalin, J., 112, 195
Stevin, S., 127, 178
Suleiman, the Magnificent, 145

Tacitus, 189
Tannery, P., 181
Teilhard de Chardin, P., 118, 194, 197
Thomas, Saint, see Aquinas
Thomson, J. J., 96, 171
Thomson, W., see Kelvin
Truman, H. S., 171
Tschirnhausen, E. W. von, 40
Toynbee, A., 174
Tuchman, B. W., 228
Turner, E. J., 41

Ueberweg, F., 40

Vasco da Gama, 61, 227
Voltaire, 16, 64, 72, 79, 167, 202, 226
Vourveris, C., 170

Warburton, W., 30
Ward, S., 217
Watson, J. B., 79-80, 86-7, 91
Webster, J., 217
Wein, H., 14
Weinberg, S., 121
Weiss, A. P., 87
Wells, H. G., 119
Weyl, H., 14
Wheeler, J. A., 213
Whewell, W., 47, 157, 178
Whittaker, E. T., 15, 138, 171
Wiedmann, F., 38
Wigner, E. P., 160
Williams, L. P., 42, 196
Wilson, E. O., 197
Wöhler, F., 219
Wolfe, G., viii
Wolff, Chr., 51
Wyrouboff, G., 187

Zöllner, J. F. K., 10

Note on the Author

Stanley J. Jaki, a Hungarian-born Catholic priest of the Benedictine order, is Distinguished Professor at Seton Hall University, South Orange, New Jersey. With doctorates in theology and physics, he has for the past twenty-five years specialized in the history and philosophy of science. The author of twenty-five books and over seventy articles, he served as Gifford Lecturer at the University of Edinburgh and as Fremantle Lecturer at Balliol College, Oxford. He has lectured at major universities in the United States, Europe, and Australia. He is *membre correspondant* of the Académie Nationale des Sciences, Belles-Lettres et Arts of Bordeaux, and the recipient of the Lecomte du Nouy Prize for 1970 and of the Templeton Prize for 1987.